WILLIAM BLAKE: THE CRITICAL HERITAGE

THE CRITICAL HERITAGE SERIES

GENERAL EDITOR: B. C. SOUTHAM, M.A., B. LITT. (OXON.)

Formerly Department of English, Westfield College, University of London

---

For a list of books in the series see the back end paper

WILLIAM BLAKE

THE CRITICAL HERITAGE

Edited by

G. E. BENTLEY, Jr
Professor of English,
University of Toronto

ROUTLEDGE & KEGAN PAUL: LONDON AND BOSTON

First published in 1975
by Routledge & Kegan Paul Ltd
Broadway House, 68–74 Carter Lane,
London EC4V 5EL and
9 Park Street,
Boston, Mass. 02108, USA
Copyright G. E. Bentley Jr 1975
No part of this book may be reproduced in
any form without permission from the
publisher, except for the quotation of brief
passages in criticism
ISBN 0 7100 8234 7

Set in 'Monotype' Bembo
and printed in Great Britain by
W & J Mackay Limited, Chatham

General Editor's Preface

The reception given to a writer by his contemporaries and near-contemporaries is evidence of considerable value to the student of literature. On one side we learn a great deal about the state of criticism at large and in particular about the development of critical attitudes towards a single writer; at the same time, through private comments in letters, journals or marginalia, we gain an insight upon the tastes and literary thought of individual readers of the period. Evidence of this kind helps us to understand the writer's historical situation, the nature of his immediate reading-public, and his response to these pressures.

The separate volumes in the *Critical Heritage Series* present a record of this early criticism. Clearly, for many of the highly productive and lengthily reviewed nineteenth- and twentieth-century writers, there exists an enormous body of material; and in these cases the volume editors have made a selection of the most important views, significant for their intrinsic critical worth or for their representative quality—perhaps even registering incomprehension!

For earlier writers, notably pre-eighteenth century, the materials are much scarcer and the historical period has been extended, sometimes far beyond the writer's lifetime, in order to show the inception and growth of critical views which were initially slow to appear.

In each volume the documents are headed by an Introduction, discussing the material assembled and relating the early stages of the author's reception to what we have come to identify as the critical tradition. The volumes will make available much material which would otherwise be difficult of access and it is hoped that the modern reader will be thereby helped towards an informed understanding of the ways in which literature has been read and judged.

B.C.S.

To JULIA and SARAH

Contents

Part II   Writings

CONTENTS

Plates

12 'The Skeleton Re-Animated', Blair, *The Grave* (1808), title page (reproduced by permission of the Huntington Library, San Marino, California), designed by Blake, etched by Schiavonetti

13 'The Soul hovering over the Body', Blair, *The Grave* (1808), p. 16 (a proof reproduced by permission of the Huntington Library, San Marino, California), designed by Blake, etched by Schiavonetti

14 'Death's Door', Blair, *The Grave* (1808), p. 32 (a proof reproduced by permission of the Huntington Library, San Marino, California), designed by Blake, etched by Schiavonetti

15 'Death of the Strong Wicked Man', Blair, *The Grave* (1808), p. 12 (a proof reproduced by permission of the Huntington Library, San Marino, California), designed by Blake, etched by Schiavonetti

16 *Jerusalem* (1804–?1820) copy H, Plate 76 (reproduced by permission of the Syndics of the Fitzwilliam Museum, Cambridge, England), designed and etched by Blake

17 Virgil, *Pastorals* (1821), p. 15 (reproduced by permission of the Trustees of the British Museum), designed and cut on wood by Blake

18 'The Hiding of Moses', *Remember Me!* (1825) at p. 32 (reproduced by permission of Princeton University, Princeton, New Jersey), designed and engraved by Blake

19 'There were not found Women fair as the Daughters of Job', *Illustrations of The Book of Job* (1826), Plate 20 (GEB collection), designed and engraved by Blake

20 '[A devil] seiz'd on his arm, And mangled bore away the sinewy part', *Blake's Illustrations of Dante* (1838), Plate 3 (GEB collection), designed and engraved by Blake about 1827

Preface

Blake's contemporaries thought of him primarily as 'an engraver who might do tolerably well, if he was not mad'.[1] He was not widely known, and most contemporary comments about Blake's work survive in manuscript, not in print. Strictly speaking, there are no reviews at all of books written by Blake, though there are comments on his poems as published in accounts of him by Malkin and by others, and his *Descriptive Catalogue* is criticized at length in the reviews of his exhibition (1809).

As a consequence, this volume must be rather different from other volumes in the Critical Heritage series. In the first place, Blake was not simply an author like Byron or Coleridge; he was a designer and an engraver as well, and his contemporaries knew him much better in these capacities than they did as a poet. Therefore, contemporary discussions of Blake are given under four headings: I 'Blake's life'; II 'Writings'; III 'Drawings'; IV 'Engraved designs'. These are followed by Part V, 'General essays on Blake', giving in substance the contemporary essays devoted entirely to Blake's life, whether critical or not, except for the anecdotal account of J. T. Smith, which is distributed under several heads.

In the second place, the greatest number of contemporary comments on Blake is in manuscript, not in print, and consequently it is necessary to give considerably more context than is usual in the Critical Heritage series.

In the third place, most of these documents up to 1831 were printed in *Blake Records* (1969), in chronological order, with full documentation of manuscript sources, explanation of biographical minutiae, and so on. The great majority of the contemporary accounts of Blake here are simply repeated from *Blake Records*.[2] I ignore here minor misquotations of Blake and trifling errors of fact in the comments of early critics.

[1] B. H. Malkin, *A Father's Memoirs of his Child* (1806); see *Blake Records* (1969), p. 424.

[2] Quotations for which no source is given may be identified by turning to the chronologically appropriate section of *Blake Records*. The comments on pp. 79, 113n, 115, 135n, 155n, 220–69 do not appear in *Blake Records*. Further, the sections in the Introduction for periods after 1863 are largely adapted from the essay on 'Blake's Reputation and Interpreters' in *Blake Books* (forthcoming).

Parts I–IV record critical comments on Blake's life, writings, drawings, and engraved designs made during his lifetime (1757–1827), with a few comments by surviving friends such as Samuel Palmer (1805–81) or by critics of the next generation such as Ruskin (1819–1900). Criticism of Blake's character is included because this seems to have been as widely known as his art or his poetry and to have vitally affected interpretation of his poetry. Part VI on 'References to William Blake 1831–62' is organized on different principles: it is neither selective nor divided by genre but includes in chronological order all the references to Blake which I know. I have not attempted to record the torrents of Blake criticism which poured forth after 1863, when the floodgates were opened by Alexander Gilchrist's *Life of William Blake, 'Pictor Ignotus'*.

A large proportion of the book is about Blake's art rather than about his writings, and consequently it is necessary to have extensive reproductions, to indicate what his contemporaries were criticizing. The works reproduced here are primarily those upon which his contemporary reputation was based.

G. E. BENTLEY, JR

Dutch Boys Landing
Mears, Michigan

Acknowledgments

The manuscripts of most of the documents quoted here from *Blake Records* (1969) are in the British Museum (chiefly Hayley, Flaxman, and Cumberland MSS.), Dr Williams's Library (Crabb Robinson's papers), the Linnell Papers of Mrs Joan Linnell Ivimy Burton (*née* Ivimy), and the collection of Mr Paul Mellon (Tatham's 'Life of Blake' and Rogers's letter, n.d. [*c.* 1832]). To all of these I can only repeat my hearty sense of obligation expressed in *Blake Records*.

In addition, I have had the privilege of quoting for the first time here from manuscripts in the Bodleian Library (Christina Rossetti poem, 12 April 1848), Houghton Library, Harvard University (Ruskin letter, n.d. [?1840]), the collection of Sir Geoffrey Keynes (C. W. Dilke letter, 27 September 1844), the Library of Congress (Gilchrist letter, 24 October 1861), the James Marshall Osborn Collection (Yale) (Hayley letter, 19 May 1801), Sheffield Public Library (Cromek letter, 17 April 1807), Turnbull Library (Wellington, New Zealand) (Allingham MSS., 17 January 1851), Yale University Library (Palmer letter, 24 July 1862), and my own collection (Schiavonetti letter, 21 July 1807).

For permission to reproduce drawings or engravings, I am indebted to the Pierpont Morgan Library, New York (Plates 1–2), the Syndics of the Fitzwilliam Museum, Cambridge, England (Plates 3, 16), Mrs Landon K. Thorne (Plate 4), the Trustees of the British Museum (Plates 5, 8, 10, 17), the Ashmolean Museum, Oxford (Plate 7), the Petworth Collection (Plate 11), the Huntington Library, San Marino, California (Plates 12–15), and Princeton University Library (Plate 18). To all of these I express my cordial thanks. Plates 6, 9, 19–20 are my own.

Introduction

BLAKE'S CRITICAL REPUTATION 1780–1863

William Blake had three professional careers which brought him to the notice of contemporary connoisseurs:[1] first as a competent engraver, for which he was trained for seven years (1772–9) as an apprentice under Basire; second as an original and powerful designer, an 'inventor' of graphic ideas, for which he studied at the Royal Academy from 1779; and third as an untutored author of appealing lyrics, of bewildering Prophecies, and of outrageous criticism. His ability as an engraver was probably creditably known all his working life throughout the small professional world concerned with reproductive engravings; it was a socially and professionally humble world from which not many comments survive. His 'extravagant' designs were increasingly known from about 1796 to connoisseurs in London, to a few patrons of watercolour painting, and to buyers of the illustrated editions of Blair's *Grave* (1808, 1813). His poetry was almost entirely ignored until after his death; none of his books of poetry was reviewed during his lifetime, and the few surviving casual judgments stress their wildness and originality.

THE ENGRAVER

Blake's most stable reputation was probably as an engraver—competent, cheap, and faithful, especially in 'bold etchings shadowed on a small scale, in which Blake has succeeded admirably sometimes', as his friend the great sculptor John Flaxman wrote in 1804 (No. 17e). Almost all his professional life he could secure creditable engraving commissions when he chose, and numbers of judges may have believed, as Flaxman did, that Blake was 'the best engraver of outlines' (No. 17e). For example, Flaxman commented that in the engraved portrait of Cowper after Romney in Hayley's *Life . . . of William Cowper* (1803) 'my friend Blake has kept the spirit of the likeness most perfectly' (No. 25d), and Samuel Greatheed agreed that it excelled in 'correctness' (that is, faithfulness), though not in 'delicacy of execution' (No. 28d).

When, however, Blake was engraving his own designs, the public reaction was more mixed; in general the public at large was indifferent or hostile to the subtlety and independence of his technique, and the praise came mostly from a small group of artists and friends. When Blake tried wood-engraving for the first and only time with his designs for Thornton's school edition of Virgil (1821), the wood-engravers greeted his work with 'a shout of derision. . . . "This will never do" ' (No. 31a), and the description which accompanied the designs apologized because 'they display less of art than genius' (No. 31c). Blake's young disciples, on the other hand, were deeply influenced and moved by the Virgil designs. Edward Calvert told his son that 'there is a spirit in them, humble enough and of force enough to move simple souls to tears' (No. 31d), and Samuel Palmer called them 'models of the exquisitest pitch of intense poetry' (No. 31e).

The circulation of the works on which Blake's reputation as an engraver chiefly depended was very limited. The *Night Thoughts* (1797) was a failure, with only four of nine Nights published; Hayley's *Ballads* (1802) sold only a little more than one hundred copies, and the new edition (1805) was never republished; and the *Job* (1826) sold only a few score copies before Blake died in 1827. Works bearing his less ambitious engraving work, such as Hoole's translation of Ariosto's *Orlando Furioso*, Lavater's *Aphorisms*, Enfield's *Speaker*, Bonnycastle's *Mensuration* and Hayley's *Triumph of Temper* went through repeated editions, but Blake's engravings elicited no comment which is known to have survived, and often in later editions Blake's engravings were replaced by the works of other men.

Blake's greatest finished work as an engraver was probably his series of twenty-one illustrations to the Book of Job (1826), commissioned by his friend John Linnell. It sold very slowly—about six copies a year for fifty years—but the narrow circle of admirers praised it generously. Sir Edward Denny could 'only say that it is a *great work* . . . truly sublime . . . [*with*] exquisite beauty & marvellous grandeur' (No. 33d). Allan Cunningham called it 'one of the noblest of all his productions . . . always simple, and often sublime' (No. 39 ¶42). Others, however, had reservations. The Quaker poet Bernard Barton remarked that 'There is a dryness and hardness in Blake's manner of engraving which is very apt to be repulsive to print-collectors in general. . . . The extreme beauty, elegance, and grace of several of his marginal accompaniments' indicate that 'he could have clothed his imaginative creations in a garb more attractive to ordinary mortals' (No. 33h). And F. T. Palgrave, as an undergraduate, told his mother in 1845 that 'they show immense power and originality. Though often quite out of drawing and grotesque . . . every stroke seems to do its utmost in expression, and to show that one mind both planned and executed them' (No. 33i).

The widespread belief in the twentieth century that Blake is one of the greatest engravers since the Renaissance is one which would simply have bewildered most connoisseurs of Blake's time.

THE DESIGNER

Blake's greatest ambitions were probably as a designer, but his peculiar power and vaulting spiritual aspirations were only truly appreciated by a few artists, mostly his own friends. His disciple Frederick Tatham (No. 42) claimed that some of his

pictures are of the most sublime composition & artistlike workmanship . . . little inferior in depth, tone & colour to any modern Oil picture in the Country. . . . his pictures mostly are not very deep, but they have an unrivalled tender brilliancy. . . . [He] has produced as fine works, as any ancient painter.

His admirers repeatedly compared him with Michelangelo. In 1783 George Romney said that 'his historical drawings rank with those of M! Angelo' (No. 9b), the artists John Flaxman, Henry Fuseli, and John Thomas Smith said that in time 'Blake's finest works will be as much sought after and treasured . . . as those of Michel Angelo are at present' (No. 16d), and the miniaturist Ozias Humphry said in 1808 that his design of 'The Last Judgment' 'is one of the most interesting performances I ever saw; & is, in many respects superior to the Last Judgment of Michael Angelo' (No. 16z). In 1803 William Hayley told a potential patron that Blake's 'great original powers' as an artistic inventor are 'perhaps unequal'd among the Br[itish] Artists' (No. 16j), and Charles Lamb wrote to a friend in 1824 that 'His pictures . . . have wonderful power and spirit, but hard and dry, yet with grace' (No. 39 ¶35). Allan Cunningham remarked in his 1830 biography that Blake 'was a most splendid tinter, but no colourist' (No. 39 ¶51). John Ruskin asserted in 1849 that the 'two magnificent and mighty' artistic geniuses of the nineteenth century were William Blake and J. M. W. Turner (No. 16gg).

Such splendid praise was, however, uncommon. Crabb Robinson remarked somewhat sweepingly in 1810 that 'professional connoisseurs know nothing of him' (No. 36), and in 1828 J. T. Smith maintained that 'the uninitiated eye was incapable of selecting the beauties of Blake; his effusions were not generally felt' (No. 16bb). There was a general reluctance to consider Blake seriously at the most respected heights of art, as a designer or painter of large 'historical' pictures. His friend John Flaxman warned in 1800 that Blake would be 'miserably deceived' if he placed 'any dependence on painting large pictures, for which he is not qualified, either by habit or study' (No. 16s). Lady Hesketh complained in 1802 that 'the Countenance[s] of his women and Children are . . . less than pleasing'; in particular, 'the faces of his babies are *not young*, and this I cannot pardon!' (No. 24h). The *British Critic* in 1796 execrated the 'detestable taste' of Blake's 'depraved fancy . . . which substitutes deformity and extravagance for force and expression' (No. 19a), and the *Analytical Review* said that his frontispiece to Burger's *Leonora* (1796) was 'ludicrous, instead of terrific' (No. 19b). The spiritualist Garth Wilkinson described some Blake designs which he saw in 1838 as 'most unutterable and abominable. . . . Blake was inferior to no one who ever lived, in terrific tremendous power, . . . [but] his whole inner man must have been in a monstrous and deformed condition' (No. 16ff).

The Blake designs about which most contemporary comments have survived are those engraved for Young's *Night Thoughts* (1797), Blair's *Grave* (1808), *Job* (1826), and Dante (1827). The 537 watercolours for *Night Thoughts* were evidently widely known among London artists before they were engraved by Blake and published in 1797, and their extravagance offended the painter Hoppner, who 'ridiculed the absurdity of his designs. . . . They were like the conceits of a drunken fellow or a madman' (No. 22b). Cunningham remarked that the nudity 'alarmed fastidious people' (No. 39 ¶19). Crabb Robinson in 1810 found the designs 'of very unequal merit'; they were sometimes 'preposterous' but 'frequently exquisite' (No. 36). The novelist Bulwer Lytton said in 1830 that Young's poem was 'illustrated in a manner at once so grotesque, so sublime', that they seem to balance genius and insanity (No. 22f). When the drawings were auctioned (unsuccessfully) in 1821 and 1826, however, the catalogue said that they were, 'perhaps, unequalled for the boldness of conception and spirit of execution' (No. 22g); 'a more extraordinary, original, and sublime production of art has seldom, if ever, been witnessed since the days of the celebrated *Mich. Agnolo*' (No. 22h). In fact, no review of the engravings was ever published, and the edition was a commercial failure.

The public success, or at least sale, of the edition of Blair's *Grave*

(1808, 1813) was, however, a very different matter, perhaps in part because Blake's designs were etched by the fashionable engraver Louis Schiavonetti. Their notoriety was caused at least in part by the vigour with which they were advertised. In the Prospectus, Blake's friend Fuseli said that Blake's genius in the designs 'play[s] on the very Verge of legitimate Invention', but that the 'Wilderness' is 'often redeemed by Taste, Simplicity, and Elegance', and that the *Grave* designs should serve as models for artists (No. 29c). Charles Lamb called it 'a splendid edition' in 1824 (No. 39 ¶35), and the designs affected W. B. Scott's father 'in the profoundest way . . . nearly every one of the prints he looked upon as almost sacred' (No. 29k). The poet David Scott (W. B. Scott's brother) said about 1850 that they were 'the most purely elevated in their relation and sentiment' 'of any series of designs which art has produced' (No. 29l). The art critic W. P. Carey wrote in 1817 that they 'abound in images of domestic gentleness and pathos; in varied grace, and unadorned elegance of form' (No. 29r).

Other private buyers probably found, as James Montgomery did, that the nudity depicted in several of the 'splendid illustrations' was 'hardly of such a nature as to render the book proper to lie on a parlour table for general inspection', and other designs manifested a 'solemn absurdity' in representing spirits with ordinary bodies (No. 29m). The published reviews were either tepid or hostile. The *Monthly Review* found 'the grouping . . . frequently pleasing, and the composition well arranged' (No. 29q), and Robert Hunt in the *Examiner* complained vigorously of Blake's attempt to depict spirits with bodies. Not only is the result often 'absurd', but the figures are sometimes shown 'in most indecent attitudes', reaching even to 'obscenity'; 'In fine, there is much to admire, but more to censure in these prints' (No. 29n). The *Anti-jacobin Review* launched a broadside against Blake's pretensions; though the designs were 'tolerably well drawn' and show some 'chasteness, simplicity', they are often 'absurd', and 'the full expression of nudity' is 'objectionable'; in sum, 'Though occasionally invigorated by an imagination chastened by good taste, we regard them in general as the offspring of a morbid fancy' (No. 29p). Despite such bitter strictures, the *Grave* plates were the designs by which Blake was best known for perhaps the next sixty years, with editions in 1808 (two), 1813, 1826, 1847, 1858, ?1874.

Blake's last great series of designs, those for Dante, were left incomplete at his death, but their spiritual ambition made a powerful effect upon those who saw them. The lawyer Crabb Robinson said that 'they evince a power of grouping & of throw^g grace & interest over conceptions most monstrous & disgusting'; 'They were too much above me' (No. 34c). Blake's disciples the artists Samuel Palmer and Frederick Tatham, on the other hand, were profoundly moved by them; Palmer called them the 'sublimest design[s]' imaginable (No. 34a), and Tatham said they were 'such designs, as have never been done by any Englishman at any period or by any foreigner since the 15th Century, & then his only competitor was Michael Angelo' (No. 34e). All these comments on Dante, however, were in manuscript; there was no published description of them until almost forty years after Blake's death.

THE AUTHOR

Blake was scarcely known as an author during his lifetime, and much of what is today thought of as his greatest and most characteristic work was then dismissed as incomprehensible. Of Blake's dozen published books of poetry, the only ones which were discussed were *Poetical Sketches, Songs of Innocence and of Experience, Thel, Urizen, America, Europe,* and *Jerusalem,* and often the critics were as much concerned with the designs as with the text. None of the books was reviewed until half a century after it was written, long after Blake's death. By a curious chance, *Poetical Sketches,* the one least characteristic of Blake, received a disproportionate amount of comment, probably because it was more available and conventional than the others.

All Blake's writings are uncommon today, and none survive in more than about twenty-six copies sold or given away by Blake. Of his works in conventional typography, only about fifty copies were printed of *Poetical Sketches* (1783), and some of these Blake had still not disposed of when he died; *The French Revolution* (1791) got no further than a single proof copy; and the *Descriptive Catalogue* (1809) presumably was bought only by persons attending Blake's exhibition, of whom only about half a dozen can be identified. *Poetical Sketches* and *Descriptive Catalogue* achieved, however, a wider circulation through quotation in reviews and biographies of Blake.

The circulation of works in illuminated printing was much more limited. Each had to be laboriously etched on copper, printed, coloured by hand, and bound by Blake, and few copies of any were produced. Blake evidently printed only four copies of *Jerusalem* (1804–?20), and his most popular work, *Songs of Innocence and of Experience* (1794), is known in only some 27 surviving contemporary copies. Blake only once publicly advertised his works, in an illuminated prospectus (1793), no copy of which has survived, and evidently he sold chiefly to friendly artists who had heard of his illuminated writings through other artists. Blake's works in illuminated printing must have been hard to find and expensive to buy. In the circumstances, the extent of contemporary comment is surprising.

Most critics found, as Blake's disciple Frederick Tatham did, that 'His poetry . . . was mostly unintelligible' (No. 42). A few of the best judges praised it highly in private. Wordsworth 'was pleased with Some of them' (Blake's poems) (No. 8d) and copied out four of them in 1807 (No. 8c), and the poet Walter Savage Landor maintained in 1838 that Blake was 'the greatest of poets', though mad (No. 8d). Unfortunately, this praise was private, while the most damaging statement appeared publicly in the *Antijacobin Review*; it said in 1808 (No. 29p) that his poetical dedication 'To the Queen' in Blair's *Grave*

is one of the most abortive attempts to form a wreath of poetical flowers that we have ever seen. Should he again essay to climb the Parnassian heights, his friends would do well to restrain his wanderings by the strait waistcoat. Whatever licence we may allow him as a painter, to tolerate him as a poet would be insufferable.

Lyrics

The poems by Blake which his contemporaries found most accessible were the lyrics in *Poetical Sketches* (1783) and *Songs of Innocence and of Experience* (1794). The former was on the whole conventional, not to say imitative, printed in ordinary type and without decorations, and generally was of modest pretensions. The preface stressed that the poems in it were by 'an untutored youth' and were unrevised, but that they nevertheless showed some 'poetical originality' (No. 9a). B. H. Malkin, who reprinted some of them in his account of Blake (1806), praised their 'simple and pastoral gaity' (No. 35), but Malkin's reviewers on the whole found little to commend in them. The *British Critic* labelled them 'idle and superfluous' (No. 7b), the *Monthly Review* said Blake was 'certainly very inferior' to 'a mere versifier' like Isaac Watts (No. 7c), and the *Monthly Magazine* remarked that Blake's poetry 'does not rise above mediocrity' (No. 7d). The closest these journalistic critics could come to praise was the statement in the *Annual Review* that they 'are certainly not devoid of merit' (No. 7e). In 1830 Allan Cunningham thought the poems were 'rude sometimes and unmelodious, but full of fine thought and deep and peculiar feeling', though the prose is 'wild and incoherent' (No. 39 ¶3, 7), and Frederick Tatham concluded that they were 'more rude than refined, more clumsy than delicate'; two are 'equal to Ben Johnson', but 'others although well for a lad are but moderate. His blank verse is prose cut in slices, & his prose inelegant, but replete with Imagery' (No. 42).

The *Songs of Innocence and of Experience* were a much more novel production which, according to J. J. G. Wilkinson, their first editor (1839), contained 'nearly all that is excellent in Blake's Poetry; and great, rare, and manifest is the excellence that is here. The faults are equally conspicuous' (No. 12h). In 1828 Richard Thomson remarked that they were 'wild, irregular, and highly mystical, but of no great degree of elegance or excellence' (No. 12a), and Edward Quillinan wrote in 1848 that some are 'very like nonsense-verses', though 'others have a real charm in their wildness & oddness' (No. 12i). Malkin praised especially 'Holy Thursday' (from *Songs of Innocence*) which expressed 'with majesty and pathos, the feelings of a benevolent mind' (No. 35), and Crabb Robinson said in 1810 that, while the designs are 'often grotesque', 'the poems deserve the highest praise and the gravest censure'. In *Songs of Innocence*, 'Some are childlike songs of great beauty', but 'many . . . are excessively childish', while in *Songs of Experience* some are 'of the highest beauty and sublimity' and some 'can scarcely be understood even by the initiated'. He singled out 'The Tyger' as 'truly inspired and original' (No. 36), and Charles Lamb, who had heard it recited, found it 'glorious' (No. 39 ¶35), but William Beckford called it 'trash'. Allan Cunningham called the *Songs* 'a work original and natural, and of high merit, both in poetry and in painting'; in particular it is coloured with 'a rich and lustrous beauty' (No. 39 ¶12, 17). The great critic William Hazlitt 'was much struck with them' in 1811 and said they were 'beautiful . . . & only too deep for the vulgar' (No. 12b), and Coleridge commented in detail on the poems and their designs in a letter of 1818, praising particularly 'The Divine Image', 'The Little Black Boy', and 'Night' as giving him pleasure 'in the highest degree' (No. 12d). Almost all this praise is from men of very considerable independence of taste.

Criticism
The only text by Blake which was dignified by its own contemporary review, the only work by Blake published in anything like the ordinary way, is his *Descriptive Catalogue* (1809). All contemporaries seem to have found it disjointed and aggressively assertive. Crabb Robinson, who

went to the exhibition it advertised, was 'deeply interested' in it (No. 14b); he described the catalogue as 'fragmentary utterances on art and religion, without plan or arrangement', but 'even amid these aberrations gleams of reason and intelligence shine out' (No. 36). He took Charles Lamb to see the pictures and gave him a copy of the catalogue. Lamb 'was delighted with the Catalogue' (No. 14b), particularly with what he called 'a most spirited criticism on Chaucer, but mystical and full of vision' (No. 39 ¶35). Southey, who also saw the exhibition, merely remarked that the catalogue was 'very curious' (No. 14c), and Blake's friend George Cumberland described it in 1809 as 'part vanity part madness—part very good sense' (No. 14e). Allan Cunningham thought it 'a wild performance, overflowing with oddities and dreams of the author', 'utterly wild and mad' (No. 39 ¶30, 32), and Robert Hunt evidently agreed with him, for he wrote a savage review in the *Examiner* in which he described Blake as 'an unfortunate lunatic, whose personal inoffensiveness secures him from confinement' and the *Catalogue* as 'a farrago of nonsense, unintelligibleness, and egregious vanity, the wild effusions of a distempered brain' (No. 14f). Clearly Blake failed in his attempt with his exhibition and *Descriptive Catalogue* to secure from the public a sympathetic hearing for his ideas on art.

The Prophecies
If Blake's lyrics and criticism had divided the critics as to whether they represented 'the highest beauty' or 'trash', the Prophecies united them in bewilderment. Some saw beauty in the designs, but none claimed to understand the texts. Perhaps the best that could be managed was J. T. Smith's comment of 1828 that 'his later poetry, if it may be so called, attached to his plates, . . . was not always wholly uninteresting' (No. 15c). In 1839 Garth Wilkinson was able to see 'some glimmer of meaning' in *Thel*, though he thought it showed strains of the madness which marked Blake's other verse (No. 10). The anonymous critic in the *London University Magazine* (1830) found the illuminations of *Thel* 'charming' and 'fairy-like' and the 'beautiful whole' a 'fanciful production of a rich imagination' (No. 40). None of the critics of *America* and *Europe* pretended to understand the poetry at all. Allan Cunningham in 1830 spoke of the plates as merely 'plentifully seasoned with verse' (No. 39 ¶45), and in 1810 Crabb Robinson said they formed a 'mysterious and incomprehensible rhapsody', 'wholly inexplicable'; indeed, he could not decide whether the text was 'intended to be in prose or verse' (No. 36). Richard Thomson in 1828 found *America* 'mystical in a very high

degree', and in *Europe* he praised the 'strength and splendour of colouring'; the frontispiece of 'The Ancient of Days' in particular is 'an uncommonly fine specimen of art' (No. 13).

The only critic to mention *Urizen* was Allan Cunningham, who said firmly that its 'wild verses' surpass 'all human comprehension'; 'what he meant by them even his wife declared she could not tell, though she was sure they had a meaning, and a fine one'. He was probably thinking primarily of the designs when he wrote that the book leaves 'a powerful, dark, terrible . . . impression . . . on the mind—and it is in no haste to be gone' (No. 39 ¶18).

If the comparatively simple *Urizen* baffled critics, it is little wonder that the great *Jerusalem* proved similarly incomprehensible. Robert Southey called it 'a perfectly mad poem' in 1811 (No. 15a), and Allan Cunningham said it was a 'strange' and 'exclusively wild' work, in which 'The crowning defect is obscurity . . . the whole seems a riddle which no ingenuity can solve', though many of the very admirable 'figures may be pronounced worthy of Michael Angelo' (No. 39 ¶25). Even Frederick Tatham, who was spurred to sympathy for the work by having the magnificent and unique coloured copy to sell, could find little to praise in the verse, though the 'designs are possessed of some of the most sublime Ideas, some of the most lofty thoughts, some of the most noble conceptions possible to the mind of man' (No. 42).

Blake's contemporaries thus were willing to accept him as a fine if eccentric engraver and as a designer whose works balanced uncertainly on the treacherous ground between extravagance and sublimity. His lyrical poetry was praised for its simple, pastoral qualities, but his prophetic works were fairly uniformly dismissed as incomprehensibly wild. His great invention of illuminated printing, uniting designs and text on the same etched page, provided a vehicle in which his strange verses could make their way into the world under cover of the beauty of the designs. To most of Blake's contemporaries, his poetry evidently seemed interesting but absurd; scarcely any could have conceived of him as a great poet.

Such in general was the public estimation of Blake's poetry and designs until 1863, when Alexander Gilchrist's *Life of William Blake, 'Pictor Ignotus'* made Blake's name known almost overnight throughout the English-speaking world.

BLAKE STUDIES 1863–1974

LIFE

The facts of Blake's life derive largely from accounts of him by his contemporaries, such as B. H. Malkin (1806), Henry Crabb Robinson (1808–27), J. T. Smith (1828), Allan Cunningham (1830), and Frederick Tatham (?1832), which were written in or shortly after his lifetime. These were supplemented from the memories of the young friends of his last years, some of whom survived him for half a century and more and preserved his memory ever green, men such as John Linnell, Samuel Palmer, Edward Calvert, and George Richmond, who told their friends and families much about Blake.[2] A number of these accounts were reprinted with little editorial sophistication by Alfred Symons and J. A. Wittreich, Jr, and all are incorporated in *Blake Records* (1969),[3] along with hundreds of others, making it perhaps the most convenient and reliable place to find records of Blake's life.

While Blake was still virtually unknown, Alexander Gilchrist assiduously searched out his surviving friends beginning about 1855, and after Gilchrist's death in 1861, his widow Anne enlisted the support of a kind of syndicate of the Pre-Raphaelite Brotherhood, including D. G. Rossetti, W. M. Rossetti, and Swinburne. When the resulting *Life of William Blake, 'Pictor Ignotus'* was published in 1863, Blake was immediately elevated from obscurity to fame and notoriety. Most of the major reviews published accounts of it, some of them at enormous length, and Blake's stature as a major poet, artist, engraver, and thinker was securely established. Gilchrist's biography has remained the closest thing we have to a 'standard biography', despite a significant amount of minor supplementary information which has come to light since 1863, and the work was reprinted, usually with significant improvements, in 1880; 1907, 1922, 1928 (ed. Graham Robertson); 1942 and 1945 (ed. Ruthven Todd); 1969. There are a number of awkward drawbacks to Gilchrist's biography, however; for one thing, the emphases necessary to a pioneering work are no longer relevant; for another, twentieth-century readers tend to be indifferent to arguments (like Gilchrist's) about Blake's madness and to be deeply interested in his mythological system, which Gilchrist and the Rossettis largely ignored; for another, Gilchrist regularly omitted the sources of his information. This last defect is largely corrected in the learned annotations in Ruthven Todd's editions of Gilchrist (1942, 1945) and in *Blake*

Records (1969), which reprints the factual parts of Gilchrist.[4]

Gilchrist's book roused great enthusiasm about Blake, but the next serious work on Blake's life did not appear until thirty years later. Then in 1893 E. J. Ellis and the poet W. B. Yeats published a Memoir of Blake in their edition of his *Works* (1893; vol. I, pp. 1–172), which Ellis expanded in his antonymically entitled *Real Blake* (1907), postulating that the poet was the son of a renegade Irishman named O'Neill. Though there is no biographical fact to support the theory, it enjoyed a long and active life,[5] but today it has about the status of the 'Bacon was Shakespeare' controversy.

The most responsible and ambitious formal biography of Blake since Gilchrist is that by Mona Wilson (1927, revised by Miss Wilson in 1948 and by Sir Geoffrey Keynes in 1971). This is judicious, balanced, and up-to-date. For all but the most recondite purposes, the biographical facts of Blake's life may be found in Gilchrist (1863, rev. ed. 1945), in Wilson (1927, rev. ed. 1971), and in *Blake Records* (1969).[6] Indeed, the facts of Blake's life now seem so clearly established that interest is turning toward his posthumous reputation.[7]

ENGRAVINGS

Among his creative works, Blake's engravings were best known to his contemporaries, as the surviving comments quoted below clearly indicate. Consequently, it is somewhat surprising that this aspect of his work is the one least examined and criticized today. A great deal of work remains to be done here.

W. M. Rossetti included catalogues of Blake's engravings in the second volume of Gilchrist's *Life* (1863, 1880, 1907), and these were verified, extended, and consolidated in A. G. B. Russell's *Engravings of William Blake* (1912) (ignoring works in illuminated printing). Similar extensions of knowledge were made by Keynes in his great *Bibliography* (1921—see below), in Keynes and Wolf's *William Blake's Illuminated Books: a Census* (1953), in Laurence Binyon's *Engraved Designs of William Blake* (1926), in Keynes's *Engravings by William Blake: the Separate Plates* (1956), and in R. Easson and R. Essick, *William Blake: Book Illustrator*, vol. I (1972); the last, the most elaborate treatment of the subject, deals chiefly with commercial book illustrations, as do *William Blake Engraver* (catalogue by Charles Ryskamp of an exhibition in Princeton, 1969) and the relevant portion of G. E. Bentley, Jr, and M. K. Nurmi, *A Blake Bibliography* (1964). Equally

1 'The Little Black Boy' from *Songs of Innocence* (1789) (*Songs*, copy V) which pleased Coleridge 'in the highest degree' (No. 12d)

The Author & Printer Will™ Blake. 1789.

2 Titlepage of *Thel* (C) (1789) which the *London University Magazine* critic (1830) thought showed the 'utmost elegance in design' (No. 40)

What time the thirteen Governors that England sent con- -vene
In Bernards house; the flames coverd the land, they rouze they
cry
Shaking their mental chains they rush in fury to the sea
To quench their anguish; at the feet of Washington down falln
They grovel on the sand and writhing lie: while all
The British soldiers thro' the thirteen states sent up a howl
Of anguish: threw their swords & muskets to the earth & ran
From their encampments and dark castles seeking where to hide
From the grim flames; and from the visions of Orc: in sight
Of Albions Angel; who enrag'd his secret clouds opend
From north to south, and burnt outstretch'd on wings of wrath covring
The eastern sky, spreading his awful wings across the heavens;
Beneath him rolld his numerous hosts, all Albions Angels camp'd
Darkend the Atlantic mountains & their trumpets shook the valleys
Armd with diseases of the earth to cast upon the Abyss,
Their numbers forty millions, mustring in the eastern sky.

3 *America* (P) (1793) Plate 15 which Richard Thomson said was a 'very fine specimen' (No. 13)

4 The Ancient of Days, frontispiece to *Europe* (G) (1794), which Richard Thomson called 'uncommonly fine' (No. 13)

O! how I dreamt of things impossible,
Of Death affecting Forms least like himself;
I've seen, or dreamt I saw the Tyrant dress,
Lay by his Horrors, and put on his Smiles;

Treacherous he came an unexpected Guest,
Nay, though invited by the loudest Calls
Of blind Imprudence, unexpected still;
And then, he dropt his Mask.

Alter'd from Young.

Blake inv. Perry. sc.

5 Frontispiece to Burger's *Leonora* (1796) which the *British Critic* condemned as
'distorted, absurd' (No. 19a) and the *Analytical Review* as 'ludicrous' (No. 19b)

Heart-buried in the rubbish of the world—
The world, that gulph of souls, immortal souls,
Souls elevate, angelic, wing'd with fire
To reach the distant skies, and triumph there
On thrones, which shall not mourn their masters changed,
Though we from earth; ethereal, they that fell.
Such veneration due, O man! to man.
    Who venerate themselves, the world despise.
For what, gay friend, is this escutcheon'd world,
Which hangs out death in one eternal night?
A night, that glooms us in the noon-tide ray,
And wraps our thought, at banquets, in the shroud.
Life's little stage is a small eminence,
Inch-high the grave above; that home of man,
Where dwells the multitude; we gaze around;
We read their monuments; we sigh; and while
We sigh, we sink; and are what we deplored:
Lamenting, or lamented, all our lot!
    Is death at distance? no: he has been on thee;
And given sure earnest of his final blow.
Those hours, which lately smiled, where are they now?
Pallid to thought, and ghastly! drown'd, all drown'd
In that great deep, which nothing disembogues;
And, dying, they bequeath'd thee small renown:
The rest are on the wing; how fleet their flight!
Already has the fatal train took fire;
A moment, and the world's blown up to thee;
The sun is darkness, and the stars are dust.
    * 'Tis greatly wise to talk with our past hours,
And ask them, what report they bore to heaven;

6 ' 'Tis greatly wise to talk with our past hours', Young, *Night Thoughts* (1797) which Bulwer Lytton thought 'very solemn' (No. 22f)

7 (*right*) Blake's miniature (1801) of Cowper after Romney, which horrified Lady Hesketh because of its indication of Cowper's madness, though she believed 'the miniature is very well executed' (No. 25b); for Blake's engraving of the same portrait, see Plate 9

8 (*below*) Frontispiece to 'The Eagle', the second of Hayley's *Ballads* (1802); Lady Hesketh complained that the baby lacks 'Infantine Graces . . and this I cannot pardon!' (No. 24h)

9 Portrait of Cowper engraved by Blake after Romney for Hayley's *Life . . . of William Cowper* (1803) (second edition); Flaxman said that in it Blake 'has kept the spirit of the likeness most perfectly'(No. 25d) and Lady Hesketh wrote: 'I admire Romneys head of all things' (No 25f); for Blake's miniature of the same subject, see Plate 7

10 Frontispiece engraved by Cromek after Blake's marginal design of T. W. Malkin for B. H. Malkin's *Father's Memoirs of his Child* (1806); *The Literary Journal* 'praise[d] his design' (No. 7a), but the *British Critic* complained that Blake mistook 'extravagance for genius... though the kneeling figure is elegant, and that of the child is passable' (No. 7b)

11 'Vision of the Last Judgment' (1808), Blake's finished watercolour for the
Earl of Egremont, which J. T. Smith thought 'excellent' (No. 16bb), and Ozias
Humphry said was 'one of the most interesting performances I ever saw' (No.
16z)

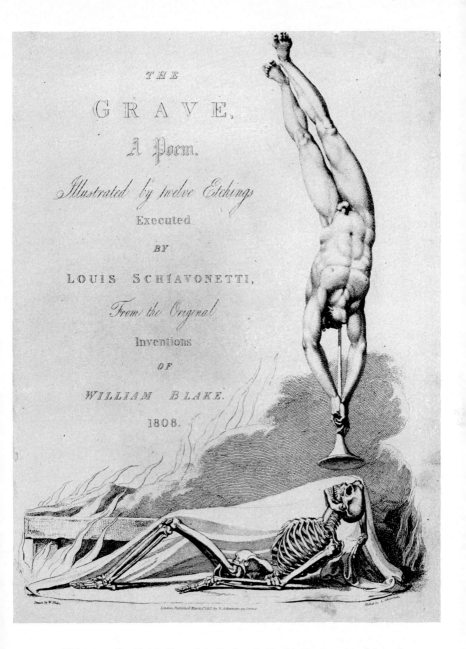

12 Title page for Blair's *Grave* (1808); the *Antijacobin Review* objected to the 'nudity' (No. 29p) and James Montgomery to the 'solemn absurdity' of the design (No. 29m)

13 'The Soul hovering over the Body, reluctantly parting with Life' for Blair's *Grave* (1808), which Robert Hunt labelled 'absurd' (No. 29n)

14 'Death's Door' for Blair's *Grave* (1808), which the *Antijacobin Review* said was 'well depicted' (No. 29p) and which Cunningham called 'one of the best' of the series (No. 39, ¶27)

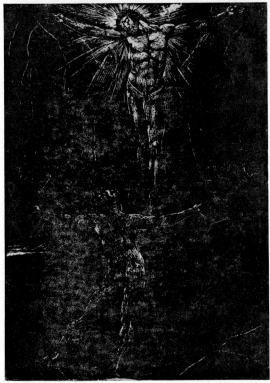

15 'Death of the Strong Wicked Man' for Blair's *Grave* (1808); Cunningham said it was 'fearful and extravagant' (No. 39, ¶24), and the *Antijacobin Review* said the depiction of the soul was an 'outrage done to nature and probability' (No. 29p)

16 *Jerusalem* (H) (1804–?20) Plate 76, one of the 'stupendous' and 'sublime' designs singled out by Tatham (No. 42)

17 Virgil, *Pastorals* (1821) p.15; Samuel Palmer called the series 'models of the exquisitest pitch of intense poetry' (No. 31e)

18 'The Hiding of Moses'
in *Remember Me!* (1825),
which the accompanying
text said could have been
accomplished only by 'an
artist possessing the
imagination and abilities of
Mr. Blake' (No. 32)

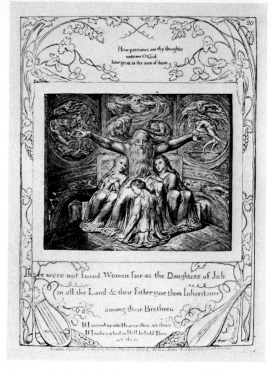

19 *Job* (1826) Plate 20;
Cunningham called *Job* 'one
of the noblest of all his
productions' (No. 39, ¶42),
and F. T. Palgrave said:
'every stroke seems . . . to
show that one mind both
planned and executed them'
(No. 33i)

20 *Dante* (1838) Plate 3; Palmer called the series of designs the 'sublimest designs' imaginable (No. 34a), but Crabb Robinson found the 'conceptions most monstrous & disgusting' (No. 34c)

important, the engravings are extensively reproduced in *William Blake's Engravings*, ed. G. Keynes (1950), in the *Separate Plates* (above),[8] and in *William Blake: Book Illustrator* (above—the intention is to reproduce in the three volumes all Blake's commercial book engravings).

Aside from these scholarly works, very little has been written about Blake as an engraver. The chief exceptions are R. N. Essick, 'Blake and the traditions of reproductive engraving', *Blake Studies*, vol. v (1972), pp. 59-103; Ruthven Todd, 'The techniques of William Blake's illuminated printing', *Print Collector's Quarterly*, vol. xxix (1948), pp. 25-36; G. E. Bentley, Jr, 'The printing of Blake's *America*', *Studies in Romanticism*, vol. vi (1966), pp. 46-57; and Bo Lindberg, *William Blake's Illustrations to the Book of Job* (1973) (see elbow, p. 15). The craft by which Blake earned his bread all his life is surprisingly little understood or appreciated among his admirers today.

ART

If Blake was best known to his contemporaries as a craftsman, an engraver, the creative skill by which he was best known was his draughtsmanship, his drawings. Since patronage of Blake was very limited, and he held only one exhibition of his own works, in 1809, his drawings were comparatively little known, and the ones which reached the widest public, those for Blair's *Grave* (1808, 1813, 1826), were conveyed through the distorting medium of Schiavonetti's fashionable etchings. Until a half-century after his death, it was scarcely possible to form an extensive idea of Blake's art except in the private collections of men like Thomas Butts.[9]

Blake's art was first made accessible to a wide public through a series of great exhibitions on both sides of the Atlantic. The most important of these were at the Burlington Fine Arts Club in London (1876—333 entries; 1927—91 entries); at the Boston Museum of Fine Arts (1880—160 entries; 1891—234 entries); at the Carfax Galleries in London (1904—41 entries; 1906—106 entries); at the Grolier Club of New York (1905—148 entries; 1919-20—61 entries); at the National Gallery, London (1913—114 entries; moved to Manchester, 1914—176 entries; to Nottingham, 1914—138 entries; to Edinburgh, 1914—141 entries); at the Franco–Britannique exhibition in Paris (1937—94 entries) and Vienna (1937—65 entries); at the very extraordinary Philadelphia Museum exhibition (1939—283 entries); at the British Council exhibition of 1947 shown in Brussels (42 entries), Zürich (41 entries), London (84 entries), and Paris (43 entries); at the National Gallery, Washington (1957—163 entries); and at the British Museum (1957—199 entries). Such remarkable exhibitions had an extraordinarily vivifying effect upon Blake's reputation, and fostered the increasingly rapid migration of his works into public collections.

The greatest public collections of Blake's art today are undoubtedly those in the Tate Gallery (London), the British Museum (London), the Huntington Library (San Marino, California), the Fitzwilliam Museum (Cambridge, England), the Rosenwald Collection (Jenkintown, Pennsylvania), the Pierpont Morgan Library (New York), and Harvard University (Houghton Library and Fogg Museum, Cambridge, Massachusetts). Of these, worthy catalogues have been printed for the Huntington, Tate, Fitzwilliam, and (in part) Morgan collections,[10] and handlists exist for the British Museum and Rosenwald Collections.[11] On these collections and catalogues all serious work on Blake's art depends.

The first important catalogue of Blake's art was that compiled by W. M. Rossetti for the second volume of Gilchrist's *Life* (1863, expanded 1880, rev. W. G. Robertson, 1907); no comprehensive work of a similar kind has since been published, but Martin Butlin of the Tate Gallery is now completing a comprehensive catalogue raisonné under the patient sponsorship of the Blake Trust. Other very useful catalogues of Blake's art are G. Keynes, *Tempera Paintings* (1951), Sir Geoffrey Keynes, *William Blake's Illustrations to the Bible* (1957), and R. N. Essick, 'A finding list of reproductions of Blake's art', *Blake Newsletter*, vol. III (1969, 1970), pp. 24–41, 64–70, and supplement pp. 1–23, 1–21, 1–3. With the aid of such catalogues, the Blake student can find most of the important Blake designs in public collections.

Even the most industrious student, however, cannot visit or hold in mind the extended riches of these great collections. He must therefore depend upon reproductions for much of his work. The most important books illustrating Blake's art are *Illustrations of the Divine Comedy of Dante* (1922—102 plates; 1968—109 plates); *William Blake's Designs for Gray's Poems*, ed. H. J. C. Grierson (1922—116 plates, mostly in monochrome), ed. G. Keynes (1972—116 plates in colour); *Heads of the Poets*, ed. T. Wright (1925—18 plates); Milton, *Poems in English*, ed. G. Keynes (1926—53 plates); *Illustrations to Young's Night Thoughts*, ed. G. Keynes (1927—30 plates out of 537 designs); *Illustrations of the Book of Job*, ed. G. Keynes and L. Binyon (1935),[12] ed. P. Hofer (1937—the

'New Zealand' set); Bunyan, *The Pilgrim's Progress*, ed. G. Keynes (1941—29 plates); and *The Blake-Varley Sketchbook of 1819*, ed. M. Butlin (2 vols, 1969).

To these specialized series should be added *The Drawings and Engravings*, ed. L. Binyon (1922, 1967—108 plates); *The Paintings*, ed. D. Figgis (1925—100 plates); and *Pencil Drawings*, ed. G. Keynes ([first series], 1927—82 plates, second series, 1956—57 plates; 1970—92 plates, mostly from 1927 and 1956), plus of course the very full illustrations in the collection-catalogues above. Except for the hundreds of unprinted *Night Thoughts* drawings in the British Museum Print Room, most of Blake's important series of designs have now been reproduced extensively.

There were, of course, appreciations of Blake's art published in the nineteenth century, but the first work of much scholarly importance on the subject was Joseph Wicksteed's *Blake's Vision of the Book of Job* (1910, rev. ed. 1924). Its most important thesis, applied persuasively to *Job* but somewhat tendentiously to earlier works, is that Blake uses the right side (especially hands and feet) to represent the spiritual and the left for the material. Most other books on Blake's art have attempted rather to survey new ground than to argue a thesis. A. S. Roe, in *Blake's Illustrations to the Divine Comedy* (1953), surveys and reproduces the great Dante series competently, but rather blurs the issue by reading the designs frequently as illustrations of Blake's own myth as well as Dante's. Two of Blake's most perplexing works, *The Gates of Paradise* and *The Arlington Court Picture*, are dealt with earnestly by G. W. Digby, *Symbol and Image in William Blake* (1957), attempting to apply modern psychology to Blake's art. Perhaps the most satisfactory book on Blake's visual work as a whole is Sir Anthony Blunt's *The Art of William Blake* (1959), a series of lectures which yet brings the erudition of a great art-historian to bear upon Blake, placing him firmly in the European iconographic traditions. In a dissertation-turned-book, like Roe's, Irene Taylor, in *Blake's Illustrations to the Poems of Gray* (1971), reproduces and for the first time analyses extensively this great series. The last, and in many ways the most scholarly and impressive of these books about Blake's art, is Bo Lindberg's *William Blake's Illustrations to the Book of Job* (1973), which is extraordinarily learned in many languages and traditions and which defines and analyses the problems of *Job* in a masterful way which is likely to make subsequent studies of it redundant; in particular, Lindberg demonstrates that virtually every detail of Blake's *Job* is consciously derived from ancient traditions of Job iconography.

With Blunt and Lindberg, in particular, Blake's art has found scholars worthy of its vaulting achievement.[13]

WRITINGS

Most of Blake's works were etched, printed, coloured, bound, and sold by Blake himself, clearly in very small numbers—the most common is *Songs of Innocence and of Experience* (1794) in some twenty-three complete contemporary copies, while several survive only in unique copies —and even his conventionally printed works, such as *Poetical Sketches* (1783) and *Descriptive Catalogue* (1809), were limited issues of which only about a score of copies can be traced today. Consequently it was very difficult to be acquainted with Blake's poetry during his lifetime, and his popularity depends very largely upon reprints of his works by other men. Malkin, Smith, and Cunningham printed a few poems, but the only book devoted to Blake's poetry published before 1863 was an edition of the *Songs* of 1839. Then D. G. Rossetti organized a very extensive selection of Blake's lyrics, particularly from Blake's *Notebook* which he owned, in the second volume of Gilchrist's great *Life of William Blake, 'Pictor Ignotus'* (1863) which made Blake's poetry sensationally well known. Rossetti unashamedly shook up Blake's verse to make it more conventional in structure, and his texts are always of dubious accuracy, but their historical importance is enormous.

The first need of Blake critics was to have texts of his works put into their hands. R. H. Shepherd and W. M. Rossetti provided separate editions of the lyrics in 1874, but the most ambitious Blake edition of the nineteenth century was the three-volume one of Ellis and Yeats in 1893, which not only presented for the first time many of Blake's prophetic works, such as the great unfinished epic *The Four Zoas*, but provided hundreds of lithographs of the illuminated works. The very great historical importance of their edition, however, was much mitigated by the occasionally grotesque inaccuracy of the text and the unreliability of the lithographs. No one today can use Ellis and Yeats's texts or reproductions with confidence.[14]

Reliable texts
The twentieth century saw great changes in the fidelity with which Blake's texts were presented, first with meticulously accurate editions by John Sampson of his *Poetical Works* (conventional lyrics chiefly) in 1905 and culminating in the great edition of Blake's *Writings* in three volumes by Geoffrey Keynes published in 1925. The Keynes edition

provided texts of meticulous verbal accuracy for all Blake's writings, together with notes on variants and generous illustrations. In various one-volume modifications, first shorn of notes and variants for a popular audience (1927 ff.) and then with the notes and variants triumphantly restored and amplified (1957 ff.), the Keynes edition has remained the most widely used edition of Blake in the twentieth century. Its chief drawback for scholars, a consistent normalization of Blake's very irregular punctuation, is rectified in the great edition of Blake's *Poetry and Prose* (1965 ff.) created by D. V. Erdman with the assistance of a team of scholars assembled to make the equally important *Concordance* (1967). Today, careful Blake critics cite either Keynes or Erdman, and frequently both together.

A few more editions deserve mention, chiefly for their annotations. D. J. Sloss and J. P. R. Wallis provided fresh texts of Blake's *Prophetic Writings* (2 vols, 1926), together with a huge and somewhat misleading index to his mythological system. One of the earliest really useful annotated editions was that of F. W. Bateson's *Selected Poems* (1957); a number of the poems in the Erdman edition (1965 ff.) are voluminously annotated by Harold Bloom, and exceedingly helpful notes are provided by W. H. Stevenson in his edition of *The Poems* (1971, text by Erdman, with punctuation added by Stevenson). Except for editions of individual works by Blake,[15] no other texts are worth much critical confidence.

Bibliographies

Because most of Blake's works were made by his unique process of illuminated printing, in which each copy differs, often in important ways, from every other, and because even the works in conventional typography were altered from copy to copy by Blake, bibliographical details concerning his works are particularly important to an understanding of him. No critic can deal seriously and reliably with Blake's works without understanding something of the bibliographical details —such as that the poems in the *Songs of Innocence and of Experience* were arranged in at least thirty-four orders. The first real *Bibliography of William Blake* is the very great work of Geoffrey Keynes (1921), on which all subsequent knowledge has been based. It has been modified in minute particulars here and there, chiefly by Keynes himself and most notably in the Keynes and Wolf census of *William Blake's Illuminated Books* (1953), but the broad outline of our knowledge is that which Keynes established in 1921.[16]

Facsimiles

Because most of Blake's works are illuminated by his own designs, and because each copy differs from every other, it is particularly important for students of Blake to examine either originals or facsimiles of them, preferably several copies. The production of facsimiles began vigorously in the nineteenth century, chiefly the hand-coloured lithographs of William Muir and his family, and their importance has been increasingly recognized by serious Blake critics. In the twentieth century, the Blake Trust has produced a series of beautiful, reliable, and very dear facsimiles which have brought the feel of the originals to enormous numbers of enthusiasts. The facsimiles which have been published thus far are:

Ahania (1892 [A][17])
All Religions are One (1926 [A], 1970 [A][18])
America (1876 [copy F?],[19] 1887 [R & A],[17] 1947, 1963 [M],[18] 1969 [C or D], 1970 [K])
The Book of Los (1886 [A][17])
The Book of Thel (1876 [D],[19] 1884 [D],[17] 1920 [J?], 1924, 1928 [D], 1933, 1966 [O],[18] 1971 [M])
Europe (1876 [D?],[19] 1887 [A, D, c],[17] 1931 [D], 1969 [B, G, K][18])
First Book of Urizen (1876 [D],[19] 1888 [B],[17] 1929 [A], 1958 [G],[18] 1966 [G], 1969 [G])
For Children: the Gates of Paradise ([1942?], 1968 [D][18])
For the Sexes: the Gates of Paradise (1888,[17] [1897?] [D?], 1925 [B], 1968 [F][18])
Jerusalem ([[1877?] [D], [1951] [E],[18] 1952 [C],[18] 1955 [C][18])
Letters . . . to Thomas Butts, ed. G. Keynes (1926)
Marriage ([1868] [F], 1885 [A],[17] 1927 [I], 1960 [D],[18] 1963 [I], 1968 [I], 1970 [I])
Milton (1886 [A],[17] 1967 [D][18])
Notebook, ed. G. Keynes (1935, 1970), ed. D. V. Erdman (1973)
On Homer's Poetry (1886 [C][17])
The 'Order' of the *Songs* (1885)[17]
Pickering Manuscript (1972)
Poetical Sketches ([1890], 1926, 1927)
The Song of Los (1876 [A or D],[19] 1890 [A][17])
Songs of Experience (1927 [A?], 1927 [A, T], 1935)
Songs of Innocence (1884 [D],[17] 1923 [*Songs* (T)], 1926 [*Songs* (A)], 1927 [*Songs* (A)], 1954 [L][18])
Songs of Innocence and of Experience (1876 [a],[19] 1883–5 [U],[17] 1923, 1941, 1947 [b], 1955 [Z],[18] 1967 [Z])
There is No Natural Religion (1886 [A, L],[17] 1948 [D], 1971 [C, F–G, L][18])
Tiriel, ed. G. E. Bentley, Jr (1967)
Vala or The Four Zoas, ed. G. E. Bentley, Jr (1963)
Visions of the Daughters of Albion (1876 [B],[19] 1884 [A],[17] 1932 [A], 1959 [C][18])

Nineteenth-century critics

The most important of Blake's nineteenth-century critics, after Gilchrist had made his poetry public property in 1863, were A. C. Swinburne, in his *William Blake: A Critical Essay* (1868), and Ellis and Yeats, in their edition of his *Writings* (1893), in separate editions by Yeats (1893) and Ellis (1906), in separate essays, and in Ellis's *Real Blake* (1907). Swinburne's book was remarkable for its surging superlatives, claiming that *The Marriage of Heaven and Hell* ranks 'as about the greatest [work] produced by the eighteenth century' and that the *Poetical Sketches* are 'better than any [other] man could do then'. Ellis and Yeats were far more learned than Swinburne, and their work is filled with references to secret cosmological knowledge, to the Kabbala and the Illuminati and their significance in Blake's work; Blake, they claim, was drinking at long-forgotten or concealed springs of knowledge and mythology. Most scholars today would probably agree that their impulse was promising but their learning unsystematic and often unpersuasive.[20] There were of course scores of essays and books on Blake contemporaneous with those of Swinburne, Ellis and Yeats, but few of them contain either facts or criticism which need detain twentieth-century scholars long.

Monuments of twentieth-century criticism

The foundations and form of contemporary criticism of Blake were established chiefly by three men: S. Foster Damon, Northrop Frye, and D. V. Erdman. The first, in his *William Blake: His Philosophy and Symbols* (1924), brought great learning in mysticism and the occult to bear on the entire range of Blake's writings and art (the latter largely ignored by Swinburne, Ellis and Yeats), and established analogies with Blake's works which have proved seminal ever since. Damon's work in *William Blake* (1924) and in his *Blake Dictionary* (1965) is deliberately encyclopaedic and has been enormously influential, though occasionally it is more assertive than demonstrative.

Northrop Frye's *Fearful Symmetry: A Study of William Blake* (1947) is comprehensive, profound, and magisterial; it is the foundation of Frye's own revolutionary critical system and of the most fruitful subsequent discussions by others of Blake's 'system'. Its learning is immense and unobtrusive, and its analysis of Blake's development lucid and witty. Frye is particularly concerned with a tradition of archetypal symbolism, for instance with Blake's Orc Cycle, and he stresses throughout Blake's consistent attempt to create one comprehensive mythological system.

D. V. Erdman's *Blake: Prophet Against Empire* (1954, rev. ed. 1969) is a very different and more limited kind of work but in its way almost as impressive and influential. Erdman attempts 'to trace through nearly all of his works [chiefly literary] a more or less clearly discernible thread of historical reference', and in the process he has demonstrated, often conclusively, Blake's frequent and deliberate responses to contemporary history and politics. Blake was neither worldly nor out of touch with his times; his profundity did not prevent him from utilizing the facts and sympathies of his day in his poetry. Within this sphere, *Blake: Prophet Against Empire* is an enormously useful work.

Scholarship and twaddle about Blake have multiplied at such a pace in the post-war years that it is scarcely possible here to do more than glance at a few of the more important and influential books. Even so, it will be necessary to treat them under several subheadings, 'Religion', 'Psychology', 'Sources', 'Influence', 'General Criticism', and 'Collections of Essays', in order to deal with all the kinds of material.

Religion
The earliest extended separate account of Blake's religious ideas appeared in Helen White's *Mysticism of William Blake* (1927, 1964), which concluded that 'he is not a great mystic in any sense that means anything', a conclusion generally assumed without discussion today.[21] A similarly specialized work was J. G. Davies's *Theology of William Blake* (1948, 1965), which argues, curiously, that Blake was an orthodox Anglican, but is yet useful in dismissing the claims that Blake's family was Swedenborgian when he was a boy.[22]

Margaret Bottrall, in *The Divine Image, A Study of Blake's Interpretation of Christianity* (1950), agrees with Davies that 'Blake's Christianity was essentially and soundly Christian', but a contrary and more persuasive conclusion about Blake's orthodoxy is reached by H. N. Fairchild in the Blake chapter of his *Religious Trends in English Poetry* (1949), vol. III, pp. 66–137, and is carried yet further by T. T. J. Altizer, *The New Apocalypse: The Radical Christian Vision of William Blake* (1967): 'Blake was the first Christian atheist.' Somewhat less doctrinaire conclusions on a related subject are reached by A. A. Ansari, in *Arrows of Intellect: A Study in William Blake's Gospel of the Imagination* (1965), which deals especially with Wordsworth, Locke, and Blake's philosophical ideas, and by Kathryn Kremen, in *The Imagination of the Resurrection: The Poetic Continuity of a Religious Motif in Donne, Blake, and Yeats* (1972), pp. 129–259, which is a reading of the theological passages in Blake's poetry. Naturally most general books on Blake also deal with his religious ideas, but today they tend to do so in the context of his myth rather than of his life.

Psychology

An obviously related subject is Blake's psychology, for most of the major psychological 'discoveries' of the twentieth century have been found adumbrated in Blake's poetry. Unfortunately, most of the psychologists are self-taught amateurs, and the professionals are rather worse. W. P. Witcutt's *Blake: A Psychological Study* (1946, 1966) begins a promising argument that Blake can be profitably illuminated by Jung. A wonderfully perverse work on the subject is Margaret Rudd's *Organized Innocence: The Story of Blake's Prophetic Books* (1956), a paraphrase of 'Blake's own psychological drama' in the 'one long narrative' formed by *Vala, Milton,* and *Jerusalem*. And finally a Jungian analyst, June K. Singer in *The Unholy Bible: A Psychological Interpretation of William Blake* (1970) analyses his sexual life as deduced from his writings in wonderful detail and with a stout disregard for plain facts. The great promises of psychology have yet to bear sweet fruit in Blake studies.

Sources

An author as difficult and heterodox as Blake seems to call to something deep in many scholars to identify the sources of his ideas, to help put him into a meaningful context and explain his work. The earliest study of this kind of much note was the essay by Henry G. Hewlett, 'Imperfect genius: William Blake', *Contemporary Review*, vol. xxviii (1876), pp. 756–84, vol. xxix (1877), pp. 207–28, which argued that Blake was scarcely doing more than imitating ineffectively the artificial archaism of Ossian and Chatterton.

Suggested and prolific arguments on Blake's sources were made by the French critic Denis Saurat, in *Blake and Milton* (1920), *Blake and Modern Thought* (1929), and *William Blake* (1954). In the second of these, which is the best of them, he claims that 'there was not one absurdity in Europe at the end of the eighteenth century that Blake did not know'; he is particularly stimulating and useful on the Kabbala, Hindu mythology, and Druidism,[23] and frequently his scholarship and accuracy are commendable. Perhaps the most satisfying book devoted to a study of Blake's sources is Milton O. Percival's *William Blake's Circle of Destiny* (1938), particularly in finding parallels and sources in the writings of the alchemists, the Kabbalists, and Biblical scholars. A similarly rewarding work is Margaret Ruth Lowery's *Windows of the Morning: A Critical Study of William Blake's Poetical Sketches* (1940), particularly in its then-novel conclusion 'that, contrary to all previous comment on Blake, the influence of the [eighteenth] century is more extensive than that of the Elizabethan period'.

Learned but incomplete essays on Blake's debt to Swedenborg and to Boehme and the alchemists were published in Jacques Roos, *Aspects littéraires du mysticisme philosophique et l'influence de Boehme et de Swedenborg au début du romanticisme: William Blake, Novalis, Ballanche* (1951), pp. 25-194, and in Désirée Hirst, *Hidden Riches: Traditional Symbolism from the Renaissance to Blake* (1964), but much remains to be done in this difficult area.

A much more speculative thesis appears in A. L. Morton's *The Everlasting Gospel: A Study in the Sources of William Blake* (1958), which deals with the Muggletonians and other seventeenth-century radical dissenters and their relationship to Blake.

An exceedingly problematic theme, the influence on Blake of Plato and the neo-Platonists via his contemporary, Thomas Taylor, has been repeatedly but unpersuasively argued, chiefly by George Harper, *The Neoplatonism of William Blake* (1961), and, rather more stridently, by Kathleen Raine, *Blake and Tradition* (2 vols, 1968). Despite occasionally convincing points, and the recent (1972) discovery of evidence that Blake did, after all, know Taylor, most scholars are likely still to return a Scottish verdict of Not Proven to the charge that Blake was extensively and directly influenced by Taylor or Plato.

Influence

Blake has been claimed, sometimes convincingly, as an important influence on authors as diverse as G. B. Shaw, D. H. Lawrence, Joyce Cary, Dylan Thomas, and D. G. Rossetti. Most ink has flowed, however, in tracing the effect of his thought on W. B. Yeats; the relationship was tentatively explored in Margaret Rudd, *Divided Image: A Study of William Blake and W. B. Yeats* (1953) and in Virginia Moore 'Blake as a Major Doctrinal Influence' on Yeats in *The Unicorn* (1954) and defined, as satisfactorily as such a problem admits of definition, in Hazard Adams, *Blake and Yeats: The Contrary Vision* (1955). But no one has yet attempted to describe with confidence the extent of Blake's influence on all subsequent authors.

General criticism

There are scores of books and literally thousands of articles dealing with

Blake's poetry generally, and naturally, among such a welter, comparatively little will generously reward a critic's serious attention. The best of them, in their time, are probably those that follow.

An Introduction to the Study of Blake (1927, 1952, 1967) by Max Plowman is clear and engagingly enthusiastic, though it has few claims to originality. Middleton Murry's William Blake (1933, 1936, 1964), on the other hand, is vigorously original, as in his claim that Blake was simultaneously a profound 'Christian' and 'a great Communist'. Both works were much admired by a generation of Blake students. A more lastingly useful introduction to Blake appeared in Jacob Bronowski's William Blake 1757–1827: A Man without a Mask (1945; expanded in William Blake and Revolution, 1969) which applies deftly and convincingly a wide range of relevant and little-used information to show how Blake's contemporary economic and political background directed and thwarted his work. Mark Schorer's William Blake: The Politics of Vision (1946) surveys similar terrain, particularly the radical circle round Joseph Johnson, at considerably greater length.[24]

In his Piper and the Bard: A Study of William Blake (1959), Robert F. Gleckner deals with Blake's earlier poetry (to 1794), stressing the narrative point of view in the Songs in a way which has since become a critical commonplace. A work similarly restricted in scope is Hazard Adams's ambitious, long, and successful William Blake: A Reading of the Shorter Poems (1963), including an annotated list, poem by poem, of criticism of Blake's lyrics.[25] Harold Bloom, a follower of Frye, analyses Blake's more difficult poems in a sophisticated, allusive way which many readers find rewarding, in his Visionary Company (1961), pp. 1–119, Blake's Apocalypse (1963), and the notes to the Erdman edition of Blake's Poetry and Prose (1965), pp. 807–89.

A subject which is deservedly receiving increasing attention was initiated in an extensive way in Jean Hagstrum, William Blake, Poet and Painter: An Introduction to the Illuminated Verse (1964); future studies of the central subject of the relationship of text and design in Blake's work are likely to begin where Hagstrum's Introduction leaves off. A yet more successful specialized work is Alicia Ostriker's Vision and Verse in William Blake (1965), which illuminates Blake's poetic techniques with great sensitivity. Finally, one of the most successful general studies of recent years is Morton Paley, Energy and The Imagination: A Study of the Development of Blake's Thought (1970), which displays convincingly the reciprocal decline in importance of Orc (Energy) and rise of Los (Imagination) in Blake's myth.[26] With studies such as these, Blake scholarship has achieved a consensus from which future studies can proceed with confidence.

Collections of essays

The tide of interest in Blake has fostered the creation of journals devoted to him, to volumes reprinting criticism, and to volumes of original essays. Chief among the journals are *Blake to Whitman* (Tokyo, 1931–2), the *Blake Newsletter* (ed. M. D. Paley, 1967 ff.), and *Blake Studies* (ed. R. and K. Easson, 1968 ff.), of which the second best rewards consultation. Reprints of essays (occasionally revised) may be found in Sir Geoffrey Keynes, *Blake Studies* (1949, expanded 1971); *Discussions of William Blake*, ed. J. E. Grant (1961); *Twentieth Century Interpretations of Songs of Innocence and of Experience*, ed. M. D. Paley (1969); *The Tyger*, ed. W. Weathers (1969); *Songs of Innocence and Experience* [*sic*], ed. M. Bottrall (1970); *Critics on Blake*, ed. J. O'Neill (1970), and *The Visionary Hand: Essays for the Study of William Blake's Art and Aesthetics*, ed. R. N. Essick (1973); only the first and last have any significant independent merit. Collections of original essays were printed in *The Divine Vision: Studies in the Poetry and Art of William Blake*, ed. V. de S. Pinto (1957), in *William Blake: Essays for S. Foster Damon*, ed. A. H. Rosenfeld (1969), in *Blake's Visionary Forms Dramatic*, ed. D. V. Erdman and J. E. Grant (1970), in *Blake's Sublime Allegory: Essays on the Four Zoas, Milton, Jerusalem*, ed. S. Curran and J. A. Wittreich, Jr (1973), and in *William Blake: Essays in Honour of Sir Geoffrey Keynes*, ed. M. D. Paley and M. Phillips (1973), which contain important essays by Frye (Pinto), Butlin (Rosenfeld), Miner (Rosenfeld), Paley (Curran and Wittreich), and Bindman (Paley and Phillips). Such anthologies have the advantage occasionally of collecting in one place the most recent advances of scholarship or of critical fashion.

NOTES

1 Such reputation as Blake had was almost exclusively British; a few German readers may have seen Crabb Robinson's 1811 article in *Vaterländisches Museum* (No. 36), but no known comments in North America appeared until after his death.

2 See A. T. Story, *The Life of John Linnell* (2 vols, 1892), A. H. Palmer, *The Life and Letters of Samuel Palmer* (1892), [S. Calvert], *A Memoir of Edward Calvert Artist* (1893), and *The Richmond Papers*, ed. A. M. W. Stirling (1926).

3 A. Symons, *William Blake* (1907), reprinting Malkin, Robinson, Smith, Cunningham, and five others, with an original and useful biography by Symons; J. A. Wittreich, Jr, ed., *Nineteenth Century Accounts of William Blake* (1970), reprinting Malkin, Robinson, Smith, Cunningham, Tatham, and Yeats in facsimile; G. E. Bentley, Jr, *Blake Records* (1969).

4 For other aspects of major importance in Gilchrist's book concerning reprints of Blake's writings and catalogues of his works, see pp. 14–16.

5 It is credulously adopted by J. G. Davies in *The Theology of William Blake* (1948), and forms the basis for the wonderful flights of Elizabeth O'Higgins in the *Dublin Magazine* (1950–2, 1956).

6 Some minor advances in Blake biography may be found in Herbert Jenkins, *William Blake* (1925) (a collection of his previously published essays), Thomas Wright, *Life of William Blake* (2 vols, 1929) (an eccentric, unreliable work embodying much new information with great ingenuity), Morchard Bishop [Oliver Stoner], *Blake's Hayley* (1951) (incorporating a great deal of new information about Hayley), and H. M. Margoliouth, *William Blake* (1951) (especially enterprising about Blake's early life).

7 For example, Louis W. Crompton, 'Blake's Nineteenth-Century Critics' (University of Chicago, thesis, 1954), D. Dorfman, *Blake in the Nineteenth Century* (1969), and S. R. Hoover, 'William Blake in the Wilderness: A Closer Look at his Reputation—1827–1863' in M. D. Paley and M. Phillips, eds, *William Blake: Essays in Honour of Sir Geoffrey Keynes* (1973), pp. 310–48.

8 Omitting, however, most of the separate plates designed by others but engraved by Blake.

9 The Butts Collection, including perhaps half the finished separate drawings Blake made, was sold at Sotheby's on 26 March 1852, at Foster & Son's on 9 June 1853 and 8 March 1854, at Sotheby's on 24 June 1903 and 19 December 1932; much of it was acquired by W. Graham Robertson, whose collection was separately catalogued (1952) and sold at Christie's on 22 July 1949.

10 C. H. C. Collins Baker, *Catalogue of William Blake's Drawings and Paintings in the Huntington Library* (1938; rev. R. R. Wark, 1957); M. Butlin, *William Blake (1757–1827): A Catalogue of the Works of William Blake in the Tate Gallery* (1957, rev. ed. 1971); *William Blake: Catalogue of the Collection in the Fitzwilliam Museum, Cambridge*, ed. D. Bindman (1970); G. E. Bentley, Jr, *The Blake Collection of Mrs. Landon K. Thorne* (1971—the Thorne Collection has now gone to the Morgan Library).

11 L. Binyon, *Catalogue of Drawings by British Artists and Artists of Foreign Origin Working in Great Britain, Preserved in the Department of Prints and Drawings in the British Museum* (1898), vol. I, pp. 124–31; [P. Morgan,] 'A Handlist of Works by William Blake in the Department of Prints & Drawings of The British Museum', ed. G. E. Bentley, Jr, *Blake Newsletter*, vol. v (1972), pp. 223–58; [M. Schild,] *The Rosenwald Collection: A Catalogue of Illustrated Books and Manuscripts, . . . The Gift of Lessing J. Rosenwald to the Library of*

Congress [ed. F. R. Goff] (1954), pp. 186–96. *N.B.* there is no similar catalogue of the drawings in the Rosenwald Collection given to the National Gallery.

12 Including all the sketches, watercolours, proofs, and finished plates.

13 Blake's Milton designs have been well served in a number of useful essays, notably in M. R. Pointon, *Milton and English Art* (1970), pp. 135–66. Two recent books on Blake's art of striking negligibility are Kathleen Raine, *William Blake* (1970), with reproductions of unfortunate colour, and Ruthven Todd, *William Blake the Artist* (1971) with novel reproductions but a text mechanically derived from elsewhere.

14 The same strictures apply to the text in the E. J. Ellis edition of Blake's *Poetical Works* (2 vols, 1906).

15 Notably the Keynes edition of Blake's *Letters* (1968); the first collection of Blake's *Letters* was made by A. G. B. Russell in 1906.

16 G. E. Bentley, Jr, and M. K. Nurmi, in *A Blake Bibliography* (1964), attempted to bring the Keynes bibliography up to date chiefly in its coverage of Blake's commercial engravings and of Blake criticism and scholarship.

17 Part of 'The Edition of the Works of Wm. Blake' produced by Wm Muir.

18 A Blake Trust publication, edited by Geoffrey Keynes.

19 Part of *Works by William Blake* (1876).

20 Kathleen Raine, a devoted believer in Yeats (see p. 23), would doubtless prove an exception to this statement.

21 The work of many scholars before 1940, particularly Foster Damon, was informed by the opposite conclusion.

22 This subject is dealt with definitively by D. V. Erdman, 'Blake's early Swedenborgianism. A twentieth century legend', *Comparative Literature*, vol. v (1953), pp. 247–57.

23 A. L. Owen, *The Famous Druids* (1962), pp. 224–50, is the best work on the subject. Blake and the eighteenth-century mythologists are dealt with responsibly by E. B. Hungerford, *Shores of Darkness* (1941) and in Ruthven Todd, *Tracks in the Snow* (1947).

24 Schorer's book has consistently been highly valued in North America and largely ignored by other scholars.

25 Three short works which are particularly successful with Blake's early poetry are Stanley Gardner, *Infinity on the Anvil: A Critical Study of Blake's Poetry* (1954), his *Blake* (1968), and John Holloway, *Blake: The Lyric Poet* (1968); on the other hand, D. H. Gillham, *Blake's Contrary States* (1966) is pedestrian, and E. D. Hirsch, Jr, *Innocence and Experience: An Introduction to Blake* (1964), is often betrayed by biographical and bibliographical facts in trying to trace autobiographical elements in the *Songs*.

26 Other general works which deserve mention are Bernard Blackstone, *English Blake* (1949, 1966), particularly for its original but probably wrong section on the *Island in the Moon*, and John Beer, *Blake's Humanism* (1968) and his *Blake's Visionary Universe* (1969), which often relate Blake usefully to his literary background.

Note on the Text

The great majority of the references to Blake here are repeated, by permission, from *Blake Records* (Oxford, Clarendon Press, 1969), where they are organized by date.

PART I   BLAKE'S LIFE

B is still an object of interest exclusively to men of imaginative taste and psychological curiosity—

Crabb Robinson, 1 March 1852[1]

---

1. General comments

1826, 1827, 1855

(a) Crabb Robinson introduced Blake to Dorothy Wordsworth in a letter of 19 February 1826:

I gave your brother some poems in MS by him[2] and they interested him—As well they might, for there is an affinity between them As there is between the regulated imagination of a wise poet And the incoherent dreams of a poet—Blake is an engraver by trade—a painter and a poet also whose works have been the subject of derision to men in general, but he has a few admirers and some of eminence have eulogised his designs—he has lived in obscurity & poverty, to which the constant hallucinations in which he lives have doomed him—I do not mean to give you a detailed account of him—A few words will serve to inform you of what class he is. He is not so much a disciple of Jacob Bohmen & Swedenborg as a fellow Visionary—He lives as they did in a world of his own. Enjoying constant intercourse with the world of spirits—He receives visits from Shakespeare Milton Dante Voltaire &c &c &c And has given me repeatedly their very words in their conversations— His paintings are copies of what he sees in his Visions—his books—(& his MSS. are immense in quantity) are dictations from the Spirits—he told me yesterday that when he writes—it is for the Spirits only—he sees the words fly about the room the moment he has put them on paper And his book is then published—A man so favoured of course has sources of wisdom & truth peculiar to himself—I will not pretend to

---

[1] *Blake Records* (1969), p. 549.
[2] These are probably poems by Blake copied out by Robinson.

give you an account of his religious & philosophical opinions—They are a strange compound of Christianity Spinosism & Platonism—[1] . . . tho' in great poverty, he is so perfect a gentleman with such genuine dignity & independence—Scorning presents & of such native delicacy in words &c &c &c that I have not scrupled promising introducing him & M^r W: together—[2]

Years later Robinson wrote in his Reminiscences:

Wordsworth said after reading a number [of] . . . Songs of Innocence & Experience—'Shewing the two opposite states of the Human Soul' [—] [']There is no doubt this poor man was mad, but there is something in the madness of this man which interests me more than the Sanity of Lord Byron & Walter Scott![']—The German painter *Gotzenberger* . . . said . . . 'I saw in England many men of talents, but only three men of Genius Coleridge, Flaxman & Blake—And of these, Blake was the greatest[.']—[3]

Robinson summarized his position in his diary account of his first meeting with Blake on 10 December 1825:

I feel great admiration & respect for him[;] he is certainly a most amiable man. A good creature[.] And of his poetical & pictorial genius there is no doubt I believe in the minds of judges—Wordsworth & Lamb like his poems & the Aders his paintings[.]

(b) When John Linnell applied to the Royal Academy for a pension for Catherine Blake just after Blake's death, on 14 August 1827, he probably took with him his memorandum of

'The Case of Mrs. Blake Widow of Wm. Blake
Historical Painter & Engraver'

—setting forth, W.B. as man of first rate talent in the art of design, &c —states his more popular works,—*Blair's G[rave]. Young N[ight].* Thoughts, the *Cant[erbury]. P[ilgrims].;—Book of Job—.* He always lived a temperate life, beloved by his friends,—in perfect harmony with his wife, never had but small prices for his works, & so though he lived

---

[1] In his diary for 10 December 1825 Robinson wrote: 'on my asking in what light he viewed the great question concerning the Divinity of Jesus Christ he said—["]*He is the only God*["]—But then he added—["]And so am I and so are you["] '.

[2] Blake and Wordsworth never met.

[3] *Blake Records* (1969), p. 536.

with the utmost economy, he could not save anything— & has left nothing for his widow but a few Plates & drawings which if sold would produce nothing adequate to defray even present expenses.

(c) And finally Blake's young disciple Samuel Palmer wrote to Alexander Gilchrist on 23 August 1855:

I regret that the lapse of time has made it difficult to recal many interesting particulars respecting Mr. Blake, of whom I can give you no connected account; nothing more, in fact, than the fragments of memory; but the general impression of what is great remains with us, although its details may be confused; and Blake, once known, could never be forgotten.

His knowledge was various and extensive, and his conversation so nervous and brilliant, that, if recorded at the time, it would now have thrown much light upon his character, and in no way lessened him in the estimation of those who know him only by his works.

In him you saw at once the Maker, the Inventor; one of the few in any age: a fitting companion for Dante. He was energy itself, and shed around him a kindling influence; an atmosphere of life, full of the ideal. To walk with him in the country was to perceive the soul of beauty through the forms of matter; and the high gloomy buildings between which, from his study window, a glimpse was caught of the Thames and the Surrey shore, assumed a kind of grandeur from the man dwelling near them. Those may laugh at this who never knew such an one as Blake; but of him it is the simple truth.

He was a man without a mask; his aim single, his path straightforwards, and his wants few; so he was free, noble, and happy.

His voice and manner were quiet, yet all awake with intellect. Above the tricks of littleness, or the least taint of affectation, with a natural dignity which few would have dared to affront, he was gentle and affectionate, loving to be with little children, and to talk about them. 'That is heaven,' he said to a friend, leading him to the window, and pointing to a group of them at play.

Declining, like Socrates, whom in many respects he resembled, the common objects of ambition, and pitying the scuffle to obtain them, he though that no one could be truly great who had not humbled himself 'even as a little child.' This was a subject he loved to dwell upon, and to illustrate.

His eye was the finest I ever saw: brilliant, but not roving, clear and intent, yet susceptible; it flashed with genius, or melted in tenderness. It could also be terrible. Cunning and falsehood quailed under it, but it was never busy with them. It pierced them, and turned away. Nor was the mouth less expressive; the lips flexible and quivering with feeling. I can yet recal it when, on one occasion, dwelling upon the exquisite beauty of the parable of the Prodigal, he began to repeat a part of it; but at the words, 'When he was yet a great way off, his father saw him,' could go no further; his voice faltered, and he was in tears.

I can never forget the evening when Mr. Linnell took me to Blake's house, nor the quiet hours passed with him in the examination of antique gems, choice pictures, and Italian prints of the sixteenth century. Those who may have read some strange passages in his *Catalogue*, written in irritation, and probably in haste, will be surprised to hear, that in conversation he was anything but sectarian or exclusive, finding sources of delight throughout the whole range of art; while, as a critic, he was judicious and discriminating.

No man more admired Albert Dürer; yet, after looking over a number of his designs, he would become a little angry with some of the draperies, as not governed by the forms of the limbs, nor assisting to express their action; contrasting them in this respect with the draped antique, in which it was hard to tell whether he was more delighted with the general design, or with the exquisite finish and the depth of the chiselling; in works of the highest class, no mere adjuncts, but the last development of the design itself.

He united freedom of judgment with reverence for all that is great. He did not look out for the works of the purest ages, but for the purest works of every age and country—Athens or Rhodes, Tuscany or Britain; but no authority or popular consent could influence him against his deliberate judgment. Thus he thought with Fuseli and Flaxman that the Elgin Theseus, however full of antique savour, could not, as ideal form, rank with the very finest relics of antiquity. Nor, on the other hand, did the universal neglect of Fuseli in any degree lessen his admiration of his best works.

He fervently loved the early Christian art, and dwelt with peculiar affection on the memory of Fra Angelico, often speaking of him as an inspired inventor and as a saint; but when he approached Michael Angelo, the Last Supper of Da Vinci, the Torso Belvidere, and some of the inventions preserved in the Antique Gems, all his powers were concentrated in admiration.

When looking at the heads of the apostles in the copy of the *Last Supper* at the Royal Academy, he remarked of all but Judas, 'Every one looks as if he had conquered the natural man.' He was equally ready to admire a contemporary and a rival. Fuseli's picture of *Satan building the Bridge over Chaos* he ranked with the grandest efforts of imaginative art, and said that we were two centuries behind the civilisation which would enable us to estimate his *Ægisthus.*

He was fond of the works of St. Theresa, and often quoted them with other writers on the interior life. Among his eccentricities will, no doubt, be numbered his preference for ecclesiastical governments. He used to ask how it was that we heard so much of priestcraft, and so little of soldiercraft and lawyercraft. The Bible, he said, was the book of liberty and Christianity the sole regenerator of nations. In politics a Platonist, he put no trust in demagogues. His ideal home was with Fra Angelico: a little later he might have been a reformer, but after the fashion of Savonarola.

He loved to speak of the years spent by Michael Angelo, without earthly reward, and solely for the love of God, in the building of St. Peter's, and of the wondrous architects of our cathedrals. In Westminster Abbey were his earliest and most sacred recollections. I asked him how he would like to paint on glass, for the great west window, his 'Sons of God shouting for Joy,' from his designs in the *Job.* He said, after a pause, 'I could do it!' kindling at the thought.

Centuries could not separate him in spirit from the artists who went about our land, pitching their tents by the morass or the forest side, to build those sanctuaries that now lie ruined amidst the fertility which they called into being.

His mind was large enough to contain, along with these things, stores of classic imagery. He delighted in Ovid, and, as a labour of love, had executed a finished picture from the *Metamorphoses,* after Giulio Romano. This design hung in his room, and, close by his engraving table, Albert Dürer's *Melancholy the Mother of Invention,* memorable as probably having been seen by Milton, and used in his *Penseroso.* There are living a few artists, then boys, who may remember the smile of welcome with which he used to rise from that table to receive them.

His poems were variously estimated. They tested rather severely the imaginative capacity of their readers. Flaxman said they were as grand as his designs, and Wordsworth delighted in his *Songs of Innocence.* To the multitude they were unintelligible. In many parts full of pastoral sweetness, and often flashing with noble thoughts or terrible imagery, we must regret that he should sometimes have suffered fancy to trespass within sacred precincts.

Thrown early among the authors who resorted to Johnson, the book-seller, he rebuked the profanity of Paine, and was no disciple of Priestley; but, too undisciplined and cast upon times and circumstances which yielded him neither guidance nor sympathy, he wanted that balance of the faculties which might have assisted him in matters extraneous to his profession. He saw everything through art, and, in matters beyond its range, exalted it from a witness into a judge.

He had great powers of argument, and on general subjects was a very patient and good-tempered disputant; but materialism was his abhor-rence: and if some unhappy man called in question the world of spirits, he would answer him 'according to his folly,' by putting forth his own views in their most extravagant and startling aspect. This might amuse those who were in the secret, but it left his opponent angry and bewil-dered.

Such was Blake, as I remember him. He was one of the few to be met with in our passage through life, who are not, in some way or other, 'double minded' and inconsistent with themselves; one of the very few who cannot be depressed by neglect, and to whose name rank and station could add no lustre. Moving apart, in a sphere above the attraction of worldly honours, he did not accept greatness, but confer it. He ennobled poverty, and, by his conversation and the influence of his genius, made two small rooms in Fountain Court more attractive than the threshold of princes.[1]

2. External events

1757-1812

Blake's father kept a modest stocking shop near Soho Square, and the poet lived most of his life (except for 1800–3) in the neighbourhood. William Blake, born on 28 November 1757, was the third of seven children. The most important member of the family, so far as William was concerned, was his much younger brother Robert, who died at the

[1] A. Gilchrist, *Life of William Blake* (1863), vol. I, pp. 301–4.

age of nineteen in 1787 and who appeared to the poet regularly there-after in visions.

Blake was apprenticed to a careful antiquarian-engraver named James Basire in 1772, and on completion of his apprenticeship in 1779 he be-came a journeyman engraver, by which profession he lived for the rest of his life. For a brief time (1784–5) he kept a print shop, and he ex-hibited a few pictures, at the Royal Academy in 1780, 1784, 1785, 1799, 1800, 1808, at his brother's hosiery shop in 1809 (a one-man show), and at the Water Colour Society in 1812. In his profession he enjoyed a modest success, particularly during the decade 1790–1800, when he was first encouraged to design his own engravings for commercial works.

3. Politics

1804, 1805

During his early manhood his political sympathies were with the radi-cals, with Paine and Horne Tooke and Joseph Johnson. (a) His friend Samuel Greatheed wrote on 27 January 1804:

I knew our friend's eccentricity, and understood, that, during the crisis of the French Revolution, he had been one of its earnest partisans. . . .

However, his only active involvement in politics occurred when he was living (1800–3) in the seaside village of Felpham under the patronage of William Hayley. (b) His patron explained what happened in a letter of 3 August 1805:

The Fact simply was that a brutal quarrelsome soldier (a degraded sar-gent) intruded into the garden of Blake's Cottage, & refused to quit it— Blake who has courage, agility, & strength, seized the abusive Intruder, & pushed Him (over several paces of ground) to the door of *his Quarters*. The vindictive soldier, provoked to Frenzy, swore He would *have the artist hanged*, & actually engaged a comrade to swear also, in league with Himself, that Blake had uttered the most horrible seditious Expressions.

—our dear Rose made an Eloquent speech in the Cause of the poor artist entangled in the snare of these perjured Wretches; but it was *not the Eloquence* of *an advocate*, that saved the innocent man on his trial, & Heaven seemed to show, in a striking manner, that He was to *owe his security* to *different defenders*: for our beloved Barrister, who had caught his fatal Cold in the Evening of the preceding day, felt the Faculties of his admirable Head *desert him*, before *He concluded*; & failed to reply, (as He otherwise would have done,) to the art and malevolence of the opposite Counsel—yet *his client* was *safe*—for Providence had graciously raised Him a little host of honest & friendly rustic Witnesses, particularly one benevolent, clear-headed woman, (the wife of a millers servant) whose garden adjoined to Blakes, & who, by her shrewd Remarks, clearly proved *several impossibilities* in the *false accusation*.

In truth this diligent & quiet artist was cordially regarded by his rustic neighbours; & the citizens of Chichester (as I probably told you at the time) were loud in the honest exultation of their joy in his acquittal.

4. Visions

1761–1825

The feature of Blake's life which his contemporaries found most piquant was his visions. These appeared to him from his earliest years. (a) His wife remarked once,

'You know, dear, the first time you saw God was when You were four years old And he put his head to the window and set you ascreaming'.[1]

On another occasion, when he was eight or ten,

Sauntering along [on Peckham Rye, by Dulwich Hill], the boy looks up, and sees a tree filled with angels, bright angelic wings bespangling every bough like stars. Returned home he relates the incident, and only through

[1] *Blake Records* (1969), pp. 542–3, quoting Crabb Robinson's reminiscences.

his mother's intercession escapes a thrashing from his honest father, for telling a lie. Another time, one summer morn, he sees the haymakers at work, and amid them angelic figures walking.[1]

Once in Westminster Abbey, where he worked as an apprentice, he had another vision:

The aisles and galleries of the old building (or sanctuary) suddenly filled with a great procession of monks and priests, choristers and censer-bearers, and his entranced ear heard the chant of plain-song and chorale, while the vaulted roof trembled to the sound of organ music.[2]

Blake carefully distinguished these visions from ghosts, though of course his contemporaries did not.

'Did you ever see a ghost?' asked a friend. 'Never but once,' was the reply. And it befel thus. Standing one evening at his garden-door in Lambeth, and chancing to look up, he saw a horrible grim figure, 'scaly, speckled, very awful,' stalking downstairs towards him. More frightened than ever before or after, he took to his heels, and ran out of the house.[3]

(b) Thomas Phillips reported that Blake sat to him for his portrait in 1807:

in order to obtain the most unaffected attitude, and the most poetic expression, [he] engaged his sitter in a conversation concerning the sublime in art. 'We hear much,' said Phillips, 'of the grandeur of Michael Angelo; from the engravings, I should say he has been over-rated; he could not paint an angel so well as Raphael.' 'He has not been over-rated, Sir,' said Blake, 'and he could paint an angel better than Raphael.' 'Well, but' said the other, 'you never saw any of the paintings of Michael Angelo; and perhaps speak from the opinions of others; your friends may have deceived you.' 'I never saw any of the paintings of Michael Angelo,' replied Blake, 'but I speak from the opinion of a friend who could not be mistaken.' 'A valuable friend truly,' said Phillips, 'and

---

[1] A. Gilchrist, *Life of William Blake* (1863), vol. I, p. 7; see *Blake Records* (1969), p. 7. In his 'Life of Blake', Tatham wrote: 'Blake asserted from a Boy that he did see them [visions], even when a Child his mother beat him for running in & saying that he saw the Prophet Ezekiel under a Tree in the Fields' (*Blake Records* [1969], p. 519).

[2] A paraphrase of a lost letter by Blake given in [Oswald Crawfurd], 'William Blake: artist, poet, and mystic', *New Quarterly Magazine*, vol. II (1874), p. 475; see *Blake Records* (1969), p. 13.

[3] A. Gilchrist, *Life of William Blake* (1863), vol. I, p. 128; see *Blake Records* (1969), p. 54.

who may he be I pray?' 'The arch-angel Gabriel, Sir,' answered Blake.
'A good authority surely, but you know evil spirits love to assume the
looks of good ones; and this may have been done to mislead you.'
'Well now, Sir,' said Blake, 'this is really singular; such were my own
suspicions; but they were soon removed—I will tell you how. I was one
one day reading Young's Night Thoughts, and when I came to that
passage which asks "who can paint an angel," I closed the book and
cried, "Aye! who can paint an angel?" A voice in the room answered,
"Michael Angelo could." "And how do *you* know," I said, looking
round me, but I saw nothing save a greater light than usual. "I *know*,"
said the voice, "for I sat to him: I am the arch-angel Gabriel." "Oho!"
I answered, "you are, are you: I must have better assurance than that of
a wandering voice; you may be an evil spirit—there are such in the land."
"You shall have good assurance," said the voice, "can an evil spirit do
this?" I looked whence the voice came, and was then aware of a shining
shape, with bright wings, who diffused much light. As I looked, the
shape dilated more and more: he waved his hands; the roof of my study
opened; he ascended into heaven; he stood in the sun, and beckoning to
me, moved the universe. An angel of evil could not have *done that*—it
was the arch-angel Gabriel.' The painter marvelled much at this wild
story; but he caught from Blake's looks, as he related it, that rapt poetic
expression which has rendered his portrait one of the finest of the English
school.

(c) The best known accounts of Blake's visions concerned those he saw
about 1819–25 in the company of John Varley, who persuaded Blake to
draw what he saw.

Sometimes Blake had to wait for the Vision's appearance; sometimes,
it would come at call. At others, in the midst of his portrait, he would
suddenly leave off, and, in his ordinary quiet tones and with the same
matter-of-fact air another might say 'It rains,' would remark, 'I can't
go on,—it is gone! I must wait till it returns;' or, 'It has moved. The
mouth is gone;' or, 'he frowns; he is displeased with my portrait
of him.'[1]

The most sensational was that of The Ghost of a Flea, which

is covered with coat of armour, similar to the case of a flea, and is represented slowly pacing in the night, with a thorn attached to his right

[1] A. Gilchrist, *Life of William Blake* (1863), vol. I, pp. 251–2; see *Blake Records* (1969),
p. 260.

hand, and a cup in the other, as if ready to puncture the first person whose blood he might fancy, like Satan prowling about to seek whom he could devour. Blake said of the flea, that were that lively little fellow the size of an elephant, he was quite sure, from the calculations he had made of his wonderful strength, that he could bound from Dover to Calais in one leap.[1]

Blake made no effort to conceal his experiences, nor did he broadcast them. For instance,

At one of Mr. Ader's parties—at which Flaxman, Lawrence, and other leading artists were present—Blake was talking to a little group gathered round him, within hearing of a lady whose children had just come home from boarding school for the holidays. 'The other evening,' said Blake, in his usual quiet way, 'taking a walk, I came to a meadow, and at the farther corner of it I saw a fold of lambs. Coming nearer, the ground blushed with flowers; and the wattled cote and its woolly tenants were of an exquisite pastoral beauty. But I looked again, and it proved to be no living flock, but beautiful sculpture.' The lady, thinking this a capital holiday-show for her children, eagerly interposed, 'I beg pardon, Mr. Blake, but *may* I ask *where* you saw this?' '*Here*, madam,' answered Blake, touching his forehead.[2]

As Blake wrote in one of his last letters, on 12 April 1827, 'in The Real Man The Imagination which Liveth for Ever . . . I am stronger & stronger as this Foolish Body decays'.

---

[1] J. T. Smith, *Nollekens and his Times* (1828); see *Blake Records* (1969), p. 467.
[2] A. Gilchrist, *Life of William Blake* (1863), vol. I, pp. 319–20; see *Blake Records* (1969), p. 301.

5. Madness

1841, 1805, 1830

(a) Such visions of course persuaded most of Blake's contemporaries that he was mad, as in this fictitious dialogue in which Astrophel argues with Evelyn that opium doesn't make a poet: Look at Shakespeare;

Look on the wild pencillings of Blake . . .

Ev. A most unhappy comparison, Astrophel. The difference between Shakspere and Blake is *antipodean*. Blake was a visionary, and thought his fancies real—he was mad. Shakspere was a philosopher, and knew all his fancy was but imagination, however real might be the facts he wrought from.[1]

(b) When Lady Hesketh learned that Hayley was still patronizing Blake after the trial for sedition, she wrote in horror to Johnny Johnson on 31 July 1805:

My hair stands on end to think that Hayley & Blake are as dear friends as ever! He talks of him as if he was an Angel! How can you Johnny suffer our poor friend to be thus impos'd upon?—I don't doubt he will poison him in his Turret or set fire to all his papers, & poor Hayley will consume in his own Fires.

Such views were also held by those better qualified to judge. (c) On 27 April 1830 Caroline Bowles wrote to Robert Southey:

I am longing to see some of Blake's engravings from his own extraordinary designs, of which I first heard from yourself. . . . Mad though he might be, he was gifted and good, and a most happy being. I should have delighted in him.

(d) Southey, who had met Blake, replied on 8 May:

Much as he is to be admired, he was at that time so evidently insane, that the predominant feeling in conversing with him, or even looking

1 W. C. Dendy, *The Philosophy of Mystery* (1841), p. 90; see *Blake Records* (1969), p. 489, n. 1.

40

at him, could only be sorrow and compassion. His wife partook of his insanity in the same way (but more happily) as Taylor the pagan's wife caught her husband's paganism. And there are always crazy people enough in the world to feed and foster such craziness as his. . . .

The exhibition of his pictures, which I saw at his brother's house near Golden-square, produced a like melancholy impression. The colouring of all was as if it had consisted merely of black and red ink in all inter-mixture. Some of the designs were hideous, especially those which he considered as most supernatural in their conception and likenesses. In others you perceived that nothing but madness had prevented him from being the sublimest painter of this or any other country. You could not have delighted in him—his madness was too evident, too fearful. It gave his eyes an expression such as you would expect to see in one who was possessed.

Whoever has had what is sometimes called the vapours, and seen faces and figures pass before his closed eyes when he is lying sleepless in bed, can very well understand how Blake saw what he painted. I am sure I can, from this experience; and from like experience can tell how sounds are heard which have had no existence but in the brain that produced them.

(e) However, those who knew Blake well stoutly defended his sanity.

James Ward [the painter], who had often met Blake in society and talked with him, would never hear him called mad. . . . 'I saw nothing but sanity,' declares . . . Mr. Calvert . . . 'saw nothing mad in his conduct, actions or character.' . . . Mr. Finch—summed up his recollections thus: 'He was not mad, but perverse and wilful . . .' 'There was nothing mad about him,' emphatically exclaimed to me Mr. Cornelius Varley.[1]

(f) Seymour Kirkup wrote:

I was much with him from 1810 to 1816, when I came abroad, and have remained in Italy ever since. . . . His high qualities I did not prize at that time; besides, I thought him mad. I do not think so now.[2]

---

[1] A. Gilchrist, *Life of William Blake* (1863), vol. I, pp. 323, 324; see *Blake Records* (1969), p. 268.

[2] *Blake Records* (1969), p. 221.

6. 'He is always in Paradise'

1825–60

Blake's manner was certainly not that of a madman. (a) In his diary for 10 December 1825 Crabb Robinson wrote:

The tone & manner are incommunicable[.] There is a natural sweetness & gentility ab! Blake which are delightful And when he is not referring to his Visions he talks sensibly & acutely[.]

(b) Blake's young friend Samuel Palmer wrote:

If asked . . . whether I ever knew among the intellectual a happy man, Blake would be the only one who would immediately occur to me.[1]

(c) A woman whom Thomas Woolner met at a party about 1860 told him this story of herself:

the Lady was thought very beautiful when a child, and was taken to an evening party and there presented to Blake, he looked at her very kindly for a long while without speaking, and then stroking her head and long ringlets said 'May God make this world to you, my child, as beautiful as it has been to me'. She thought it strange at the time, she said, that such a poor old man, dressed in such shabby clothes, could imagine the world had ever been so beautiful to him as it must be to her, nursed in all the elegancies and luxury of wealth; but in after years she understood well enough what he meant and treasured the few words he had spoken to her.[2]

(d) And Seymour Kirkup wrote many years later:

His excellent old wife was a sincere believer in all his visions. She told me seriously one day, 'I have very little of Mr. Blake's company; he is always in Paradise.'[3]

---

[1] A. Gilchrist, *Life of William Blake* (1863), vol. I, p. 309; see *Blake Records* (1969), p. 312, n. 2.

[2] *Blake Records* (1969), pp. 274–5.

[3] *Blake Records* (1969), p. 221.

His death was consistent with his life. (e) He told Crabb Robinson on 7 December 1826: 'I cannot consider death as any thing but a removing from one room to another'. (f) His last commission was for colouring his print of 'The Ancient of Days' for his devoted disciple Frederick Tatham, who wrote:

After he had worked upon it he exclaimed 'There I have done all I can[;] it is the best I have ever finished[.] I hope M.r Tatham will like it.['] He threw it suddenly down & said [']Kate you have been a good Wife, I will draw your portrait.['] She sat near his Bed & he made a Drawing, which though not a likeness is finely touched & expressed. He then threw that down, after having drawn for an hour & began to sing Hallelujahs & songs of joy & Triumph which M.rs Blake described as being truly sublime in music & in Verse. He sang loudly & with true extatic energy and seemed too happy that he had finished his course, that he had run his race, & that he was shortly to arrive at the Goal, to receive the prize of his high & eternal calling. . . . His bursts of gladness made the room peal again. The Walls rang & resounded with the beatific Symphony. It was a prelude to the Hymns of Saints. It was an overture to the Choir of Heaven. It was a chaunt for the response of Angels.[1]

[1] *Blake Records* (1969), pp. 527–8.

PART II   WRITINGS

7. Reviews of Malkin's account of Blake (1806)

1806, 1807

Blake was scarcely known to his contemporaries as an author, and, among those who did so know him, it was largely poets and his friends who relished his poetry. His first poems were printed in 1783, but no comment on them, public or private, is known until B. H. Malkin reprinted, in his *Father's Memoirs of his Child* (1806), Blake's 'How Sweet I Roamed' and 'I Love the Jocund Dance' from *Poetical Sketches* (1783), 'Laughing Song', 'Holy Thursday', and 'The Divine Image' from *Songs of Innocence* (1789), and 'The Tyger' from *Songs of Experience* (1794). Most of the reviewers of Malkin's book remarked impatiently upon the poetry which he had given. (a) For example, the *Literary Journal* for 1806 said:

we cannot extend our approbation of the irrelevant panegyric upon Mr. William Blake, painter and engraver. . . .
To relieve our readers with a lighter subject, with a touch, indeed, of the ridiculous—let us refer to Mr. William Blake. With the professional occupations of painting and engraving, in which this gentleman is engaged, we have nothing to do; except, indeed, to praise his design prefixed to this volume. The portrait of the child is very interesting.—[1]
But what can Mr. Malkin mean by introducing his friend to us as a poet? He allows that Mr. Blake's attempts are 'unfinished and irregular' —and he asserts him to have ventured on the 'ancient simplicity'— *illa priorum simplicitas*—but with due submission to the judgment of our readers, should we not say that Mr. Blake has successfully heightened the 'modern nonsense?' We conclude our critique with an extract:

[1] The frontispiece 'portrait' is by R. M. Paye; only the design surrounding it is by Blake.

44

LAUGHING SONG....[1]

(b) The second review of Malkin to mention Blake, in the *British Critic* for September 1806, extends the same conclusions. It said that Malkin's book

is one of the most idle and superfluous works that we have ever seen. . . .

In a very long and elaborate address to a valuable friend, by way of dedication, another supposed prodigy is celebrated, the designer of the frontispiece to the book. He is celebrated both as an artist and as a poet; but so little judgment is shown, in our opinion, with regard to the proofs of these talents, that we much doubt whether the encomium will be at all useful to the person praised. As an artist, he seems to be one of those who mistake extravagance for genius; as is testified even by his angel in the frontispiece, though the kneeling figure is elegant, and that of the child is passable. As a poet, he seems chiefly inspired by that,
>   —Nurse of the didactic muse,
>   Divine Nonsensia.—
>   *Loves of the Triangles.*[2]

(c) The account in the *Monthly Review* for October 1806 was marginally more charitable:

In the long dedication to Mr. Johnes of Hafod, a biographical notice is inserted of Mr. William Blake the artist, with some selections from his poems, which are highly extolled: but if Watts seldom rose above the level of a mere versifier, in what class must we place Mr. Blake, who is certainly very inferior to Dr. Watts?[3]

(d) The *Monthly Magazine* for 25 January 1807 agreed laconically:

The poetry of Mr. Blake, inserted in the dedication, does not rise above mediocrity; as an artist he appears to more advantage.[4]

(e) The most generous account was that in the *Annual Review* for 1807, which did not

[1] Anon., 'Art. II. *A Father's Memoirs of his Child.* By Benjamin Heath Malkin . . .', *Literary Journal*, 2nd S., vol. II (July 1806), pp. 28, 34–5; see *Blake Records* (1969), p. 622.

[2] Anon., 'Art. 40. *A Father's Memoirs of his Child. By Benjamin Heath Malkin, Esq., M.A., F.A.S.* Royal 8vo. 172 pp. 10s. 6d. Longman and Co. 1806', *British Critic*, vol. XXVIII (September 1806), p. 339; see *Blake Records* (1969), p. 181. [John Hookham Frere,] 'The Loves of the Triangles', appeared in the *Antijacobin*, vol. III (16 April 1798), p. 170.

[3] [Christopher Lake Moody,] 'Art. 37. *A Father's Memoirs* . . .', *Monthly Review*, n.s., vol. LI (October 1806), p. 217; see *Blake Records* (1969), p. 181.

[4] Anon., 'Half-yearly retrospect of domestic literature', *Monthly Magazine*, supplementary number, vol. XXII (25 January 1807), p. 633; see *Blake Records* (1969), p. 182.

however entirely approve the manner in which the author has executed his task. In the first place, the dedication occupies nearly a third of the whole volume, and includes the life and poems of Mr. Blake the artist. What connection this has with the main object of the work, it is difficult to conjecture, unless indeed it is introduced, because Mr. Blake once approved [on pp. 33-4 of Malkin's book] the drawings of Master Malkin. The poems are certainly not devoid of merit, one specimen we shall give our readers.

'SONG.' ['I Love the Jocund Dance', see p. 154 below][1]

8. General comments

1807–38

Unfortunately for Blake, all this pejorative criticism was very public, while the better-judged praise of his contemporaries was normally private. (a) For example, George Cumberland wrote to Blake on 18 December 1808:

A gentleman of my acquaintance to whom I was shewing your incomparable etchings last night, was so charmed with them, that he requested me to get him a compleat Set of all you have published in the way of *Books* coloured as mine are;[2]—at the same time he wishes to know what will be the price of as many as you can spare him, if all are not to be had, being willing to wait your own time in order to have them as those of mine are.

(b) To this comprehensive order Blake replied discouragingly on 19 December:

I am very much obliged by your kind ardour in my cause & should immediately Engage in reviewing my former pursuits of printing if I

---

1 Anon., 'Art XIV. *A Father's Memoirs of his Child . . .*', *Annual Review . . .* for 1806, vol. v (1807), pp. 379–81; see *Blake Records* (1969), p. 623.

2 Cumberland owned *Thel* (A), *Songs* (F), *America* (F), *Visions* (B), *Song of Los* (D), *For Children* (C), *Poetical Sketches* (D), *Descriptive Catalogue*, and *Europe* (D).

had not now so long been turned out of the old channel into a new one that it is impossible for me to return to it without destroying my present course[.] New Vanities or rather new pleasures occupy my thoughts[.] New profits seem to arise before me so tempting that I have already involved myself in engagements that preclude all possibility of promising any thing.

(c) When Wordsworth read Malkin's book in the spring of 1807, he was sufficiently impressed by Blake's poems to have 'I Love the Jocund Dance', 'Laughing Song', 'Holy Thursday', and 'The Tyger' copied out in a commonplace book.[1] (d) Crabb Robinson reported in his diary for 24 May 1812 a walk across the fields to Hampstead Heath with Wordsworth:

[Wordsworth said] that there is insanity in Lord B[yron]'s family and that he believes Lord By to be somewhat cracked—I read W. some of Blake's poems[;] he was pleased with Some of them and consid^d B[lake] as hav^g the elements of poetry—a thousand times more than either Byron or Scott.

Next winter, on 12 January 1813, Crabb Robinson reported that he returned home from Coleridge's lecture:

Mrs Kenny[,] Barnes & Barron Field there—The usual gossiping chat— F & B. both interested by Blake's poems of whom they knew nothing before[.]

Robinson's last report of a general response to Blake's poetry is in his diary account for 20 May 1838:

My breakfast party went off very well indeed as far as talk was concerned—I had with me *Landor, Milnes*, & Serj^t *Talfourd*[.] A great deal of rattling on the part of W.S.L.: He maint^d Blake to be the greatest of poets—That Milnes is the greatest poet now living in England and that Scotts Marmion is superior to all Wordsworth & Byron—and the description of the battles better than anything in Homer!!! but Blake furnished the chief matter for talk.[2]

(e) On another occasion,

At an old bookseller's in Bristol he [Landor] picked up some of the writings of Blake, and was strangely fascinated by them. He was

---

[1] *Blake Records* (1969), p. 430.
[2] *Blake Records* (1969), p. 229, n. 3.

anxious to have collected as many more as he could, and enlisted me [John Forster] in the service; but he as much wanted patience for it as I wanted time, and between us it came to nothing. He protested that Blake had been Wordsworth's prototype, and wished they could have divided his madness between them; for that some accession of it in the one case, and something of a diminution of it in the other, would very greatly have improved both.[1]

9. *Poetical Sketches* (1783)

1828, 1784

(a) Blake's earliest poetry was evidently circulated, not as printed books or as manuscripts, but as songs. According to J. T. Smith, about 1784 at the house of A. S. Mathew.

I have often heard him [Blake] read and sing several of his poems. He was listened to by the company with profound silence, and allowed by most of the visitors to possess original and extraordinary merit.[2]

This indeed was the occasion of the printing of Blake's first work, for, as Smith, explained elsewhere, Mrs Mathew

was so extremely zealous in promoting the celebrity of Blake, that upon hearing him read some of his early efforts in poetry, she thought so well of them, as to request the Rev. Henry [i.e., A. S.] Mathew, her husband, to join Mr. Flaxman in his truly kind offer of defraying the expense of printing them; in which he not only acquiesced, but, with his usual urbanity, wrote the following advertisement, which precedes the poems.

The following sketches were the production of an untutored youth, commenced in his twelfth, and occasionally resumed by the author till his twentieth year;

---

[1] J. Forster, *Walter Savage Landor* (1869), vol. II, pp. 322–3; see *Blake Records* (1969), p. 229n.
[2] J. T. Smith, *A Book for a Rainy Day* (1845), p. 81; see *Blake Records* (1969), p. 26.

since which time, his talents having been wholly directed to the attainment of excellence in his profession, he has been deprived of the leisure requisite to such a revisal of these sheets, as might have rendered them less unfit to meet the public eye.

Conscious of the irregularities and defects to be found in almost every page, his friends have still believed that they possessed a poetical originality, which merited some respite from oblivion. These, their opinions, remain, however, to be now reproved or confirmed by a less partial public.

The annexed Song is a specimen of the juvenile playfulness of Blake's muse, copied from page 10 of these Poems.*

SONG. ['How sweet I roam'd . . .']

But it happened, unfortunately, soon after this period, that in consequence of his unbending deportment, or what his adherents are pleased to call his manly firmness of opinion, which certainly was not at all times considered pleasing by every one, his visits were not so frequent.[1]

(b) The only known manuscript reference to the book is in a letter from John Flaxman to William Hayley of 26 April 1784:

I have left a *Pamphlet of Poems* with Mr Long who he will transmit to Eartham; they are the writings of a MR BLAKE you have heard me mention, his education will plead sufficient excuse to your Liberal mind for the defects of his work & there are few so able to distinguish & set a right value on the beauties as yourself, I have beforementioned that Mr Romney thinks his historical drawings rank with those of M^l Angelo; he is at present employed as an engraver, in which his encouragement is not extraordinary—Mr Hawkins a Cornish Gentleman has shewn his taste & liberality in ordering Blake to make several drawings for him, & is so convinced of his uncommon talents that he is now endeavouring to raise a subscription to send him to finish [his] studies in Rome[;] . . . his generosity is such he would bear the whole charge of Blakes travels—but he is only a younger brother, & can therefore only bear a large proportion of the expence[.]

This tactful attempt to raise a subscription failed, and Blake never left England.

* The whole copy of this little work, entitled 'Poetical Sketches, by W.B.' containing seventy pages, octavo, bearing the date of 1783, was given to Blake to sell to friends, or publish, as he might think proper [Smith's note].
[1] J. T. Smith, *Nollekens and his Times* (1828); see *Blake Records* (1969), pp. 456–7.

10. *The Book of Thel* (1789)

1839

One of the few contemporary accounts of Blake's first illuminated Prophecy, *The Book of Thel* (1789), was in Garth Wilkinson's letter of 17 July 1839:

I received the Designs, etc., of Blake's from Mr Clarke; comprising, I fancy, all those you saw. I almost wish I had not seen them. The designs are disorder rendered palpable and powerful, and give me strongly the impression of their being the work of a madman. Insanity seems stamped on every one of them; and their hideous forms and lurid hellish colouring, exhale a very unpleasant sphere into my mind; so much so, that I confess I should not like to have the things long in my house. . . . I felt puzzled what to say of the man who was compounded of such heterogeneous materials as to be able at one time to write the 'Songs of Innocence' and at another 'The Visions of the Daughters of Albion.' 'The Book of Thel' is, partly, an exception to the general badness or unintelligibility of his verse and designs. I *can* see some glimmer of meaning in it, and some warmth of religion and of goodness; but beginning to be obscured and lost under the infatuating phantasies which at length possessed its author. I should say sanity predominates in it, rather than that the work was a sane one. Some of the single lines are grand and expressive.[1]

[1] C. J. Wilkinson, *James John Garth Wilkinson* (1911), pp. 30–1.

11. *The French Revolution* (1791)

1827

The only known reference before the twentieth century to the unique copy of Blake's *French Revolution* is apparently the one in a letter of 10 October 1827 from Blake's enthusiastic young disciple Samuel Palmer, in which he says vainly:

I wish I could get that terrific poem on the French Revolution.

12. *Songs of Innocence and of Experience* (1789, 1794)

1811–63

(a) It was not only the poems in *Poetical Sketches* which Blake set to music, as J. T. Smith reported:

Much about this time [?1785], Blake wrote many other songs, to which he also composed tunes. These he would occasionally sing to his friends; and though, according to his confession, he was entirely unacquainted with the science of music, his ear was so good, that his tunes were sometimes most singularly beautiful, and were noted down by musical professors.[1]

He evidently did not want a commercial publisher for his songs, but preferred to combine his two arts of poetry and design, if he could. His contemporary, J. T. Smith, wrote:

[1] J. T. Smith, *Nollekens and his Times* (1828); see *Blake Records* (1969), p. 457.

Blake, after deeply perplexing himself as to the mode of accomplishing the publication of his illustrated songs, without their being subject to the expense of letter-press, his brother Robert stood before him in one of his visionary imaginations, and so decidedly directed him in the way in which he ought to proceed, that he immediately followed his advice, by writing his poetry, and drawing his marginal subjects of embellishments in outline upon the copper-plate with an impervious liquid,[1] and then eating the plain parts or lights away with aquafortis considerably below them, so that the outlines were left as a stereotype. The plates in this state were then printed in any tint that he wished, to enable him or Mrs. Blake to colour the marginal figures up by hand in imitation of drawings.[2]

Probably the first work he published in his new method of Illuminated Printing was his *Songs of Innocence* (1789), which were later complemented by his *Songs of Experience* (1794). These too were largely ignored, and those of Blake's contemporaries who noticed them were often most struck by the designs rather than by the poetry. J. T. Smith, for example, wrote:

As to Blake's system of colouring, which I have not hitherto noticed, it was in many instances most beautifully prismatic. In this branch of the art he often acknowledged Apelles to have been his tutor, who was, he said, so much pleased with his style, that once when he appeared before him, among many of his observations, he delivered the following:—'You certainly possess my system of colouring; and I now wish

---

1 In his copy of Smith's book, Blake's friend John Linnell wrote:

The liquid mentioned by Mr Smith with which he says Blake used to Draw his subjects in outline on his copper plates was nothing more I believe than the usual stopping as it is called used by engravers made chiefly of pitch and diluted with Terps. The most extraordinary facility seems to have been attained by Blake in writing backwards & that with a brush dipped in a glutinous liquid for the writing is in many instances highly ornamental & varied in character as may be seen in his Songs of Innocence and . . . Jerusalem[.]

George Cumberland wrote that '*Blake* . . . alone excels in that art' of writing backwards ('Hints on various modes of printing from autographs', *Journal of Natural Philosophy*, vol. XXVIII[January 1811]; see *Blake Records* [1969], p. 212n).

2 J. T. Smith, *Nollekens and his Times* (1828); see *Blake Records* (1969), p. 460. A. Gilchrist, *Life of William Blake* (1863), vol. I, p. 69, adds: 'On his rising in the morning, Mrs. Blake went out with half a crown, all the money they had in the world, and of that laid out 1s. 10d. on the simple materials necessary for setting in practice the new revelation' (see *Blake Records* [1969], p. 32).

you to draw my person, which has hitherto been untruly delineated.'

I must own that until I was favoured by Mr. Upcott with a sight of some of Blake's works, several of which I had never seen, I was not so fully aware of his great depth of knowledge in colouring. Of these most interesting specimens of his art, which are now extremely rare, and rendered invaluable by his death, as it is impossible for any one to colour them with his mind, should the plates remain. Mr. Richard Thomson, another truly kind friend, has favoured me with the following descriptive lists.

SONGS OF EXPERIENCE. The author and printer, W. Blake. Small octavo; seventeen plates, including the title-page. Frontispiece, a winged infant mounted on the shoulders of a youth. On the title-page, two figures weeping over crosses [*i.e. corpses*].

Introduction. Four Stanzas on a cloud, with a night-sky behind, and beneath, a figure of Earth stretched on a mantle.

Earth's Answer. Five Stanzas; a serpent on the ground beneath.

The Clod and the Pebble. Three Stanzas; above, a headpiece of four sheep and two oxen; beneath, a duck and reptiles.

A Poison Tree. Four Stanzas. The tree stretches up the right side of the page; and beneath, a dead body killed by its influence.

The Fly. Five Stanzas. Beneath, a female figure with two children.

Holy Thursday. Four Stanzas. Head-piece a female figure discovering a dead child. On the right-hand margin a mother and two children lamenting the loss of an infant which lies beneath. Perhaps this is one of the most tasteful of the set.

The Chimney-Sweeper. Three Stanzas. Beneath, a figure of one walking in snow towards an open door.

London. Four Stanzas. Above, a child leading an old man through the street; on the right-hand, a figure warming itself at a fire. If in any instance Mr. Blake has copied himself, it is in the figure of the old man upon this plate, whose position appears to have been a favourite one with him.

The Tiger. Six Stanzas. On the right-hand margin, the trunk of a tree; and beneath, a tiger walking.

A Little Boy Lost. Six Stanzas. Ivy-leaves on the right-hand, and beneath, weeping figures before a fire, in which the verses state that the child had been burned by a Saint [*i.e. 'Priest'*].

The Human Abstract. Six Stanzas. The trunk of a tree on the right-hand margin, and beneath, an old man in white drawing a veil over his head.

The Angel. Four Stanzas. Head-piece, a female figure lying beneath a tree and pushing from her a winged boy.

My Pretty Rose Tree. Two Stanzas: Succeeded by a small vignette, of a figure weeping, and another lying reclined at the foot of a tree. Beneath, are two verses more, entitled, *Ah! Sun Flower*; and a single stanza, headed *The Lilly*.

Nurse's Song. Two Stanzas. Beneath, a girl with a youth and a female child at a door surrounded by vine-leaves.

A Little Girl Lost. Seven Stanzas; interspersed with birds and leaves, the trunk of a tree on the right-hand margin.

['] The whole of these plates are coloured in imitation of fresco. The poetry of these songs is wild, irregular, and highly mystical, but of no great degree of elegance or excellence, and their prevailing feature is a tone of complaint of the misery of mankind.[1]

(b) The earliest known comment on the *Songs* as Blake issued them (as opposed to Malkin's reprints) is in Crabb Robinson's diary for 10 March 1811:

—had a call from Turner & from W. Hazlitt. I shewed W. H. Blake's Young. He saw no merit in them as designs[.] I read him some of the Poems—He was much struck with them & expressed himself with his usual strength & singularity[.] [']They are beautiful,['] he said, ['] & only too deep for the vulgar[;] he has no sense of the ludicrous & as to a God a worm crawling in a privy is as worthy an obj! as any other, all being to him indifferent[.] So to Blake the Chimney Sweeper &c[.] He is ruined by vain struggles to get rid of what presses on his brain— he attempts impossibles—[.'] I added—['] he is like a man who lifts a burthen too heavy for him; he bears it an instant, it then falls on & crushes him[.']

W. H. preferred the Chimney Sweeper.

(c) Elsewhere Hazlitt commented:

Flaxman is . . . a profound mystic. This last is a character common to many other artists in our days—Loutherbourg, Cosway, Blake, [*William*] Sharp, Varley, &c.—who seem to relieve the literalness of their professional studies by voluntary excursions into the regions of the preternatural, pass their time between sleeping and waking, and whose ideas are like a stormy night, with the clouds driven rapidly across, and the blue sky and stars gleaming between![2]

(d) In 1818 Coleridge borrowed from Charles Augustus Tulk a copy (J) of the *Songs*, about which he wrote in a letter of 6 February 1818:

I have this morning been reading a strange publication—viz. Poems

[1] J. T. Smith, *Nollekens and his Times* (1828); see *Blake Records* (1969), pp. 468–70.
[2] [William Hazlitt], *The Plain Speaker* (1826), vol. I, pp. 223–4; see *Blake Records* (1969), p.332.

with very wild and interesting pictures, as the swathing, etched (I suppose) but it is said—printed and painted by the Author, W. Blake. He is a man of Genius—and I apprehend, a Swedenborgian—certainly, a mystic *emphatically*. You perhaps smile at *my* calling another Poet, a *Mystic*; but verily I am in the very mire of commonplace common-sense compared with Mr Blake, apo- or rather anacalyptic Poet, and Painter!

It was probably about a week later that he wrote to Tulk:

I return you Blake's poesies, metrical and graphic, with thanks. With this and the Book I have sent a rude scrawl as to the order in which I was pleased by the several poems. . . .

Blake's Poems.

I begin with my Dyspathies that I may forget them: and have uninterrupted space for Loves and Sympathies. Title page and the following emblem contain all the faults of the Drawings with as few beauties, as could be in the compositions of a man who was capable of such faults+such beauties.—The faults—despotism in symbols, amounting in the Title page to the μισητέον [odium], and occasionally, irregular unmodified Lines of the Inanimate, sometimes as the effect of rigidity and sometimes of exossation—like a wet tendon. So likewise the ambiguity of the Drapery. Is it a garment—or the body incised and scored out? The *Limpness* (= the effect of Vinegar on an egg) in the upper one of the two prostrate figures in the Title page, and the *eye*-likeness of the twig posteriorly on the second,—and the strait line down the waist-coat of pinky goldbeater's skin in the next drawing, with the I don't know whatness of the countenance, as if the mouth had been formed by the habit of placing the tongue, not contemptuously, but stupidly, between the lower gums and the lower jaw—these are the only *repulsive* faults I have noticed. The figure, however, of the second leaf (abstracted from the *expression* of the countenance given it by something about the mouth and the interspace from the lower lip to the chin) is such as only a Master learned in his art could produce.

N.B. I signifies, [']It gave me great pleasure.['] Ŧ [']still greater.['] —Ħ [']and greater still.['] ө, [']in the highest degree.['] o, [']in the lowest.[']*

Shepherd I. Spring I (last Stanza Ɪ). Holy Thursday Ħ[.] Laughing Song Ŧ[.] Nurses Song I[.] The Divine Image ө[.] The Lamb Ŧ[.]

[*] o means that I am perplexed—and have no opinion.

The little Black Boy ⊖: yea ⊖+o! Infant Joy Ħ. (N.b. for the 3 last lines I should wish—'When wilt thou smile,['] or—[']O smile, o smile! I'll sing the while—.['] For a Babe two days old does not, cannot *smile*— and innocence and the very truth of Nature must go together. Infancy is too holy a thing to be ornamented—.)] Echoing Green I (the figures Ɨ, and of the second leaf Ħ[)]. The Cradle Song I[.] The School boy Ħ. Night ⊖[.] On another's Sorrow I[.] A Dream?—The little Boy lost I (the drawing Ɨ)[.] The little boy found I. The Blossom o.— The Chimney Sweeper o. The V[oice] of the ancient Bard o.

Introduction I. Earth's Answer Ɨ. Infant Sorrow I[.] The Clod and the Pebble I[.] The Garden of Love Ɨ. The fly I[.] The Tyger Ɨ[.] A little Boy lost Ɨ[.] Holy Thursday I.—P. 13. O.[1] Nurse's Song O. The little girl lost. And found (the ornaments most exquisite! the poem, I)[.] Chimney Sweeper in the Snow o. To Tirzah—and The Poison Tree I and yet o. A little girl lost—o. (I would have had it omitted—not for the want of innocence in the poem, but for the too probable want of it in many readers[)]. London I[.] The sick Rose I[.] *The little Vagabond*—Tho' I cannot approve altogether of this last poem and have been inclined to think that the error, which is most *likely* to beset the Scholars of Em. Sw[edenborg] is that of utterly demerging the tremendous incompatibilities with an evil will that arise out of the essential Holiness of the abysmal Aseity in the Love of the eternal *Person*—and thus giving temptation to *weak* minds to sink this Love itself into *good nature*—yet still I disapprove the mood of mind in this wild poem so much less than I do the servile, blind-worm, wrap-rascal Scurfcoat of FEAR of the *modern Saints* (whose whole Being is a Lie, to themselves as well as to their Brethren) that I should laugh with good conscience in watching a Saint of the new stamp, one of the Fixt Stars of our eleemosynary Advertisements, groaning in wind-pipe! and with the whites of his Eyes upraised, at the *audacity* of this poem!— Anything rather than *this* degradation★ of Humanity, and therein of the incarnate Divinity!—

S.T.C.

(e) Only about twenty-six copies of the *Songs* survive, and Blake clearly had difficulty finding customers. His friend Linnell

---

★ with which how can we utter 'Our Father'?

1 Coleridge comments on the poems in the order they are found in Tulk's copy of the *Songs*(J). This 'P. 13' seems to cover both 'My Pretty Rose Tree', 'Ah! Sun Flower', and 'The Lilly' (all on one plate), and 'The Angel', which would be pp. 12 and 13 if the frontispiece to *Experience* (which is now loose) were then in its proper place. Coleridge also omits 'The Human Abstract' after 'The Little Girl Lost [and] Found'.

recommended him to all he thought likely purchasers: Chantrey, who (as we said) declined the *Paradise Regained* [*at* £20], but took a highly finished copy of the *Songs of Innocence and Experience*, at 20*l*; Lord Egremont, Sir Thomas Lawrence, Mr. Tatham, and others. They considered it almost giving the money, even when they chose copies of the obviously beautiful *Songs*.[1]

(f) As Blake wrote to George Cumberland on 12 April 1827,

You are desirous I know to dispose of some of my Works & to make them Pleasin[g.] I am obliged to you & to all who do so But having none remaining of all that I had Printed I cannot Print more Except at a great loss for at the time I printed those things I had a whole House to range in[;] now I am shut up in a Corner therefore am forced to ask a Price for them that I scarce expect to get from a Stranger. I am now Printing a Set of the Songs of Innocence & Experience for a Friend at Ten Guineas which I cannot do under Six Months consistent with my other Work, so that I have little hope of doing any more of such things.

(g) Perhaps the most common attitude among the more judicious of Blake's contemporaries is that found in a letter from Edward FitzGerald to W. B. Donne of 25 October 1833:

I have lately bought a little pamphlet which is very difficult to be got, called The Songs of Innocence, written and adorned with drawings by W. Blake (if you know his name) who was quite mad, but of a madness that was really the elements of great genius ill-sorted: in fact, a genius with a screw loose, as we used to say. I shall shew you this book when I see you: to me there is particular interest in this man's writing and drawing, from the strangeness of the constitution of his mind. He was a man that used to see visions: and made drawings and paintings of Alexander the Great, Caesar, etc., who, he declared, stood before him while he drew.[2]

(h) The biographical facts in J. J. G. Wilkinson's 'Preface' to his edition of Blake's *Songs of Innocence and of Experience* (1839) derive from

---

[1] A. Gilchrist, *Life of William Blake* (1863), vol. I, p. 357; see *Blake Records* (1969), p. 339.

[2] *Letters and Literary Remains of Edward FitzGerald*, ed. W. A. Wright (1889), vol. I, pp. 25–6. On 19 November 1833 he wrote: 'I take pleasure in reading things I don't wholly understand. . . . I think there is a greater charm in the half meanings and glimpses of meaning that come in through Blake's wilder visions' than in Shakespeare (*Letters*, ed. Cohen [1960], p. 6).

Cunningham's life, but the critical section (pp. xvi–xxi) is independent and original:

They who would form a just estimate of Blake's powers as an Artist, have abundant opportunities of doing so, from his exquisite Illustrations to the Songs of Innocence; from his Designs to Blair's Grave, Young's Night Thoughts, and the Book of Job, in all of which, there are 'glorious shapes, expressing godlike sentiments.' These works, in the main, are not more remarkable for high original genius, than they are for sane self-possession; and shew the occasional sovereignty of the inner man, over the fantasies which obsessed the outer. Yet he, who professed as a doctrine, that the visionary form of thought was higher than the rational one; for whom the common earth teemed with millions of otherwise invisible creatures; who naturalized the spiritual, instead of spiritualizing the natural; was likely, even in these, his noblest Works, to prefer seeing Truth under the loose garments of Typical, or even Mythologic Representation, rather than in the Divine-Human Embodiment of Christianity. And accordingly, his Imagination, self-divorced from a Reason which might have elevated and chastened it, and necessarily spurning the Scientific daylight and material Realism of the nineteenth century, found a home in the ruins of Ancient and consummated Churches; and imbued itself with the superficial obscurity and ghastliness, far more than with the inward grandeur of primeval Times. For the true Inward is one and identical, and if Blake had been disposed to see it, he would have found that it was still (though doubt-less under a multitude of wrappages) extant in the present Age. On the contrary, copying the outward form of the Past, he has delivered to us a multitude of new Hieroglyphics, which contain no presumable reconditeness of meaning, and which we are obliged to account for, simply by the Artist's having yielded himself up, more thoroughly than other men *will* do, to those fantastic impulses which are common to all mankind; and which saner people subjugate, but cannot extermin-ate. In so yielding himself, the Artist, not less than the man, was a loser, though it unquestionably gave him a certain power, as all unscrupulous *passion* must, of wildness and fierce vagary. This power is possessed in different degrees, by every human being, if he will but give loose and free vent to the hell that is in him; and hence, the madness even of the meanest, is terrific. But no madness can long be considered either really Poetic or Artistical. Of the worst aspect of Blake's genius it is painful to speak. In his 'Prophecies of America,' his 'Visions of the Daughters of Albion,' and a host of unpublished drawings, earthborn might has banished the heavenlier elements of Art, and exists combined with all that is monstrous and diabolical. In the domain of Terror he here entered, the characteristic of his genius is fearful Reality. He embodies no Byronisms,—none of the sentimentalities of civilized vice, but delights to draw evil things and evil beings in their naked and final state. The effect of these delineations is greatly heightened by the antiquity which is engraven on the faces of those who do and suffer in them. We have the impression that we are looking down into the hells of the ancient people, the Anakim, the Nephilim, and the Rephaim. Their human forms are gigantic petrifactions, from which the fires of lust and intense selfish passion, have long dissipated what was animal and vital; leaving stony limbs, and countenances expressive of despair, and stupid cruelty.

In many of the characters of his mind, Blake resembled Shelley. From the opposite extremes of Christianity and Materialism, they both seem, at length, to have converged towards Pantheism, or natural-spiritualism; and it is probable, that a somewhat similar self-intelligence, or Ego-theism, possessed them both. They agreed in mistaking the forms of Truth, for the Truth Itself; and, consequently, drew the materials of their works, from the ages of type and shadow which preceded the Christian Revelation. The beauty, chasteness, and clear polish of Shelley's mind, as well as his metaphysical irreligion, took him, naturally enough, to the Philosophy and Theology of the Greeks; where he could at once enjoy the loose dogma of an Impersonal Creator, and have liberty to distribute Personality at will to the beautiful unliving forms of the visible creation. We appeal to the 'Prometheus Unbound,' his consummating Work, in proof of this assertion. The visionary tendencies, and mysticism of Blake, developing themselves, as they did, under the shelter of a religious parentage and education, carried him, on the contrary, to the mythic fountains of an elder time, and his genius which was too expansive to dwell in classic formalisms, entered into, and inhabited, the Egyptian and Asiatic perversions of an ancient and true Religion. In consequence of these allied deformities, the works of both are sadly deficient in vital heat, and in substantial or practical Truth, and fail, therefore, to satisfy the common wants, or to appeal to the universal instincts, of Humanity. Self-will in each, was the centre of the Individual, and self-intelligence, the 'Anima Mundi' of the Philosopher, and they both imagined, that they could chop and change the Universe, even to the confounding of Life with Death, to suit their own creative fancies.

The present Volume contains nearly all that is excellent in Blake's Poetry; and great, rare, and manifest, is the excellence that is here. The faults are equally conspicuous, and he who runs may read them. They amount to an utter want of elaboration, and even, in many cases, to an inattention to the ordinary rules of grammar. Yet the 'Songs of Innocence,' at least, are quite free from the dark becloudment which rolled and billowed over Blake in his later days. He here transcended Self, and escaped from the isolation which Self involves; and, as it then ever is, his expanding affections embraced universal Man, and, without violating, beautified and hallowed, even his individual peculiarities. Accordingly, many of these delicious Lays, belong to the ERA as well as to the Author. They are remarkable for the transparent depth of thought which constitutes true Simplicity—they give us glimpses of all that is holiest in the Childhood of the World and the Individual— they abound with the sweetest touches of that Pastoral life, by which the Golden Age may be still visibly represented to the iron one—they delineate full-orbed Age, ripe with the seeds of a second Infancy, which is 'the Kingdom of Heaven.' The latter half of the Volume, comprising the 'Songs of Experience,' consists, it is true, of darker themes; but they, too, are well and wonderfully sung; and ought to be preserved, because, in contrastive connexion with the 'Songs of Innocence,' they do convey a powerful impression of 'THE TWO CONTRARY STATES OF THE HUMAN SOUL.'

If the Volume gives one impulse to the New Spiritualism which is now dawning on the world;—if it leads one reader to think, that all Reality for him, in the long run, lies out of the limits of Space and Time; and that Spirits, and not bodies, and still less garments, are men; —if it gives one blow, even the faintest, to those term-shifting juggleries, which usurp the name of 'Philosophical Systems,' (and all the energies of all the forms of genuine Truth must be henceforth expended on these effects,) it will have done its work in its little day; and we shall be abundantly satisfied, with having undertaken to perpetuate it, for a few years, by the present Republication.

(i) On 27 July 1848 Edward Quillinan wrote to Crabb Robinson that the publisher Moxon had just sent Wordsworth Blake's poems and that he, Quillinan, found that some 'sound very like nonsense-verses', though 'others have a real charm in their wildness & oddness'.[1]

---

[1] *The Correspondence of Henry Crabb Robinson with the Wordsworth Circle*, ed. E. J. Morley (1927), vol. II, pp. 675–6.

(j) In an undated letter to John Flaxman's sister-in-law, Maria Denman (d. 1859), presumably about *Songs* (O) or *Innocence* (D), from which he quotes 'The Eechoing Green', John Ruskin wrote:

I cannot enough thank you for trusting me with the invaluable little volume which I return to day—nor at all express to you the pleasure I have had in looking it over;—I had, before, the deepest respect for the genius of Blake—yet I was quite ignorant of his fine feeling for colour—which is one of the ruling & lovely qualities of these noble designs—I am afraid—when I was at your house—that you thought me cold to the beauty of its treatment—but in proportion to the real power and rank of any work of art—is the necessity of separate & quiet worship of it—the incapability of tasting it in such accumulation—I saw too much—when I again—(forgive my presuming on your permission) enter your sanctuary, I shall not so wander—but shall resign myself altogether to the Resignation—or look to be warmed & fed by the Charity—alone—I have been prevented by the severity of the weather from again waiting upon you—but I hope personally to express my thanks to you for this kindness as soon as the 'sun does arise— & make happy the Skies'—[1]

13. *America* (1793) and *Europe* (1794)

1828

One of the few contemporary accounts of *America* and *Europe* is that written for J. T. Smith by Richard Thomson:

AMERICA: *a Prophecy.* Lambeth: Printed by William Blake, in the year 1793; folio; eighteen plates or twenty pages, including the frontispiece and title-page. After a preludium of thirty-seven lines commences the Prophecy of 226, which are interspersed with numerous head-pieces, vignettes, and tail-pieces, usually stretching along the

[1] Quoted from a reproduction of the letter in Houghton Library, Harvard University. Miss Denman had acquired *Songs* (O) and *Innocence* (D) from Flaxman.

left-hand margin and enclosing the text; which sometimes appears written on a cloud, and at others environed by flames and water. Of the latter subject a very fine specimen is shown upon page 13, where the tail-piece represents the bottom of the sea, with various fishes coming together to prey upon a dead body. The head-piece is another dead body lying on the surface of the waters, with an eagle feeding upon it with outstretched wings. Another instance of Mr. Blake's favourite figure of the old man entering at Death's door, is contained on page 12 of this poem. The subject of the text is a conversation between the Angel of Albion, the Angels of the Thirteen States, Washington, and some others of the American Generals, and 'Red Orc,' the spirit of war and evil. The verses are without rhyme, and most resemble hexameters, though they are by no means exact; and the expressions are mystical in a very high degree.

EUROPE: *a Prophecy*. Lambeth: Printed by William Blake, 1794; folio; seventeen plates on the leaves, inclusive of the frontispiece and title-page. Coloured to imitate the ancient fresco painting. The Preludium consists of thirty-three lines, in stanzas without rhyme, and the Prophecy of two hundred and eight; the decorations to which are larger than most of those in the former book, and approach nearest to the character of paintings, since, in several instances, they occupy the whole page. The frontispiece is an uncommonly fine specimen of art, and approaches almost to the sublimity of Raffaelle or Michel Angelo. It represents 'The Ancient of Days,' in an orb of light surrounded by dark clouds, as referred to in Proverbs viii. 27, stooping down with an enormous pair of compasses to describe the destined orb of the world,★ 'when he set a compass upon the face of the earth.'

> '—— in His hand
> He took the golden compasses, prepar'd
> In God's eternal store, to circumscribe
> This universe and all created things:
> One foot he centr'd, and the other turn'd

★ He was inspired with the splendid grandeur of this figure, by the vision which he declared hovered over his head at the top of his staircase; and he has been frequently heard to say, that it made a more powerful impression upon his mind than all he had ever been visited by. This subject was such a favourite with him, that he always bestowed more time and enjoyed greater pleasure when colouring the print, than any thing he ever produced.

Mr. F. Tatham employed him to tint an impression of it, for which I have heard he paid him the truly liberal sum of three guineas and a half. I say liberal, though the specimen is worth any price, because the sum was so considerably beyond what Blake generally had been accustomed to receive as a remuneration for his extraordinary talents. . . .

Round through the vast profundity obscure;
And said, "Thus far extend, thus far thy bounds,
This be thy just circumference, O World!"'

Paradise Lost, Book vii, line 236.

Another splendid composition in this work, are the two angels pouring out the black spotted plague upon England, on page 9; in which the fore-shortening of the legs, the grandeur of their positions, and the harmony with which they are adapted to each other and to their curved trumpets, are perfectly admirable. The subject-matter of the work is written in the same wild and singular measures as the preceding, and describes, in mystical language, the terrors of plague and anarchy which overspread England during the slumbers of Enitharmon for eighteen hundred years; upon whose awaking, the ferocious spirit Orc bursts into flames 'in the vineyards of red France.' At the end of this poem, are seven separate engravings on folio pages, without letter-press [i.e., the 'Large Book of Designs'], which are coloured like the former part of the work, with a degree of splendour and force, as almost to resemble sketches in oil-colours. The finest of these are a figure of an angel standing in the sun, a group of three furies surrounded by clouds and fire, and a figure of a man sitting beneath a tree in the deepest dejection; all of which are peculiarly remarkable for their strength and splendour of colouring. Another publication by Mr. Blake [the 'Small Book of Designs'], consisted only of a small quarto volume of twenty-three engravings of various shapes and sizes, coloured as before, some of which are of extraordinary effect and beauty. The best plates in this series are,—the first of an aged man, with a white beard sweeping the ground, and writing in a book with each hand, naked; a human figure pressing out his brain through his ears; and the great sea-serpent; but perhaps the best is a figure sinking in a stormy sea at sun-set, the splendid light of which, and the foam upon the black waves, are almost magical effects of colouring. Beneath the first design is engraven 'Lambeth, printed by W. Blake, 1794.'[1]

---

[1] J. T. Smith, *Nollekens and his Times* (1828); see *Blake Records* (1969), pp. 470–2.

14. *Descriptive Catalogue* (1809)

The book by Blake which aroused the most extensive comment among his contemporaries was evidently the *Descriptive Catalogue* (1809) of the exhibition of his own paintings which he held at his brother's house in 1809–10. (a) Blake explained the occasion for the exhibition in his advertisement for it:

The execution of my Designs, being all in Watercolours, (that is in Fresco) are regularly refused to be exhibited by the *Royal Academy*, and the *British Institution* has, this year, followed its example, and has effectually excluded me by this Resolution; I therefore invite those Noblemen and Gentlemen, who are its Subscribers, to inspect what they have excluded: and those who have been told that my Works are but an unscientific and irregular Eccentricity, a Madman's Scrawls, I demand of them to do me the justice to examine before they decide. . . . They have ex[c]luded Water-colours; it is therefore become necessary that I should exhibit to the Public, in an Exhibition of my own, my Designs, Painted in Water-colours.

(b) One of the few visitors to the exhibition was Crabb Robinson, who wrote in his diary for 23 April 1810:

I went to see a Gallery of Blakes paintings—which were exhibited by his brother a hosier in Carnaby Market—The Entrance was 2/6 Catalogue included[.] I was deeply interested by the Catalogue as well as the pictures[.] I took four—telling the brother I hoped he would let me come in again—He said—'Oh! as often as you please'—I dare say such a thing had never happened before or did afterwards[.]

Next month Robinson took Charles Lamb and his sister to the exhibition and gave 'a copy [of the *Catalogue*] to Lamb & others. . . . *Lamb* was delighted with the Catalogue—especially with the description of a painting afterwards engraved' for Chaucer's Canterbury Pilgrims.

Perhaps Robinson persuaded Southey to go to the exhibition as well. (c) Years later Southey wrote:

That painter of great but insane genius, William Blake, of whom Allan Cunningham has written so interesting a memoir, took this [Welsh] Triad for the subject of a picture, which he called The Ancient Britons. It was one of his worst pictures,—which is saying much; and he has illustrated it with one of the most curious commentaries in his very curious and very rare descriptive Catalogue of his own Pictures.[1]

Even Blake's good friends found the *Catalogue* puzzling. (d) Young George Cumberland wrote to his father on 14 October 1809:

Blakes has published a Catalogue of Pictures being the ancient method of Frescoe Painting *Restored*.—you should tell Mr Barry to get it, it may be the means of serving your Friend[;] it sells for 2/6. and may be had of J. Blake. 28. Broad St Golden Square at his Brothers—the Book is a great curiosity. He [h]as given Stothard a compleat set down—

(e) To which his father replied on 13 November:

Blakes Cat. is truly original—part vanity part madness—part very good sense—is this the work of his you recommended, and of which I gave you a Comm^n to buy *two* sets one for me and one for Mr Barrys Library?—did he sell many Pictures? and had he many subscribers to the Wife of Bath?—Tell him with my best regards if I was not among the Subscribers it was because I literally cannot afford to lay out a shilling in any thing but *Taxes & necessaries of Life*[.]

(f) The most public comment, however, was one by Robert Hunt in the *Examiner* for 17 September 1809:

Mr. Blake's Exhibition

If beside the stupid and mad-brained political project of their rulers, the sane part of the people of England resquired [*sic*] fresh proof of the alarming increase of the effects of insanity, they will be too well convinced from its having lately spread into the hitherto sober region of Art. I say hitherto, because I cannot think with many, that the vigorous genius of the present worthy Keeper of the Royal Academy [Fuseli] is touched, though no one can deny that his Muse has been on the verge of insanity, since it has brought forth, with more legitimate offspring, the furious and distorted beings of an extravagant imagination. But, when the ebullitions of a distempered brain are mistaken for the sallies of genius by those whose works have exhibited the soundest thinking

---

[1] [Robert Southey,] *The Doctor, &c* (1847), vol. VI, pp. 116–17; see *Blake Records* (1969), p. 226.

in art, the malady has indeed attained a pernicious height, and it becomes a duty to endeavour to arrest its progress. Such is the case with the productions and admirers of WILLIAM BLAKE, an unfortunate lunatic, whose personal inoffensiveness secures him from confinement, and, consequently, of whom no public notice would have been taken, if he was not forced on the notice and animadversion of the EXAMINER, in having been held up to public admiration by many esteemed amateurs and professors as a genius in some respect original and legitimate. The praises which these gentlemen bestowed last year on this unfortunate man's illustrations of *Blair's Grave*, have, in feeding his vanity, stimulated him to publish his madness more largely, and thus again exposed him, if not to the derision, at least to the pity of the public. That work was a futile endeavour by bad drawings to represent immaterially[1] by bodily personifications of the soul, while it's partner the body was depicted in company with it, so that the soul was confounded with the body, as the personifying figure had none of the distinguishing characteristics of allegory, presenting only substantial flesh and bones. This conceit was dignified with the character of genius, and the tasteful hand of SCHIAVONETTI, who engraved the work, assisted to give it currency by bestowing an exterior charm on deformity and nonsense. Thus encouraged, the poor man fancies himself a great master, and has painted a few wretched pictures, some of which are unintelligible allegory, others an attempt at sober character by caricature representation, and the whole 'blotted and blurred,'[2] and very badly drawn. These he calls an Exhibition, of which he has published a Catalogue, or rather a farrago of nonsense, unintelligibleness, and egregious vanity, the wild effusions of a distempered brain. One of the pictures represents *Chaucer's Pilgrims*, and is in every respect a striking contrast to the admirable picture of the same subject by Mr. STOTHARD, from which an exquisite print is forthcome from the hand of SCHIAVONETTI. 'In this Exhibition,' Mr. BLAKE very modestly observes, 'the grand style of art is restored; and in it will be seen *real* art, as left us by RAPHAEL and ALBERT DURER, MICHAEL ANGELO and JULIO ROMANO, stripped from the ignorances of RUBENS and REMBRANDT, TITIAN and CORREGGIO.'[3] Of the engraving which he proposes to make from his picture of the *Canterbury Pilgrims*, and to finish in a year, he as

---

1 This is obviously a misprint for 'immateriality'. In his *Notebook* (p. 62) Blake wrote of the critic 'Who cries all art is fraud & Genius a trick And Blake is an unforunate lunatic'.

2 *Descriptive Catalogue.* Most of these quotes are somewhat inaccurate.

3 Advertisement for the Catalogue.

justly, soberly, and modestly observes, 'No work of art can take longer than a year: it may be worked backwards and forwards without end, and last a man's whole life, but he will at length only be forced to bring it back to what it was, and it will be worse than it was at the end of the first twelve months. The value of this artist's year is the *criterion of society*; and as it is valued, so does society *flourish or decay*.'[1] That insanity should elevate itself to this fancied importance, is the usual effect of the unfortunate malady; but that men of taste, in their sober senses, should mistake its unmeaning and distorted conceptions for the flashes of genius, is indeed a phenomenon.

A few extracts from Mr. BLAKE's Catalogue will at once amuse the reader, and satisfy him of the truth of the foregoing remarks. Speaking of his picture of the *Ancient Britons*, in which he has attempted to represent 'the strongest man, the beautifullest man, and the ugliest man', he says—

'It has been said to the artist, take the Apollo for the model of your beautiful man, and the Hercules for your strong man, and the Dancing Fawn for your ugly man. Now he comes to his trial. He knows that what he does is not inferior to the grandest Antiques. *Superior they cannot be, for human power cannot go beyond either what he does, or what they have done; it is the gift of God, it is inspiration and vision.* He has resolved to emulate those precious remains of antiquity; he has done so, and the result you behold; his ideas of strength and beauty have not been greatly different. Poetry as it exists now on earth, in the various remains of ancient authors, Music as it exists in old tunes or melodies, Painting and Sculpture as it exists in the remains of antiquity, and in the works of more modern genius, is inspiration, and cannot be surpassed; it is perfect and eternal. Milton, Shakspeare, Michael Angelo, Rafael, the finest specimens of Ancient Sculpture and Painting, and Architecture, Gothic, Grecian, Hindoo and Egyptian, are the extent of the human mind. The human mind cannot go beyond the gift of God, the Holy Ghost. To suppose that art can go beyond the finest specimens that are now in the world, is noi [*sic*] knowing what art is; it is being blind to the gifts of the spirit.'

This picture is a complete caricature: one of the bards is singing to his harp in the pangs of death; and though the colouring of the flesh is exactly like hung beef, the artist modestly observes—

'The flush of health in flesh, exposed to the open air, nourished by the spirits of forests and floods, in that ancient happy period, which

[1] Prospectus of 'Blake's Chaucer: an Original Engraving'.

history has recorded, cannot be like the sickly daubs of Titian or Rubens. Where will the copier of nature, as it now is, find a civilized man, who has been accustomed to go naked. Imagination only can furnish us with colouring appropriate, such as is found in the frescos of Rafael and Michael Angelo: the disposition of forms always directs colouring in works of true art. As to a modern man stripped from his load of clothing, he is like a dead corpse. Hence Rubens, Titian, Corregio, and all of that class, are like leather and chalk; their men are like leather, and their women like chalk, for the disposition of their forms will not admit of grand colouring; in Mr. B.'s Britons, the blood is seen to circulate in their limbs; he defies competition in colouring.'

Mr. BLAKE, in another part says, 'Rubens is a most outrageous demon, and by infusing the remembrances of his pictures and style of execution, hinders all powers of individual thought. Corregio is a soft and effeminate, and consequently a most cruel demon, whose whole delight is to cause endless labour to whoever suffers him to enter his mind.' 'The great and golden rule of art, as well as of life, is this: That the more distinct, sharp, and wiry the bounding line, the more perfect the work of art.' Mr. BLAKE concludes thus:—

'If a man is master of his profession, he cannot be ignorant that he is so; and if he is not employed by those who pretend to encourage art, he will employ himself, and laugh in secret at the pretences of the ignorant, while he has every night dropped into his shoe, as soon as he puts it off, and puts out the candle, and gets into bed, a reward for the labours of the day, such as the world cannot give, and patience and time await to give him all that the world can give.'[1]

(g) Blake replied in a doggerel poem in his *Notebook* beginning:

> The Examiner whose very name is Hunt
> Calld Death a Madman trembling for the affront

---

[1] [Robert Hunt,] 'Mr. Blake's exhibition' (in his column called 'Fine Arts'), *Examiner*, 17 September 1809, pp. 605–6; see *Blake Records* (1969), pp. 215–18.

15. Jerusalem (1804–?20)

1811–28

For perhaps the last twenty-five years of his life, Blake worked on his most ambitious work, the one hundred illuminated plates of *Jerusalem*, composing, etching, printing, and colouring it. Even this work was scarcely noticed or treated seriously by his contemporaries. (a) On 24 July 1811 Crabb Robinson wrote:

Returned late to C. Lamb's[.] Found a very large party there—Southey had been with Blake & admired both his designs & his poetic talents; At the same time that he held him for a decided madman. Blake, he says, spoke of his visions with the diffidence that is usual with such people And did not seem to expect that he shoᵈ be believed. He showed S. a perfectly mad poem called Jerusalem—Oxford Street is in Jerusalem.[1]

(b) Blake's young friend and patron, the poisoner and dilettante Thomas Griffiths Wainewright, referred to it with a kind of respectful frivolity in his column in the new *London Magazine* for September 1820:

my learned friend Dr. Tobias Ruddicombe, M.D. is, at my earnest entreaty, casting a tremendous piece of ordnance,—*an eighty-eight pounder!* which he proposeth to fire off in your next. It is an account of an ancient, newly discovered, illuminated manuscript, which has to name 'Jerusalem the Emanation of the Giant Albion!!!' It contains a good deal anent one '*Los*,' who, it appears, is now, and hath been from the creation, the *sole* and fourfold dominator of the celebrated city of *Golgonooza*! The doctor assures me that the redemption of mankind hangs on the universal diffusion of the doctrines broached in this M.S. —But, however, this isn't the subject of this *scrinium*, scroll, or scrawl, or whatever you may call it.[2]

[1] Oxford Street is not in Jerusalem the city; Jerusalem the woman is in Oxford Street (*Jerusalem*, pl. 38).

[2] 'Mr. [Janus] Weathercock's Private Correspondence, Intended for the Public Eye. George's Coffee House, Tuesday, 8th August, 1820', *London Magazine*, vol. 1 (September 1820), pp. 299–301; see *Blake Records* (1969), pp. 265–6.

(c) Perhaps a more common judgment among those who saw *Jerusalem* was that of J. T. Smith, who wrote:

As for his later poetry, if it may be so called, attached to his plates, though it was certainly in some parts enigmatically curious as to its application, yet it was not always wholly uninteresting; and I have unspeakable pleasure in being able to state, that though I admit he did not for the last forty years attend any place of Divine worship, yet he was not a Freethinker, as some invidious detractors have thought proper to assert, nor was he ever in any degree irreligious. Through life, his Bible was every thing with him; and as a convincing proof how highly he reverenced the Almighty, I shall introduce the following lines with which he concludes his address to the Deists [on *Jerusalem*, pl. 52].

'For a tear is an intellectual thing;
And a sigh is the sword of an Angel-King;
And the bitter groan of a Martyr's woe
Is an arrow from the Almighty's bow.'

Again, at page 77, in his address to the Christians:

'I give you the end of a golden string;
Only wind it into a ball,
It will lead you in at Heaven's gate,
Built in Jerusalem's wall.'

In his choice of subjects, and in his designs in Art, perhaps no man had higher claim to originality, nor ever drew with a closer adherence to his own conception.[1]

[1] J. T. Smith, *Nollekens and his Times* (1828); see *Blake Records* (1969), pp. 457–8.

PART III   DRAWINGS

16. General comments

1780–1865

The contemporaries who respected Blake frequently praised in particular his powers of design and his dedication to his art. (a) For example, in a conversation with Crabb Robinson on 10 December 1825

He spoke with seeming complacency of himself—Said he acted by command—The spirit said to him 'Blake be an artist & nothing else. In this there is felicity[.]' His eye glistend while he spoke of the joy of devoting himself solely to divine art— [']Art is inspiration[.] When Michael Angelo or Raphael or Mr Flaxman does any of his fine things he does them in the spirit[.']—Bl said [']I shd be sorry if I had any earthly fame for whatever natural glory a man has is so much detracted from his spiritual glory[.] I wish to do nothing for profit. I wish to live for art—I want nothing whatr[.] I am quite happy[.']—

(b) Blake expressed a similar singlemindedness in his 'Laocoon' (?1820):

Christianity is Art . . .
The Whole Business of Man Is The Arts . . .
    A Poet a Painter a Musician and Architect: the Man Or Woman who is not one of these is not a Christian[.]
You must leave Fathers & Mothers & Houses & Lands if
they stand in the way of Art[.]
    Prayer is the Study of Art
    Praise is the Practise of Art . . .
    The Eternal Body of Man is The Imagination, that is, God himself
The Divine Body . . . It manifests itself in his Works of Art

(c) Blake's devotion to art made an overwhelming impression on the disciples who gathered round him late in his life.

'Never,' adds Mr. Richmond, 'have I known an artist so spiritual, so devoted, so single-minded, or cherishing imagination as he did.' Once, the young artist, finding his invention flag during a whole fortnight, went to Blake, as was his wont, for some advice or comfort. He found him sitting at tea with his wife. He related his distress; how he felt deserted by the power of invention. To his astonishment, Blake turned to his wife suddenly and said: 'It is just so with us, is it not, for weeks together, when the visions forsake us? What do we do then, Kate?' 'We kneel down and pray, Mr. Blake.'[1]

His most distinguished friends thought very highly indeed of his designs. Romney, as we have seen (No. 9b), thought 'his historical drawings rank with those of M.ͥ Angelo'. (d) In 1828 J. T. Smith reported that

Blake's talent is not to be seen in his engravings from the designs of other artists, though he certainly honestly endeavoured to copy the beauties of Stothard, Flaxman, and those masters set before him by the few publishers who employed him; but his own engravings from his own mind are the productions which the man of true feeling must ever admire, and the predictions of Fuseli and Flaxman may hereafter be verified—'That a time will come when Blake's finest works will be as much sought after and treasured up in the portfolios of men of mind, as those of Michel Angelo are at present.'[2]

Both men may have expressed the sincerest form of admiration for Blake's art by imitating it. (e) In his *Notebook* (p. 53), Blake asserted that

Flaxman cannot deny that one of the very first Monuments he did I gratuitously designd for him.

(f) Fuseli evidently acknowledged outspokenly his indebtedness to Blake. According to one account, 'Fuseli said to Flaxman "By gare Flaxman all that we do know we have acquired from Mishter Blake."'[3] According to another, 'Fuseli admired Blake very much. The former when Blake showed him a design, said—"Blake, I shall invent that myself."'[4] But the best known account is the one in which Fuseli declared that *'Blake is d——d good to steal from!'*[5]

---

[1] A. Gilchrist, *Life of William Blake* (1863), vol. I, pp. 297–8; see *Blake Records* (1969), pp. 293–4.

[2] J. T. Smith, *Nollekens and his Times* (1828), repeated substantially in his *A Book for a Rainy Day* (1845); see *Blake Records* (1969), pp. 467, 26.

[3] Marginalia by Joseph Hogarth (*fl.* 1878); see *Blake Records* (1969), p. 467.

[4] Interview with George Richmond (1809–96); see *Blake Records* (1969), p. 39.

[5] Unsupported statement by A. Gilchrist, *Life of William Blake* (1863), vol. I, p. 52; see *Blake Records* (1969), p. 39.

The relationship between Blake and Fuseli produced good stories as well as good art. (g) George Richmond reported this exchange:

Flaxman: 'How do you get on with Fuseli? I can't stand his foul-mouthed swearing. Does he swear at you?'
Blake: 'He does.'
Flaxman: 'And what do you do?'
Blake: 'What do I do? Why—I swear again! and he says astonished, "*Vy, Blake, you are svaring!*" But he leaves off himself!'[1]

(h) And according to Cunningham,

When Blake, a man infinitely more wild in conception than Fuseli himself, showed him one of his strange productions, he said, 'Now some one has told you this is very fine.'—'Yes,' said Blake, 'the Virgin Mary appeared to me, and told me it was very fine: what can you say to that?'—'Say?' exclaimed Fuseli, 'why nothing—only her ladyship has not an immaculate taste.'[2]

(i) For Isaac D'Israeli, the father of the novelist-prime minister, the interest of Blake's art seems to have lain largely in the

infinite variety of these wonderous deleriums of his fine and wild creative imagination. Heaven, hell, and earth, and the depths below, are some of the scenes he seems alike to have tenanted; but the invisible world also busies his fancy; aereal beings which could only float in his visions, and unimaginable chimeras, such as you have never viewed, lie by the side of his sunshiny people. You see some innocent souls winding about blossoms—for others the massive sepulchre has opened, and the waters beneath give up their secrets. The finish, the extreme delicacy of his pencil, in his light gracile forms, marvellously contrast with the ideal figures of his mystic allegories; sometimes playful, as the loveliness of the arabesques of Raffaelle. Blake often breaks into the '*terribil via*' of *Michael Angelo*, and we start amid a world too horrified to dwell in. Not the least extraordinary fact of these designs is, their colouring, done by the artist's own hand, worked to his fancy; and the verses, which are often remarkable for their sweetness and their depth of feeling. I feel the imperfection of my general description. Such singular productions require a commentary.[3]

[1] *Blake Records* (1969), p. 53.
[2] A. Cunningham, life of Fuseli, in his *Lives* (1830), vol. II, p. 333; see *Blake Records* (1969), p. 480, n. 10.
[3] T. F. Dibdin, *Reminiscences of a Literary Life* (1836), p. 789; see *Blake Records* (1969), p. 244.

(j) William Hayley wrote more temperately and accurately in recommending Blake to the patronage of the Countess of Portarlington about the spring of 1803:

M.ʳ B. is an artist of great original powers and of uncommon Merit in his Inventions, in wᶜʰ Line he is perhaps unequal'd among the Br[itish]. Artists[.]

(k) Blake's habit of independence is reflected in his determination to prepare as many as possible of his artistic materials himself, and in the course of doing so he made a number of technical innovations of great consequence for his art.

He ground and mixed his water-colours himself on a piece of statuary marble, after a method of his own, with common carpenter's glue diluted, which he had found out, as the early Italians had done before him, to be a good binder. Joseph, the sacred carpenter, had appeared in vision and revealed *that* secret to him. The colours he used were few and simple: indigo, cobalt, gamboge, vermilion, Frankfort-black freely, ultamarine rarely, chrome not at all. These he applied with a camel's-hair brush, not with a sable, which he disliked. . . . the poet and his wife did everything in making the book,—writing, designing, printing, engraving,—everything except manufacturing the paper: the very ink, or colour rather, they did make.[1]

(l) A similar account, probably the basis of the one above, is given by J. T. Smith:

Blake's modes of preparing his ground, and laying them over his panels for painting, mixing his colours, and manner of working, were those which he considered to have been practised by the earliest fresco-painters, whose productions still remain, in numerous instances, vivid and permanently fresh. His ground was a mixture of whiting and carpenter's glue, which he passed over several times in thin coatings: his colours he ground himself, and also united them with the same sort of glue, but in a much weaker state. He would, in the course of painting a picture, pass a very thin transparent wash of glue-water over the whole of the parts he had worked upon, and then proceed with his finishing.

This process I have tried, and find, by using my mixtures warm, that I can produce the same texture as possessed in Blake's pictures of the

[1] A. Gilchrist, *Life of William Blake* (1863), vol. I, pp. 69–70; see *Blake Records* (1969), p. 33.

Last Judgment, and others of his productions, particularly in Varley's curious picture of the personified Flea. Blake preferred mixing his colours with carpenter's glue, to gum, on account of the latter cracking in the sun, and becoming humid in moist weather. The glue-mixture stands the sun, and change of atmosphere has no effect upon it. Every carpenter knows that if a broken piece of stick be joined with good glue, the stick will seldom break again in the glued parts.

That Blake had many secret modes of working, both as a colourist and an engraver, I have no doubt. His method of eating away the plain copper, and leaving his drawn lines of his subjects and his words as stereotype, is in my mind perfectly original. Mrs. Blake is in possession of the secret, and she ought to receive something considerable for its communication, as I am quite certain it may be used to the greatest advantage both to artists and literary characters in general.[1]

(m) Blake's disciple Frederick Tatham evidently told Alexander Gilchrist about Blake's method of colour-printing:

Blake, when he wanted to make his prints in oil ... took a common thick millboard, and drew in some strong ink or colour his design upon it strong and thick. He then painted upon that in such oil colours and in such a state of fusion that they would blur well. He painted roughly and quickly, so that no colour would have time to dry. He then took a print of that on paper, and this impression he coloured up in water-colours, re-painting his outline on the millboard when he wanted to take another print. This plan he had recourse to, because he could vary slightly each impression; and each having a sort of accidental look, he could branch out so as to make each one different. The accidental look they had was very enticing.[2]

(n) And Blake's young friend and patron John Linnell explained to Gilchrist that Blake

evidently founded his claim to the name *fresco* on the material he used, which was water-colour on a plaster ground (literally glue and whiting); but he always called it either fresco, gesso, or plaster. And he certainly laid this ground on too much like plaster on a wall. When so laid on to canvas or linen, it was sure to crack and, in some cases, for want of care and protection from damp, would go to ruin. Some of his pictures in this material on board have been preserved in good condition, and so

[1] J. T. Smith, *Nollekens and his Times* (1828); see *Blake Records* (1969), pp. 472–3.
[2] A. Gilchrist, *Life of William Blake* (1863), vol. I, p. 376; *Blake Records* (1969), pp. 33–4.

have a few even on cloth. They come nearer to *tempera* in process than to anything else, inasmuch as white was laid on and mixed with the colours which were tempered with common carpenter's glue.[1]

(o) Even as a young man, Blake's preference was for linear artists rather than for the colourists, as is indicated in an anecdote he recorded himself in his copy of Reynolds's *Works*:

I was once looking over the Prints from Rafael & Michael Angelo in the Library of the Royal Academy[.] Moser came to me & said[:] [']You should not Study these old Hard Stiff & Dry Unfinishd Works of Art. Stay a little & I will shew you what you should Study[.'] He then went & took down Le Bruns & Rubens's Galleries[.] How I did secretly rage. I also spoke my Mind. . . . I said to Moser, [']These things that you call Finishd are not Even Begun[;] how can they then, be Finishd? The Man who does not know The Beginning, never can know the End of Art[.']

He had a similar kind of encounter with the President of the Royal Academy:

'Once I remember his talking to me of Reynolds,' writes a surviving friend: 'he became furious at what the latter had dared to say of his early works. When a very young man he had called on Reynolds to show him some designs, and had been recommended to work with less extravagance and more simplicity, and to correct his drawing. This Blake seemed to regard as an affront never to be forgotten. He was very indignant when he spoke of it.'[2]

(p) At about this time, Blake entered his first picture at the Royal Academy exhibition in May 1780. Though he exhibited again at the Royal Academy in 1784, 1785, 1799, 1800, and 1808, and at the Water Colour Society in 1812, the first drawing he exhibited at a public society is the only one which received any attention in a known review, perhaps because that review was by his friend George Cumberland, who wrote:

On looking once again over the Exhibition there are a few more [pictures] which claim our attention: . . . [Last is] No. 315, the death of Earl Goodwin, by Mr. Blake; in which, though there is nothing to be

---

[1] A. Gilchrist, *Life of William Blake* (1863), pp. 368–9; *Blake Records* (1969), p. 33, n.3.
[2] A. Gilchrist, *Life of William Blake* (1863), p. 267; see *Blake Records* (1969), p. 31.

said of the colouring, may be discovered a good design, and much character.[1]

Other early friends admired his artistic talents as well. (q) On 18 June 1783 John Flaxman wrote to his wife:

M.r Hawkins paid me a visit & at my desire has employed Blake to make him a capital drawing for whose advantage in consideration of his great talents he seems desirous to employ his utmost interest[.]

Hawkins seems to have been sufficiently interested to try to send Blake to complete his artistic training in Rome (see p. 49 above).

Blake's older and more conventional patrons were less sympathetic. (r) The history of his dealings with the Reverend Dr Trusler is given in Blake's own letters for August 1799:

I attempted every morning for a fortnight together to follow your Dictate, but when I found my attempts were in vain, resolvd to shew an independence. . . . I could not do otherwise, it was out of my power! I know I begged of you to give me your Ideas & promised to build on them[;] here I counted without my host [my Genius or Angel] . . . And tho I call them [my Designs] Mine, I know that they are not mine being of the same opinion with Milton when he says That the Muse visits his Slumbers & awakes & governs his Song when Morn purples the East.

Blake felt that the 'Drawing [was] in my best manner', but Trusler nevertheless 'sent it back [at once] with a Letter full of Criticisms in which he says It accords not with his Intentions which are to Reject all Fancy from his Work'.

Your Fancy [said Trusler] from what I have seen of it, & I have seen variety at M.r Cumberlands seems to be in the other world or the World of Spirits, which accords not with my Intentions, which whilst living in This World Wish to follow the Nature of it.

Blake replied promptly on August 23rd:

I really am sorry that you are falln out with the Spiritual World Especially if I should have to answer for it. . . . That which can be made Explicit to the Idiot is not worth my care. . . . I know that This World Is a World of Imagination & Vision[.] I see Every thing I paint In This World, but Every body does not see alike. To the Eyes of a Miser a Guinea is more beautiful than the Sun. . . . To Me This World is all One continued Vision of Fancy or Imagination. . . .

[1] *Morning Chronicle and London Advertiser*, 27 May 1780; see *Blake Records* (1969), p. 17.

(s) Even Blake's best friends discouraged him from undertaking large commissions. When Blake decided to move to Felpham in 1800, partly to engrave the plates for Hayley's biography of Cowper, John Flaxman wrote to Hayley on 19 August:

You may naturally suppose that I am highly pleased with the exertion of Your usual Benevolence in favour of my friend Blake & as such an occasion offers you will perhaps be more satisfied in having the portraits engraved under your own eye, than at a distance, indeed I hope that Blake's residence at Felpham will be a Mutual Comfort to you & him, & I see no reason why he should not make as good a livelihood there as in London, if he engraves & teaches drawing, by which he may gain considerably as also by making neat drawings of different kinds but if he places any dependence on painting large pictures, for which he is not qualified, either by habit or study, he will be miserably deceived—

(t) Blake soon discerned this attitude in his patrons, and on 10 January 1802 he wrote to his friend Butts:

I find on all hands great objections to my doing any thing but the mere drudgery of business & intimations that if I do not confine myself to this I shall not live. . . . This from Johnson & Fuseli brought me down here & this from Mr H will bring me back again, for that I cannot live without doing my duty to lay up treasures in heaven is Certain & Determined. . . .

(u) Patrons who were not friends as well were able to admire his works without placing them on a standard with those of the most popular of his contemporaries. T. F. Dibdin, for instance, wrote:

I told Mr. Blake that our common friend, Mr. Masquerier, had induced me to purchase his 'Songs of Innocence,' and that I had no disposition to 'repent my bargain.' This extraordinary man sometimes—but in good sooth very rarely—reached the sublime; but the sublime and the grotesque seemed, somehow or the other, to be for ever amalgamated in his imagination; and the choice or result was necessarily doubtful. Yet there are few books of which I love to turn over the leaves, more assiduously and carefully, than 'Young's Night Thoughts,' emblazoned by his truly original pencil. When Blake entered the arena with Stothard, as a rival in depicting the Dramatis Personae of Chaucer's Canterbury Tales, he seems to have absolutely lost his wits; his pencil was as inferior to that of the former, as his burin was to that of *Cromek* [i.e., Schiavonetti], who engraved Stothard's immortal picture.[1]

The most fashionable painters of Blake's time were of course the portrait artists like Romney, Reynolds, and Lawrence, and their humbler brethren the miniaturists such as Blake's acquaintance Richard Cosway. The most reliable course toward fame and fortune for a painter was to paint portraits, and therefore Blake's well-meaning new patron William Hayley launched him on this new career. (v) On 13 May 1801 he sent a 'little portrait' to a friend, remarking:

I have recently formed a new artist for this purpose by teaching a worthy creature (by profession an Engraver) who lives in a little Cottage very near me to paint in miniature—accept this little specimen of his Talent as a mark of Kind Remembrance from

yr sincere & affectionate Friend

W Hayley

And a few days later, on 19 May, he wrote to George Romney, asking permission to send his wife

as a present, copies (by the good enthusiastic Blake, whom I have taught, with the aid of Meyers' & yr portraits to paint miniature with considerable success) of *the two infinitely best Resemblances of* yrself, that I am so happy as to possess[.][2]

In his autobiography, Hayley was even more enthusiastic about Blake's talents as a miniaturist:

That singularly industrious man applied himself to various Branches of art—He had wonderful Talents for original design—& at Hayleys suggestion, He executed some portraits in miniature very happily, particularly a portrait of Cowpers beloved relation, the Revd Dr [John] Johnson. . . .[3]

(w) For a time, at any rate, Blake was happy with his well-meaning patron and his miniature profession, and on 10 May 1801 he wrote:

Mr Hayley acts like a Prince. I am at complete Ease. . . . Miniature is

[1] T. F. Dibdin, *Reminiscences of a Literary Life* (1836), p. 789; see *Blake Records* (1969), pp. 243–4.

[2] Quoted from a photocopy of the MS. with the James Osborn Collection at Yale; not in *Blake Records* (1969).

[3] Quoted from the MS. printed as Hayley's *Memoirs* (1823), vol. II, pp. 31–2; see *Blake Records* (1969), p. 88.

become a Goddess in my Eyes & my Friends in Sussex say that I Excell in the pursuit. I have a great many orders & they Multiply[.]

Within a year, however, Blake was persuaded that his patron Hayley, portrait miniatures, and almost all commissioned work were in the service of Mammon and not of Jesus, the Divine Imagination, and he cut himself off from all of them as far as he could do with politeness.

Some of Blake's patrons were so enthusiastic about his work that they wanted as much of it as possible. (x) In 1801 Flaxman had introduced Blake to a Mr Thomas, who had commissioned a series of illustrations to *Comus* from Blake, and in September 1805 Nancy Flaxman wrote to her husband that 'Mr T'

wishes as a great favor the loan of *Blake's Gray* to amuse himself with promising that it shall not go from his chamber or be wantonly shewn to anybody[.] *He* wishes to make a few copies from it—to keep with his Youngs Nights Thoughts & some other works he has of Blakes[.] *He* wishes to collect all B— has done, & I have a little commission to give to Blake for him—

One of the most ambitious and admired works Blake ever undertook was his 'Vision of the Last Judgment', of which there were several versions. One of these was for Blair's *Grave* (1808). (y) Another was, as Blake told his friend Ozias Humphry on 18 January 1808,

completed by your recommendation for the Countess of Egremont . . . but for you [it] might have slept till the Last Judgment. . . .

Blake wrote an elaborate description of the design for Humphry, who was going blind, with a copy for the wife of the Earl of Egremont. (z) Humphry was so impressed that he asked Blake for another duplicate, which he sent to the Earl of Buchan on 9 February 1808, with the following covering letter:

Not being able to furnish your Lordship with much amusement myself, I have ventured to inclose, (from the Author himself written expressly for the purpose) the subject of an important Composition lately made by W. Blake for the Countess of Egremont, of a final Judgment—

a Subject so vast, & multitudinous was never perhaps, more happily conceivd.—

The Size of this drawing is but small not exceeding twenty Inches by fifteen or Sixteen (*I guess*) but then the grandeur of its conception, the Importance of its subject, and the sublimely multitudinous masses,

& groups, wᶜʰ it exhibits. . . . In brief, It is one of the most interesting performanᶜᵉˢ I ever saw; & is, in many respects superior to the Last Judgment of Michael Angelo and to give due credit & effect to it, woud require a Tablet, not less than the Floor of Westminster Hall.—

I cannot see to read what I have written . . . [*because of* The unhappy Condition of my Sight.]

(aa) Blake made yet another copy, which was described by George Cumberland's son (also named George) in a letter to his father of 21 April 1815:

We call upon Blake yesterday evening[,] found him & his wife drinking Tea, durtyer than ever[;] however he received us well & shewed his large drawing in Water Colors of the last Judgement[.] *He* has been labouring at it till it is nearly as black as your Hat—the only lights are those of a *Hellish Purple*—his time is now intirely taken up with Etching & Engraving[.][1]

(bb) And at his death Blake was working on (apparently) yet another version of the same subject, as J. T. Smith reported in 1828:

His greatest pleasure was derived from the Bible,—a work ever in his hand, and which he often assiduously consulted in several languages. Had he fortunately lived till the next year's exhibition at Somerset-house, the public would then have been astonished at his exquisite finishing of a Fresco picture of the Last Judgment, containing upwards of one thousand figures, many of them wonderfully conceived and grandly drawn. The lights of this extraordinary performance have the appearance of silver and gold; but upon Mrs. Blake's assuring me that there was no silver used, I found, upon a closer examination, that a blue wash had been passed over those parts of the gilding which receded, and the lights of the forward objects, which were also of gold, were heightened with a warm colour, to give the appearance of the two metals.

It is most certain, that the uninitiated eye was incapable of selecting the beauties of Blake; his effusions were not generally felt; and in this opinion I am borne out in the frequent assertions of Fuseli and Flaxman.

[1] On a tracing of the 'Last Judgment', Tatham wrote: 'The original picture was six feet long and about five wide, and was very much spoiled and darkened by over-work; and is one of those alluded to in his [Descriptive] Catalogue as being spoiled by the spirits of departed artists, or "blotting and blurring demons."' (A. Gilchrist, *Life of William Blake* [1863], vol. II, p. 242; see *Blake Records* [1969], p. 235, n. 4).

It would, therefore, be unreasonable to expect the booksellers to embark in publications not likely to meet remuneration.[1]

Blake's drawings were the subject of an angry letter of about August 1810 written to George Cumberland by Charles Henry Bellenden Ker, whom Blake had had arrested for non-payment of an artistic debt for work delivered. (cc) Ker complained:

Blake is more knave than fool and made me pay 30 [*sic*] Guineas for 2 Drawings which on my word were never orderd and which were as [word illeg: unportus(?)] as they are infamously done[.]

This is a very uncommon view, at least of Blake's character.

At least one of Blake's contemporaries thought his greatest work was his enormous drawing of 'The Ancient Britons', which appeared in his exhibition of 1809. (dd) In 1865 Seymour Kirkup wrote that Blake [*c.* 1809]

was painting the master-piece at the time, the great fresco on canvass (an invention of his own) which made such an impression on my mind that I could draw it now, after a lapse of 55 years or more—although I was a partisan of the colourists, his opponents, & thought him mad—[2]

And a little later he wrote again:

the impression which Blake's *Ancient Britons* made on me (above all others) was so strong that I can answer for the truth of my sketch, as will be proved if the picture is ever found. . . . Blake had but little effect in the works that I remember. I should have liked the heads more English and less Grecian.[3]

(ee) Blake's warmest critical partisans were always to be found among his best friends, as George Cumberland showed in his letter to Blake of 18 December 1808:

The Holy family is like all your designs full of Genius and originality—I shall give it a handsome frame and shew it to all who come to my house.

(ff) Garth Wilkinson wrote on 6 November 1838 of the Blake drawings he saw at Frederick Tatham's:

---

[1] J. T. Smith, *Nollekens and his Times* (1828); see *Blake Records* (1969), pp. 467–8.
[2] *Blake Records* (1969), p. 220.
[3] *Blake Records* (1969), p. 220.

It was indeed a—*not* a treat, but an astonishment to me. The first painting we came to realized to me the existence of powers which I did not know are had in it. 'Twas an infernal scene, and the only really infernal thing I ever saw—'life *dies*, Death lives' might, as Elwell said, explain the character of it. It was most unutterable and abominable—a hopeless horror. Of the same kind were many of the others. On the whole, I must say the series of drawings, giving me an idea that Blake was inferior to no one who ever lived, in terrific tremendous power, also gave me the impression that his whole inner man must have been in a monstrous and deformed condition—for it teemed with monstrous and horrid productions. Those who would see Hell *before* they die, may be quite satisfied that they veritably have seen it by looking at the drawings of Blake. At the same time, all the conceptions are gigantic and appropriate, and there is an awful Egyptian death-life about all the figures.[1]

(gg) In a passage written for, but eventually omitted from, his *Seven Lamps of Architecture* (1849), John Ruskin wrote:

We have had two [geniuses] in the present century, two magnificent and mighty—William Blake and J. M. W. Turner. I do not speak of the average genius of the higher ranks of human mind . . . but of the Great Pharoses of the moving wilderness, those towering and solitary beacons whose tops are seen from above, and beyond the morning cloud and the evening horizon. We have had only two of these built for us. . . . But what have they done for us? The influence of the one is felt as much as the weight of last winter's snow: and that of the other has been so shortened by our dulness, and distorted by our misapprehension, that it may be doubted whether it has wrought among us more of good or of evil.[2]

[1] C. J. Wilkinson, *James John Garth Wilkinson* (1911), pp. 29–30.
[2] John Ruskin, *The Seven Lamps of Architecture* (vol. VIII of *The Works of John Ruskin*, ed. E. T. Cook and A. Wedderburn), (1903), p. 256n.

PART IV ENGRAVED DESIGNS

17. General comments

1791–1863

Blake was apprenticed as an engraver, and for most of his life his chief income was probably derived from his exercise of this art. His contemporaries clearly knew him best as an engraver, and his reputation was generally good, though few suggested that he was one of the great masters of his craft. In fact, however, he rarely drew much attention simply as an engraver; most of the accounts below refer to him as the engraver of his own designs. Most critics apparently felt that the oddity of his designs was to some extent compensated for by the competence of the engravings.

(a) Blake himself wrote in a letter of 12 March 1804 that

Engraving is Eternal work. . . . I curse & bless Engraving alternately because it takes so much time & is so untractable tho capable of such beauty & perfection.

(b) As Gilchrist wrote,

while engrossed in designing, he had often an aversion to resuming his graver, or to being troubled with money matters. It put him out very much when Mrs. Blake referred to the financial topic, or found herself constrained to announce, 'The money is going, Mr. Blake.' 'Oh, d— the money!' he would shout; 'it's always the money!' Her method of hinting at the odious subject became, in consequence, a very quiet and expressive one. She would set before him at dinner just what there was in the house, without any comment until, finally, the empty platter had to make its appearance: which hard fact effectually reminded him it was time to go to his engraving for a while. At that, when fully embarked again, he was not unhappy; work being his natural element.[1]

(c) The same attitude seems to be reflected in Flaxman's letter of 14 November 1805, when Blake was engaged on his designs for Blair's *Grave*:

on the Subject of Engravers you will be glad to hear that Blake has his hands full of work for a considerable time to come and if he will only condescend to give that attention to his worldly concerns which every one does that prefers living to Starving, he is now in a way to do well[.]

Blake's competence as an engraver was widely recognized, particularly as an engraver of outlines. (d) The publisher Joseph Johnson wrote on 23 July 1791 to Erasmus Darwin about his plan to have the Portland Vase copied for his *Botanic Garden*:

Blake is certainly capable of making an exact copy of the vase, I believe more so than Mr B[artolozzi]., if the vase were lent him for that purpose[.]

(e) On 2 January 1804 Flaxman urged that Hayley should choose several noble studies by Romney to be reproduced in his biography of Romney:

they are well worth etching in a bold manner which I think Blake is likely to do with great success & perhaps at an expence that will not be burthensome[.]

On 1 May 1804 he wrote again:

it might perhaps be advantageous to Romney's life, to adorn the book with two or three bold etchings shadowed on a small scale, in which Blake has succeeded admirably sometimes[.]

Even more eloquent by implication was the praise of another engraver, which Flaxman reported in a letter of 4 May 1808:

concerning the [Romney] engravings Mr Raimbach thought very modestly that Mr Blake would execute the *outlines* better than himself[.]

And finally, Flaxman recommended on 19 August 1814 to Dr T. H. Whitaker a plate by Blake: 'the engraving including the Copper plate will cost 6 Guineas if done by Mr Blake the best engraver of outlines'.

[1] A. Gilchrist, *Life of William Blake* (1863), vol. I, pp. 312–13; see *Blake Records* (1969), p. 276.

18. Salzmann, *Elements of Morality* (1791)

1791

[C. G. Salzmann,] *Elements of Morality, for the Use of Children; with an Introductory Address to Parents. Translated from the German* [by Mary Wollstonecraft]. *Illustrated by Fifty* [anonymous] *Copper Plates* [some of which are probably engraved by Blake]. *In Three Volumes.* (London, 1791.)

A review in the *Analytical Review* for January 1791 asserted:

The prints are far superior, both with respect to design and engraving, than any we have ever seen in books designed for children. . . .[1]

19. Burger, *Leonora* (1796)

1796

The first important plate which Blake designed for a book, Burger's *Leonora* (tr. J. T. Stanley), was greeted with indignation by the critics. (a) The account in the *British Critic* for September 1796 protested at

the distorted, absurd, and impossible monsters, exhibited in the frontispiece to Mr. Stanley's last edition. Nor can we pass by this opportunity of execrating that detestable taste, founded on the depraved fancy of one man of genius, which substitutes deformity and extrava-

---

[1] Anon., 'Art. XLII. *Elements of Morality* . . . Vol. i. . . .', *Analytical Review*, vol. IX (January 1791), p. 102; see *Blake Records* (1969), pp. 38–9.

gance for force and expression, and draws men and women without skins, with their joints all dislocated; or imaginary beings, which neither can nor ought to exist.[1]

(b) That in the *Analytical Review* for November 1796 was similar:

This edition is embellished with a frontispiece, in which the painter has endeavoured to exhibit to the eye the wild conceptions of the poet, but with so little success, as to produce an effect perfectly ludicrous, instead of terrific.[2]

20. Cumberland, *Thoughts on Outline* (1796)

1796

More charitable views were expressed of his engravings for his friend George Cumberland's *Thoughts on Outline* in 1796:

one thing may be asserted of this work, which can be said of few others that have passed the hands of an engraver, which is, that *Mr. Blake* has condescended to take upon him the laborious office of making them, I may say, fac-similes of my originals: a compliment, from a man of his extraordinary genius and abilities, the highest, I believe, I shall ever receive:—and I am indebted to his generous partiality for the instruction which encouraged me to execute a great part of the plates myself; enabling me thereby to reduce considerably the price of the book.[3]

[1] Anon., '[Four] Translations of Burger's Leonora', *British Critic*, vol. VIII (September 1796), p. 277; see *Blake Records* (1969), pp. 54–5.

[2] Anon., 'Art. XI. *Leonore* . . . A new Edition, 4to. 16 pages, with a Frontispiece and two Vignettes, by Blake. Price 7s. 6d. sewed. Miller. 1796', *Analytical Review*, vol. XXIV (November 1796), p. 472; see *Blake Records* (1969), p. 55.

[3] George Cumberland, *Thoughts on Outline, Sculpture and the System that Guided the Ancient Artists in Composing their Figures and Groupes* (1796), pp. 47–8; see *Blake Records* (1969), pp. 55–6.

21. Stuart and Revett, *Antiquities of Athens* (1794)

1803

James Stuart and Nicholas Revett, *The Antiquities of Athens Measured and Delineated* (1794), volume III.

Flaxman recommended Blake as an engraver for Prince Hoare's *Academic Correspondence, 1803* (1804), in a letter of 25 December 1803:

he etched & engraved some of the fine Basso Relievos in the 3ᵈ Vol of Stuart's Athens in a very masterly manner & I think he will do the bust of Ceres exactly in the manner You wish for[.]

22. Young, *Night Thoughts* (1797)

1796–1830

Edward Young, *The Complaint, and The Consolation; or, Night Thoughts* [Nights I–IV out of nine] (1797).

The most ambitious work Blake ever undertook was a commission from Richard Edwards to illustrate Young's *Night Thoughts*. (a) Despite the fact that he received what J. T. Smith called a 'despicably low . . . price' for his work,[1] he created eventually some 537 large watercolours and forty-three engravings. (b) A work of such size naturally excited

[1] J. T. Smith, *Nollekens and his Times* (1828); see *Blake Records* (1969), p. 461.

comment from artists; it was probably the *Night Thoughts* drawings which were being discussed in the conversation reported in Joseph Farington's diary, 19 February 1796:

West, Cosway & Humphry spoke warmly in favour of the designs of Blake the Engraver, as works of extraordinary genius and imagination. —Smirke differed in opinion, from what He had seen, so do I.

Farington was more explicit in his diary account for 24 June 1796:

Fuseli called on me last night & sat till 12 oClock. He mentioned Blake, the Engraver, whose genius & invention have been much spoken of. Fuseli has known him several years, and thinks He has a great deal of invention, but that 'fancy is the end, and not a means in his designs'. He does not employ it to give novelty and decoration to regular conceptions; but the whole of his aim is to produce singular shapes & odd combinations.

He is ab^t 38 or 40 years of age, and married a maid servant, who has imbibed something of his singularity. They live together with^t a servant at a very small expence.

Blake has undertaken to make designs to encircle the letter press of each page of 'Youngs night thoughts.['] Edwards the Bookseller, of Bond S^{tr} employs him, and has had the letter press of each page laid down on a large half sheet of paper. There are ab^t 900 pages.—Blake asked 100 guineas for the whole. Edwards said He could not afford to give more than 20 guineas for which Blake agreed.—Fuseli understands that Edwards proposes to select ab^t 200 from the whole and to have that number engraved as decorations for a new edition.—

Fuseli says, Blake has something of madness ab^t him. He acknowledges the superiority of Fuseli: but thinks himself more able than Stothard.—

He was probably referring to the *Night Thoughts* designs again in his diary account for 12 January 1797:

We supped together and had laughable conversation. Blakes eccentric designs were mentioned. Stothard supported his claims to Genius, but allowed He had been misled to extravagance in his art, & He knew by whom.—Hoppner ridiculed the absurdity of his designs, and said nothing could be more easy than to produce such.—They were like the conceits of a drunken fellow or a madman. 'Represent a man sitting on the moon, and pissing the Sun out—that would be a whim of as much merit.'

(c) It may have been early in 1797 that the following flyer was issued:

EDWARDS's
MAGNIFICENT EDITION
OF
YOUNG's NIGHT THOUGHTS.

EARLY in JUNE will be published, by subscription, part of the first of a splendid edition of this favorite work, elegantly printed, and illustrated with forty [eventually forty-three] very spirited engravings from original drawings by BLAKE.

These engravings are in a perfectly new style of decoration, surrounding the text which they are designed to elucidate.

The work is printed in atlas-sized quarto, and the subscription for the whole, making four parts, with one hundred and fifty engravings, is five guineas.

(d) When the work itself was published, it bore the following

ADVERTISEMENT.

In an age like the present of literature and of taste, in which the arts, fostered by the general patronage, have attained to growth beyond the experience of former times, no apology can be necessary for offering to the publick an embellished edition of an english classick; or for giving to the great work of Young some of those advantages of dress and ornament which have lately distinguished the immortal productions of Shakspeare and of Milton.

But it was not solely to increase the honours of the british press, or to add a splendid volume to the collections of the wealthy, that the editor was induced to adventure on the present undertaking. Not uninfluenced by professional, he acted also under the impulse of higher motives; and when he selected the *Night Thoughts* for the subject of his projected decoration, he wished to make the arts, in their most honourable agency, subservient to the purposes of religion; and by their allurements to solicit the attention of the great for an enforcement of religious and moral truth, which can be ineffectual only as it may not be read.

From its first appearance in the world, this poem has united the suffrages of the criticks in the acknowledgement of its superior merit. . . .

The principal charges which have been urged against this poem, and which in some degree may have affected its popularity, are the dark tints of its painting; and the obscurities which occasionally occur in it to retard the progress of the reader. . . .

On the immediate subject of the present edition of this valuable work the editor has only to say that he has shrunk from no expence in the preparing of it; and that to make it as worthy in every respect as possible of the public favour has been the object of his particular and solicitous attention. It has been regarded by him, indeed, not as a speculation of advantage, but as an indulgence of inclination;—as an undertaking in which fondness and partiality would not permit him to be curiously accurate in adjusting the estimate of profit and loss. If this edition, therefore, of the *Night Thoughts* be found deficient in any essential requisite to its perfection, the circumstance must be imputed to some other cause, than to the oeconomy or the negligence of the editor.

Of the merit of Mr. Blake in those designs which form not only the ornament of the page, but, in many instances, the illustration of the poem, the editor conceives it to be unnecessary to speak. To the eyes of the discerning it need not be pointed out; and while a taste for the arts of design shall continue to exist, the original conception, and the bold and masterly execution of this artist cannot be unnoticed or unadmired.

Dec. 22d. 1796.[1]

No contemporary reviews of the book are known, but it clearly made a strong impression on some. (e) Thomas Frognall Dibdin wrote in 1824 of the *Night Thoughts*:

Wherefore is it, that I love to read that portion of the poem, published in folio form, with the bizarre but original and impressive ornaments by BLAKE? At times, the pencil of the artist* attains the sublimity of the poet: and it is amidst the wild uproar of the wintry elements—when

---

[1] E. Young, *Night Thoughts* (1797), pp. iii–viii; see *Blake Records* (1969), pp. 56–7.

* A magnificent portrait of Mr. Blake, admirably painted by Phillips, and as admirably engraved by Schiavonetti, is prefixed to the edition of *Blair's Grave*. My friend Mr. D'Israeli possesses the largest collection of any individual of the very extraordinary drawings of Mr. Blake; and he loves his classical friends to disport with them, beneath the lighted Argand lamp of his drawing room, while soft music is heard upon the several corridores and recesses of his enchanted staircase. Meanwhile the visitor turns over the contents of the Blakëan portefeuille. Angels, Devils, Giants, Dwarfs, Saints, Sinners, Senators, and Chimney Sweeps, cut equally conspicuous figures: and the *Concettos* at times border upon the burlesque, or the pathetic, or the mysterious. Inconceivably blest is the artist, in his visions of intellectual bliss. A sort of golden halo envelopes every object impressed upon the retina of his imagination; and (as I learn) he is at times shaking hands with Homer, or playing the pastoral pipe with Virgil. Meanwhile, shadowy beings of an unearthly form hang over his couch, and disclose to him scenes . . . such as no other Mortal hath yet conceived! Mr. Blake is himself no ordinary poet.

91

piping winds are howling for entrance round every corner of the turretted chamber, and the drifted snow works its way into the window casement, however closely fastened—it is in moments LIKE THESE that I love to open that portion of the text of Young which has been embellished by the pencil of Blake. My friends will laugh . . . peradventure deride . . . but let us all be endured in these venial moments of hallucination. The soul of poetry itself (we are told) is fiction: and I would feign happiness at such moments.[1]

(f) A similarly impressionistic account of the *Night Thoughts* appears in a dialogue by Bulwer Lytton in the *New Monthly Magazine* for December 1830:

A. Of all enthusiasts, the painter Blake seems to have been the most remarkable. With what a hearty faith he believed in his faculty of seeing spirits and conversing with the dead! And what a delightful vein of madness it was—with what exquisite verses it inspired him!

L. And what engravings! I saw a few days ago, a copy of the 'Night Thoughts,' which he had illustrated in a manner at once so grotesque, so sublime—now by so literal an interpretation, now by so vague and disconnected a train of invention, that the whole makes one of the most astonishing and curious productions which ever balanced between the conception of genius and the ravings of positive insanity. I remember two or three [of his illustrations], but they are not the most remarkable. To these two fine lines—

> "'Tis greatly wise to talk with our past hours,
> And ask them what report they bore to heaven;'

he has given the illustration of one sitting and with an earnest countenance conversing with a small shadowy shape at his knee, while other shapes, of a similar form and aspect, are seen gliding heavenward, each with a scroll in its hands. The effect is very solemn. Again, the line—

> 'Till death, that mighty hunter, earths them all,'

is bodied forth by a grim savage with a huge spear, cheering on fiendish and ghastly hounds, one of which has just torn down, and is griping by the throat, an unfortunate fugitive; the face of the hound is unutterably death-like.

The verse—

> 'We censure Nature for a span too short,'

obtains an illustration, literal to ridicule.—A bearded man of gigantic

---

[1] T. F. Dibdin, *The Library Companion* (1824), p. 734; see *Blake Records* (1969), p. 289.

statu[r]e is spanning an infant with his finger and thumb. Scarcely less literal, but more impressive, is the engraving of the following:—

'When Sense runs savage, broke from Reason's chain,
And sings false peace till smother'd by the pall!'

You perceive a young female savage, with long locks, wandering alone, and exulting—while above, two bodiless hands extend a mighty pall, that appears about to fall upon the unconscious rejoicer.

A. Young was fortunate. He seems almost the only poet who has had his mere metaphors illustrated and made corporeal.[1]

When the drawings themselves were offered for sale, they were praised in terms which evidently seemed extravagant to contemporaries, for they were not purchased. (g) In Thomas Edwards's sale catalogue of 1821 they were described as

very spirited designs by Mr. Blake, many of them in the Style of Michael Angelo, they occupied nearly two years of the time of this singular and eminent Artist, which renders this work unique, as well as highly valuable . . . £300. This work is, perhaps, unequalled for the boldness of conception, and spirit of execution exhibited in the masterly designs of Mr. Blake.

(h) Its description in an auction catalogue of 10 May 1826 was yet more eloquent:

It would be difficult, if not impossible, to convey to those at a distance and who have not seen this magnificent Work, an adequate, or even a faint idea of the singular nature of these most extraordinary and sublime conceptions of our Artist; but those who have seen his truly original designs for *Blair's Grave*, may form some faint idea of the style and manner of his treating this equally eccentric and original Poem; to embody which, and give it a visible form and reality, required the skill of a great Artist, and the poetic feeling of the original author combined. How far he has succeeded, the present beautiful and sublime Commentary upon his Author, bears ample and delightful evidence; and it may truly be averred, that a more extraordinary, original, and sublime production of art has seldom, if ever, been witnessed since the days of the celebrated *Mich. Agnolo*, whose grandeur and elevation of style it greatly resembles, and this, *alone*, if he had left

[1] [Edward Bulwer Lytton,] 'Conversation with an ambitious student in ill health', *New Monthly Magazine*, vol. XXIX (1830), pp. 518–19, reprinted as *The Student* (1835), vol. II, pp. 152–5, see *Blake Records* (1969), pp. 401–2.

no other work of merit, would be sufficient to immortalize his name, and transmit it to posterity, as that of an Artist of the very highest order. This was the late Mr. Fuseli's opinion. This splendid and *unique* Work, upon which the Artist was employed for more than two years, has never been published, and this circumstance, it must be allowed adds greatly to its interest and value.[1]

(i) The same ideas are expressed more briefly in the auction catalogue of 24 May 1828:

It is scarcely possible to present the collector with an adequate, or even faint idea of the singular nature of these most extraordinary and sublime conceptions of the artist. They are in the style and manner of his designs for 'Blair's Grave.' In point of composition and design, the present production is certainly superior, and is alone sufficient to immortalize the name of *Blake* as an artist of the highest order.[2]

[1] Thomas Winstanley & Co., *Catalogue of . . . Thomas Edwards*, 10 May 1826 ff., lot 1076; see *Blake Records* (1969), pp. 330–1. The lot was withdrawn at £50. Forty-three of the designs had, of course, been engraved and published in 1797.

[2] Stewart, Wheatley, and Adlard, *Catalogue of . . . Thomas Edwards*, 15 May 1828 ff., lot 1130; see *Blake Records* (1969), p. 368. The work was withdrawn again, at £52 10s.

23. Hayley, *An Essay on Sculpture* (1800)

1800

William Hayley's *Essay on Sculpture* was designed in part to give pleasure to his dying illegitimate son Thomas, for it was to contain a portrait of the boy and an engraving by Blake of a design representing Demosthenes by him also.

(a) On 7 March 1800 Hayley mentioned in a letter that 'that worthy ingenious Engraver Blake . . . has done the outline of dear Toms Demosthenes delightfully'. The portrait, however, was a much more difficult matter, and a few weeks later Hayley wrote:

Thursday April 17 1800

My Dear Blake,

You are very good to take such pains to produce a Resemblance of our dear disabled artist—you have improved yr first plate a little, & I believe with a little more alteration it may be more like than the second outline.

The great & radical defect I conceive to be this—the engraving is a Head 3 years older than the medallion—the Features by being made *longer & more sedate* have lost the *lively sensibility* of 16 . . . —would it not give a little younger appearance to shorten the space between the nose & the upper lip a little more by representing the mouth rather more open, in the act of speaking which appears to me the Expression of the medallion? I submit the part to you & our dear Flaxman with *proper deference* to yr *superior judgment*; as I do the following Question whether the making the Dot at the corner of the mouth a little deeper, & adding a darker Touch also at the Bottom of the Eye would add a little gay juvenility to the Features without producing (what I by all means wish to avoid) a *Grin* or a *Smirk*—In short I wish the character of the engraving to *harmonise a little more*, than *it does at present*, with the following verses towards the conclusion of the Poem, which as *you* are a *kind-hearted Brother of Parnassus*, you will forgive my inserting in this letter to *explain my meaning to you*—

95

'That youth of fairest Promise, fair as May,
Pensively tender, and benignly gay,
On thy Medallion still retains a Form
In Health exulting, & with pleasure warm.
Teach Thou my Hand, with mutual love, to trace
His Mind, as perfect, as thy Lines his Face!
For Nature in that Mind' &c

(b) To this Blake replied tardily but characteristically a fortnight later, on hearing of the death of Tom:

I send the Shadow of the departed Angel, hope the likeness is improved, the lip I have again lessened as you advised & done a good many other softenings to the whole—I know that our deceased friends are more really with us than when they were apparent to our mortal part. Thirteen years ago I lost a brother & with his spirit I converse daily & hourly in the Spirit & See him in my remembrance in the regions of my Imagination. I hear his advice & even now write from his Dictate.

(c) Hayley's distress at the engraved portrait was lasting and frequently expressed, for instance in a poem of July:

Laborious artist of a liberal Heart
atone for Errors of a skillful Hand
That failed the due Resemblance to impart
To that dear Form which prompts my tear to start[.]
As truth herself let his new portrait stand
Correctly beautiful & mildly grand[!]

Hayley forgave Blake shortly after he met him in the summer of 1800, and in a letter of 22 July 1800 he described him as

a most worthy, enthusiastic Engraver, who has within these few days finished for me a small drawing (from a most wonderful portrait, as large as Life, which my dear crippled child contrived to execute of Himself in crayons) . . . He has infinite Genius with a most engaging simplicity of character. . . .

He has already made me most agreable amends for the mortification I suffered in seeing that *very unfaithful* representation of my dear child, which appears in the volume [the *Essay on Sculpture*].[1]

[1] However, on 24 August 1803, Flaxman wrote to Hayley:
on the Subject of engraving, permit me to offer an opinion concerning the medallion, you may remember how much you was disappointed in the engraving from our Dear Thomas's portrait, & consider whether there is not a possibility that You may be as little pleased with the prints from Romney's Medallion? if this should be the case you will pay an additional sum to make the Your book less acceptable . . .

24. Hayley, *Designs to a Series of Ballads* (1802)

1802

(a) One of the most curious publishing ventures with which Blake was associated was described by William Hayley in a letter to Lady Hesketh of 24 May 1802:

Do not be surprised if you receive in about a Fortnight a Bundle of Ballads, for I have a wicked project of turning your Ladyship into a Ballad Monger for the sake of serving the excellent friendly artist, who has been working long & patiently by my side on our portraits of Cowper.—He has drawn & engraved some very ingenious designs of his own to a series of singular Ballads, one of which He proposes to publish every Month with three prints annexed to it.—for the moderate price of half a crown—His first number will be ready in a week or two, delicately printed on a fine quarto paper, & if I send you one dozen to dispose of among yr friends I know you will not think yrself overloaded by

> your sincere &
> affectionate   Hermit

(b) When the first set of Ballads reached her, Lady Hesketh wrote to Hayley on 16 June:

I am ill qualified to speak of the Merits either of the Engravings or the ballad, but to me I confess they seem very worthy of each other.

(c) John Flaxman commented on 27 June: 'I think the Etchings have Spirit & Sentiment', and (d) Charlotte Collins reported on the 28th that Mr Spilsbury 'was so well pleas'd with the Engravings of the Ballad that he beg'd to become a purchaser immediately'. (e) This encouragement was followed by dolorous news from Lady Hesketh (Cowper's cousin) written on 3 July:

Dear Sir—
From my Heart I hope that London & Chichester make ample amends

to y^r ingenious Artist, for the deficiencies of Bath; which I have reason to fear is still more empty and deserted than I thought it possible it should be; even at *this* season of the year! too certain however it is that it is abandond by all those of Genius and Taste or the Elephants must have attracted more company: sorry I am to say that not more than half a dozen Names are yet to be found, so low are the Arts fallen in this sweet City of Bath. I flatter myself however that your bookseller in Pall Mall will have a long list of *Cowpers*, who I trust will gladly endeavour to attone for the deficiencies of other people. I have sent them word that I shall expect to see *all* their Names, and to have *all their Interest* exerted towards the work in hand;—and now dear Sir, may I be *forgiven* if I say, *to you* that *some* among the *very few* now here, who have any pretensions to Taste, find many defects in your friends engravings?—I know you would be much better pleased that they shou'd find fault with *You* than with *Him* whom you patronize, *yet*,—if M^r B: is but New in the world, may it be not *in reality kinder* to point out his failings, than to suffer him to think his performances faultless.—surely it may, as it may stimulate his endeavours after Perfection!—it wou'd be wrong to *name* those who have dared to Criticize what I own pleased *me* very much: but I will try if I can put under the Seal—(for I would not make you pay for a double letter) the opinion of one [? Richard Hurd] who I believe to have as much *Taste* as he has goodness, Learning, Knowledge of all kinds, both in the *polite* arts, and all others! he has likewise great knowledge of the *world*, having always liv'd in the very first Circles—He is *to be sure 82!*— and you may therefore suppose Him to be *Superannuated*;—but *indeed he is not*, & cou'd you see his little Billets to Ladys, and see the grace & even gallantry with wch he presides at our little Suppers & the Spirits he is in at Eleven at *Night* you wou'd be inclined to allow some degree of Credit to his opinion—be this as it may I will not *transcribe*, but give you that part of his note that relates to the Elephant in question, because as that is in his own hand, you will think I am sure that it would be no discredit to a man of five & Thirty! there was also a *certain Lady* [? Princess Elizabeth], of whose skill in painting &c: you and all the world have I know a high opinion;—I dont visit her, but she was lately here, & when Dr Randolph shew'd her this (perhaps with all the enthusiastic warmth which makes his manner)—She too I know (She is a woman of Quality) made objections, chiefly I believe to the design[;] the Elephant not being seen in the back ground in the same piece where the man is struggling at the windows, *she* consider'd as a defect, since no one cou'd tell how he came there? the window too shou'd have appeard in Light as a motive to influence the motions of the Elephant & all this I heard,—whether I am wrong, or not to *tell* it to *You* Time only can discover! one thing I am sure of, that I wou'd not willingly give you Pain—there, where I know you are most Vulnerable. I mean in the person of your Friends, but I cannot help fancying that some hints from you very *gently applied*, as I know you will apply them, may be *useful* to your protegéé—and if they shou'd induce Improvement, I shall applaud myself for the liberty I have taken & for having had the *courage* to tell you, what perhaps *nobody else* will! . . . Examine *yourself* dear Sir who have so much taste[;] is there not something Strikingly disproportionate in the Figure of the Horse & of some of those in the *first* Piece? *even to Me that* is not agreable at all.

(f) It was probably after hearing something like this that Blake Wrote:

The Enquiry in England is not whether a Man has talent*s* & Geniu*s* But whether he is Passive & Polite & a Virtuous Ass: & obedient to Noblemens Opinions in Art & Science. If he is; he is a Good Man; If Not he must be Starved.[1]

(g) Johnny Johnson reported more cheerfully:

> E. Dereham. July 7. 1802
> Wednesday

My dear Sir

The Elephant arrived in perfect safety—and delighted us beyond measure. By *Us* you are to understand the four personages that follow— Peggy, my Cousin Castres and Me—*Three prime Virgins*—and my sister Catherine, *an especial Wife*. In the opinion of the first Maiden, They were *exceedingly pretty*—in that of the second (to whom, as he is a Cantab, I wish I may not have ascribed more honour than he deserves) they were *interesting and novel in the extreme*—and in the judgement of the Last (who,

Were HE-*maidens* crown'd, wou'd *out-mitre* THE POPE,) They were—*what were they not?*—

(h) Lady Hesketh commented somewhat more ambivalently on the second Ballad in her letter to Hayley of 10 July:

Dear Sir, I lose as little time as possible to acquaint you of the Arrival of those Imperial birds the Eagles, who arrived safe, and alighted at my

---

[1] Marginalia to Reynolds's *Works*.

door the day before yesterday.—I dare give no opinion of them in regard to the Engravings, as I certainly place no dependence on *my own* Judgment in these matters, and have not yet been able to consult that of others—to me I own they appear more perfect than the Elephants, but that may be fancy— I have however one objection to make.—I'm afraid you will say 'tis a very *feminine one!* but will you not at the same time Join with me in opinion that yr ingenious friend pays little Respect to the 'Human Face Divine' for certainly the Countenance of his women and Children are nothing less than pleasing [*sic*]:—the *figure* of the woman hovering over her child is fine, but her *Countenance* is to me rather unpleasant, and that of the child extremely so, without any of those Infantine Graces which few babies are without, and which are to me so delightful—in short the faces of his babies are *not young*, and this I cannot pardon!

(i) On 15 July Hayley replied to Lady Hesketh's letter of the 6th:

Pray suffer no Mortal, my dear Lady, however you may give them *credit for refined Taste in art*, to *prejudice you* against the works of that too feeling artist, whose designs met with *so little Mercy* from your *octogenaire admirable*! I allow the *aimable Veillard* to be as severe as He pleases, as we happily counteract his Censure with the applause of *a more competent* but *also nameless Judge* [Flaxman], who has said, I think with *more Truth*, that there is great spirit & sentiment in the engravings, of my Friend.—To this variety of opinions I apply the lively words of the goodhumoured Goldoni on a similar subject—'Ciascuno ha la sua maniera d'operari: gli uni trovano buono, quel che altri han trovato cattivo, e ne risulta piu bene che male.'—Whatever the Merits or the Failings of my diligent & grateful artist may be, I know I shall interest your Heart & Soul in *his Favour*, when I tell you, that He resembles our beloved Bard in the Tenderness of his Heart, & in the perilous powers of an Imagination utterly unfit to take due Care of Himself.— with admirable Faculties, his sensibility is so *dangerously acute*, that the common rough Treatment which true genius often receives from *ordinary Minds* in the commerce of the World, might not only wound Him *more than it should do*, but really reduce Him to the Incapacity of an Ideot without the consolatory support of a considerate Friend.— From these excesses of Feeling, & of irregular Health (forever connected with such excess) His productions must ever perhaps be *unequal*, but in all he does, however wild or hasty, a penetrating eye will discover true Genius, & if it were possible to Keep his too apprehensive Spirit for a Length of Time *unruffled*, He would produce Works of the pencil, almost as excellent & original, as those works of the pen, which flowed from the dear poet, of whom he often reminds me by little Touches of *nervous Infirmity*, when his mind is darkend with any unpleasant apprehension.—He reminds me of him also by being a most fervent admirer of the Bible, & intimately acquainted with all its Beauties— I wish our beloved Bard had been as happy in *a Wife*, for Heaven has bestowed on this extraordinary mortal perhaps the only female on Earth, who could have suited Him *exactly*. They have been married more than 17 years & are as fond of each other, as if their Honey Moon were still shining—They live in a neat little cottage, which they both regard as the most delightful residence ever inhabited by a mortal; they have no servant:—the good woman not only does all the work of the House, but she even makes the greatest part of her Husbands dress, & assists him in *his art*—she draws, she engraves, & sings delightfully & is so truly the Half of her good Man, that they seem animated by one Soul, & that a soul of indefatigable Industry & Benevolence—it sometimes hurries them both to labour *rather too much*, & I had some time ago the pain of seeing both confined to their Bed.—I endeavour to be as kind as I can to two creatures so very interesting & meritorious, & indeed I consider it as a point of devotion to the *two dear departed angels* (Cowper & Tom!) to be so, for I am confident I could gratify their Spirits in nothing so much, as in befriending two wonderful Beings, whom they both, were they still on Earth, & possest of Health, would peculiarly delight to befriend.—

This well-intentioned letter was not likely to give much comfort to Lady Hesketh who was clearly horrified by any signs of '*nervous Infirmity*' in her cousin William Cowper or in anyone else. (j) However, she replied pacifically enough on 22 July:

The account you have so kindly sent me dear Sir of your amiable Protegéés, was not necessary to Impress me with a favorable opinion of their Merit.—I could have no doubt of the good qualities both of heart and head of those who are so distinguished by your friendship, and the affectionate Interest you take in them—it was only respecting the Gentlemans Skill as an Engraver that I took the Impertinent liberty of hinting my doubts[, in] which I say, with *Regret* that I have been but too well authorized; and indeed I hope you do not think I obtruded my own Opinion in this Subject, in which I am perfectly Incompetent to give any, except the idle one I hazarded in my last, as to the '*human face Divine*' which I really think should always be made as handsome as possible, (those of women & children particularly) unless where there is a reason for making them otherwise; I must however beg leave to observe, that this, *my only Criticism*, does not in the least impeach your friends character either as a painter or as an Engraver, for Hogarth who excell'd so much, & whose fame will never dye, made all his children frightful!...

The only printed review of the 1802 Ballads which is known demonstrates the failure of the undertaking, for it does not mention the 'Designs' which were their *raison d'être*:

Anon., 'Designs to a Series of Ballads, written by William Hayley, Esq. and founded on Anecdotes relating to Animals. 4to. Three Numbers [actually four]. pp. 39', *The Poetical Register* for 1802 (London, 1803), p. 440:

These ballads are written in a style of elegance and simplicity. They are three in number, and the subjects of them are the Elephant, the Lion, and the Eagle. It is intended to continue the publication to the extent of a quarto volume. The work is inscribed by Mr. Hayley to the inhabitants of Chichester.

25. Hayley, *Life ... of William Cowper* (1803)

1801–4

William Hayley, *The Life, and Posthumous Writings, of William Cowper, Esqr*, 3 vols (London, vols I–II, 1803, vol. III, 1804).

Within a few months of the death of William Cowper in 1800, and about the time that Blake moved to Felpham to work under Hayley's patronage, William Hayley undertook to write the biography of his lamented friend. There were voluminous materials, particularly Cowper's wonderful letters, but many of them were in the possession of Cowper's devoted cousin Lady Hesketh, who was determined that any biography should ignore aspects of his life such as his madness which were painful to the family, particularly to herself. (a) Hayley wrote to her of Blake on 25 February 1801:

this very amiable Man shall execute, under my own Inspection, all the plates for the Work; & I am persuaded He will produce a Head of Cowper, that will surprise & delight you. . . .

Hayley wanted to persuade Lady Hesketh to allow him to use Romney's portrait of Cowper (which Hayley owned), despite the hint it gave of Cowper's madness, and he therefore had Blake paint a miniature of it which he sent to her. (b) On 19 March she wrote to him in great distress:

[On one subject] I am *determin'd—absolutely determind!*—I mean the subject of the picture, which I have *this moment* receiv'd and for which I do indeed thank you; tho.' the Sight of it has in *real truth* inspired me with a degree of horror, which I shall not recover from in haste! . . . I cannot restrain my Pen from declaring that I think it *dreadful! Shocking!* and that I intreat you on my Knees not to suffer so horrible a representation of our angelic friend to be presented to the publick and to disgrace and disfigure a work I long so much to see. . . . I cannot bear to have it in my possession nor wou'd I for worlds, shew it to *any one* . . . . I must observe that I have no doubt that the *Original* from which this fatal Miniature is taken is a very fine *Picture*, considered *as a Picture*, & I even believe the miniature is very well executed . . . [but I must intreat] that you will not be so cruel as to multiply this fatal resemblance, by having the picture *engrav'd*[!]

Despite this *cri de cœur*, Hayley continued with his plan to have Blake engrave the Romney portrait, and he continued sanguine about Blake's progress. (c) On 18 October he told Cowper's cousin Johnny Johnson,

It is worth riding from Dereham to the Turret [Hayley's house in Felpham] to see the Engravings, that our good Blake is making to decorate the Book,

and on 1 November he told Lady Hesketh:

He is already far advanced in two other portraits [besides Lawrence's] for the Book in question & I think they will be excellent[.]

On 18 January 1802 Hayley sent to Flaxman one of Blake's '*unfinish'd* Engravings . . . tell us your *frank opinion* of it, in its *present unfinish'd state*'[.] (d) On 25 January Flaxman replied:

In the Engraving of Cowper I think my friend Blake has kept the spirit of the likeness most perfectly[;] the eyes are exceedingly well, & in the finishing I presume the extremities of the nose & mouth will be softened which at present appear rather harsh.

(e) By the end of the year the first two volumes were in print, and on 20 December Hayley sent a set to Lady Hesketh, with a letter in which he wrote:

I know your tender Humanity will spare my good zealous Coadjutor the Engraver, if you think He has failed in one Portrait, as I am confident you must think he has succeeded delightfully in the second—His plate from Romney has not all the merit of *his own drawing in India Ink* whence He copied it, but his print from Lawrence is infinitely superior to Bartolozzi's in *tender fidelity to the Character of the original*[.]

(f) Hayley and Blake must have been anxious about her response and relieved when she wrote on 29 December:

I admire Romneys head of all things! now it is *Softened*[;] of the engraving I pretend not to Judge, but I like it.

On 10 January 1803 she wrote again:

the only thing my Sister has particularized is the print from Romney which she dislikes as much as ever, but to which I am perfectly reconciled, as a Print I mean for my abhorrence of the Miniature is in its full force but this Engraving has an effect totally different from that[.]

And on 15 January she wrote again:

the print softens it [the Romney portrait] extremely & it has not that distracted and distracting look which prevails in the miniature[.]

(g) Blake expressed his sense of relief in his letter to his brother James of 30 January:

My Heads of Cowper for M^r H's life of Cowper have pleasd his Relations exceedingly & in Particular Lady Hesketh & Lord Cowper[;] to please Lady H was a doubtful chance who almost adord her Cousin the poet & thought him all perfection & she writes that she is quite satisfied with the portraits & charmd by the great Head in particular tho she never could bear the original Picture[.]

(h) Later, however, Lady Hesketh was more critical, for in her letter to Hayley of 20 April 1803 she wrote, apparently of the *Cowper* plates:

I shou'd be very sorry to add to the Criticisms I have already heard on the Subject of some certain engravings which I am sorry to say are not thought *quite* worthy of the work and I have been told more than once that (however *difficult* it might have been to find) M͏ʳ Hayley shou'd have endeavor'd after a pencil more nearly allied to his admirable Pen.

(i) None of the known reviews of Hayley's *Cowper* comment on the quality of the engraving work, and the latest relevant comment, on Blake's plate of Cowper's monument in volume III, is in a letter from Samuel Greatheed to Hayley of 30 April 1804: 'Friend Blake has well executed his business respecting it.'

26. Hayley, *Triumphs of Temper* (1803)

1803

William Hayley, *The Triumphs of Temper. A Poem: in Six Cantos. The Twelfth Edition, Corrected With New Original Designs, by Maria Flaxman* (London, 1803).

The only known contemporary comment on Blake's engravings for the new edition of Hayley's *Triumphs of Temper* appears in a letter of 24 August 1803 from John Flaxman to Hayley:

I hope You will excuse my partiality when I say the Sentiment of my Sister's drawings allways appeared to me, just & delicate, altho I must acknowledge there is room for amendment in the effects & drawing of her figures, these corrections might be done in the engraving but I confess the prints for Serena seem in these respects to be worse than the drawings. I am sorry for it because now there is no remedy[.]

27. Hoare, *Academic Correspondence, 1803* (1804)

1804

Prince Hoare. *Academic Correspondence, 1803. Containing Extracts, No. II., from a Correspondence with the Academies of Vienna and St. Petersburgh, on the Present Cultivation of the Arts of Painting, Sculpture, and Architecture; a Summary Report of the Transactions of The Royal Academy of London, from the Close of the Exhibition, 1802, to the Same Period, 1803. And a Description of Public Monuments, Voted by the Parliament of Great Britain, to the Memory of Distinguished Naval and Military Officers, since the Year 1798. Published by Desire of the Academy.* (London, 1804)

S.Q. complained of the only plate in Prince Hoare's *Academic Correspondence*, engraved by Blake after a design by Flaxman representing Ceres: 'Surely . . . the Royal Academy of England might have offered an engraving worthy of the subject, and of the country.'[1]

[1] S.Q., '*Academic Correspondence . . .*', *Literary Journal*, vol. III (1 February 1804), pp. 94–5. S.Q. may have been objecting not so much to the quality of the engraving as to the fact that it is in outline only.

28. Hayley, *Ballads* (1805)

1805, 1806

William Hayley. *Ballads, Founded on Anecdotes Relating to Animals, with Prints, Designed and Engraved By William Blake.* (London, 1805)

(a) Following the failure of the *Designs to a Series of Ballads* issued in quarto in 1802, Hayley arranged to have them collected in octavo, and he sent one of the first copies on 18 July 1805 to Lady Hesketh, as

a respectful offering of *gratitude to you* from a very *industrious* tho not a very *prosperous* artist—smile on his gratitude, tho you will frown on some productions of his pencil, particularly *the last*, in the little volume [of 'the Horse'], which He thinks his *best*!—so little can artists & authors judge of their own *recent* Composition[.] *As to the Failings* of the Ballads themselves, they perhaps may be allowed to *find shelter* in the *Mantle of Charity* so famous for *covering sins of all sorts*, at least they will meet with *that indulgence* from *your Good Nature*, my dear Lady, as I will whisper in *your Ear*, that I printed them *only*, that they may prove more beneficial in their *pocket size* to the diligent artist, who laboured in the Cause of dear Cowper with *more Zeal*, than *Success*—but as Addison tells us in his Cato
> 'Tis not in Mortals to *command* success'
& even your lovely princess [Elizabeth], like your zealous Hermit [Hayley], must lament, I think, that the *Hand* of an industrious artist did not *perfectly record* the wishes of her *Heart*[.]

(b) Lady Hesketh had by this time heard reports of Blake's trial for sedition and rumours concerning his sanity, and she replied on 27 July:

Surely my dear Sir you are gifted with *more* true Charity, than falls to the lot of most mortals, (or that perhaps one would wish there *should*) if you can not only forgive but continue to *protect*, and cherish, one, (whom, for y^r sake, I ever *tremble* to think of, and whom certainly I will *not name*) and now let me, before I say another word, return you a

107

thousand thanks for your sweet little work. . . . [It] has given me much Entertainment. . . . I confess I think with you that the Horse is a little extra! to say nothing of the extreme composure of the Lady, but I was never formd to Criticize any of the Sister arts, and shall leave to abler Judges to decide on the merits of the Engravings. . . .

(c) Samuel Greatheed was more tolerant when he wrote to Hayley on 21 November:

Your pretty little volume of Ballads . . . has given me, and several others hereabout much pleasure, and I hope will do good both to my friend Blake, and to many of my junior friends to whose pleasure and benefit I think it exceedingly well adapted.

The published reviews were:

(d) [Samuel Greatheed] 'Art. VIII. Ballads; by William Hayley, Esq. founded on Anecdotes relating to Animals, with Prints designed and engraved by William Blake. Small 8vo. pp. 216. Price 10s. 6d. Phillips. 1805.' Eclectic Review, vol. 1 (December 1805), p. 923.

we think that Mr. Hayley's well-known benevolence has been wisely directed, and usefully employed, in the small volume which he has now published. . . . If Esop's lion were the reviewer of this book, he would doubtless charge the Engraver, as well as the Poet, with partiality; for having represented one of his fraternity transfixed to a tree, by the poisoned arrow of a negress. The plates, of which there are five, mark the genius, if not the taste, of an artist to whom the public are indebted for an excellent likeness of Cowper, from a sketch by Lawrence, inserted in Mr. Hayley's biography of his friend. The correctness of its resemblance as much exceeds that of an engraving by Bartolozzi, which we have seen, from the same drawing, as the latter excels in delicacy of execution. We recollect, also, to have met some of the engravings of these Ballads, on a larger scale; and we think it would be likely to impress the minds of young people more strongly with the subjects if a plate by the same artist were prefixed to each tale, in any future edition.

(e) [Robert Southey] 'Art. xvii. Ballads. By William Hayley, Esq. Founded on Anecdotes relating to Animals, with Prints, designed and engraved by William Blake. 8vo. pp. 212.' Annual Review for 1805, vol. IV (1806), p. 575.

MEDIOCRITY, as all the world knows, is forbidden to poets and to punsters; but the punster has a privilege peculiar to himself,—the exceeding badness of his puns is imputed as a merit. This privilege may fairly be extended to Mr. Hayley: his present volume is so incomparably absurd that no merit within his reach could have amused us half so much. [Plate XXII, here intervene stanzas from 'The Dog'.] ... Edward, when he was in India, used, it seems, frequently to take a fearless swim, as Mr. Hayley poetically expresses himself, not being aware that there was a crocadile in the water. His custom was to leap from a high bank. One day when he was undressing, Fido did all he could to prevent him; his master, not understanding the meaning of this interruption, scolded, and at last beat him; but the dog finding all his efforts vain, and seeing Edward about to plunge in, ran before him, and leapt—into the crocadile's mouth. The poet has had the singular good fortune to meet with a painter capable of doing full justice to his conceptions; and, in fact, when we look at the delectable frontispiece to this volume which represents Edward starting back, fido *volant*, and the crocadile *rampant*, with a mouth open like a boot-jack to receive him, we know not whether most to admire the genius of Mr. William Blake or of Mr. William Hayley.[1]

29. Blair, *The Grave* (1808)

1805–63

Robert Blair, *The Grave, A Poem. Illustrated by twelve Etchings Executed by Louis Schiavonetti, From the Original Inventions of William Blake* (London, 1808).

General comments, 1805–63

The Blake designs best known to his contemporaries were those etched by Louis Schiavonetti for Robert Blair's *The Grave*, which was printed twice in 1808, in 1813, *c.* 1874 and the etchings were used for another purpose in 1826. (a) The inception of the project is described in a letter from Flaxman of 18 October 1805:

[1] The designs are not mentioned in the review in the *Poetical Register* for 1805 (1807).

Mr Cromek has employed Blake to make a set of 40 drawings from Blair's poem of the Grave 20 of which he proposes [to] have engraved by the Designer and to publish them with the hope of rendering Service to the Artist, several members of the Royal Academy have been highly pleased with the specimens and mean to encourage the work, I have seen several compositions, the most Striking are, The Gambols of Ghosts according with their affections previous to the final Judgment—A widow embracing the turf which covers her husband's grave—Wicked Strong man dying—the good old man's Soul received by Angels[.]—

(b) Blake confirmed Flaxman's account in his own letter of 27 November 1805:

Mr Cromek the Engraver came to me desiring to have some of my Designs, he namd his Price & wishd me to Produce him Illustrations of The Grave A Poem by Robert Blair, in consequence of this I produced about twenty Designs which pleasd so well that he with the same liberality with which he set me about the drawings, has now set me to Engrave them. He means to Publish them by Subscription with the Poem as you will see in the Prospectus which he sends you in the same Pacquet with the Letter. You will I know feel as you always do on such occasions, not only warm wishes to promote the Spirited Exertions of my Friend Cromek. You will be pleased to see that the Royal Academy have Sanctioned the Style of work. I now have reason more than ever to lament your Distance from London as that alone has prevented our Consulting you in our Progress, which is but of about two Months Date[.]

It will be noticed that in both letters Blake is described as the intended engraver. (c) However, the prospectus of November 1805 named Schiavonetti as the engraver:

Prospectus / of / A New and Elegant Edition / of / Blair's Grave, / illustrated with / Twelve Very Spirited Engravings / by / Louis Schiavonetti, / from Designs Invented / by William Blake; / with a Preface / containing an explanation of the artist's view in the designs, / and / a critique on the poem. / [Rule] / The Work has been honoured with the Subscriptions and Patronage of the following Gentlemen: / Benjamin West, Esq. President of the Royal Academy.

Sir William Beechey, R.A.   James Northcote, Esq. R.A.

Richard Cosway, Esq. R.A.   John Opie, Esq. Pr. in Painting.
Henry Fuseli, Esq. R.A.   Thomas Stothard, Esq. R.A.
John Flaxman, Esq. R.A.   Martin Archer Shee, Esq. R.A.
Thomas Lawrence, Esq. R.A.   Henry Thomson, Esq. R.A. and
Joseph Nollekens, Esq. R.A.   Henry Tresham, Esq. R.A.
Thomas Hope, Esq. and William Locke, Jun. Esq. / [Rule] / The
Preface will be contributed by Benjamin Heath Malkin, Esq. M.A.
F.S.A. / [Double rule] /

The Proprietor of the present Work, diffident of his own judgment
in general, and more particularly so in a Case, where private Friendship
and personal Interests might be suspected of undue Influence, was
afraid to venture on ushering this Prospectus into the World, merely
on his own Opinion. That he might know how far he was warranted in
calling the Attention of the Connoisseurs to what he himself imagined
to be a high and original Effort of Genius, he submitted the Series of
Drawings to Mr. West, and Mr. Fuseli, whose Character and Authority
in the highest Department of the Art are unquestionable. The latter
Gentleman has favoured the Proprietor with some Observations from
his elegant and classical Pen, with Permission to make them public:
they are decisive in their Testimony, and as they preclude the Possibility
of any additional Remarks, they are here subjoined in the Author's
own Words.

'The Moral Series here submitted to the Public, from its Object and
Method of Execution, has a double Claim on general attention.

'In an Age of equal Refinement and Corruption of Manners, when
Systems of Education and Seduction go hand in hand; when Religion
itself compounds with Fashion; when in the Pursuit of present Enjoyment, all Consideration of Futurity vanishes, and the real Object of
Life is lost—in such an Age, every Exertion confers a Benefit on Society
which tends to impress Man with his Destiny, to hold the Mirror up
to Life, less indeed to discriminate its Characters, than those Situations
which shew what all are born for, what all ought to act for, and what
all must inevitably come to.

The Importance of this Object has been so well understood at every
Period of Time, from the earliest and most innocent, to the latest and
most depraved, that Reason and Fancy have exhausted their Stores of
Argument and Imagery, to impress it on the Mind: animate and inanimate Nature, the Seasons, the Forest and the Field, the Bee and Ant,
the Larva, Chrysalis and Moth, have lent their real or supposed

Analogies with the Origin, Pursuits, and End of the Human Race, so often to emblematic Purposes, that Instruction is become stale, and Attention callous. The Serpent with its Tail in its Mouth, from a Type of Eternity, is become an Infant's Bauble; even the nobler Idea of Hercules pausing between Virtue and Vice, or the varied Imagery of Death leading his Patients to the Grave, owe their Effect upon us more to technic Excellence than allegoric Utility.

Aware of this, but conscious that Affectation of Originality and trite Repetition would equally impede his Success, the Author of the Moral Series before us, has endeavoured to wake Sensibility by touching our Sympathies with nearer, less ambiguous, and less ludicrous Imagery, than what Mythology, Gothic Superstition, or Symbols as far-fetched as inadequate could supply. His Invention has been chiefly employed to spread a familiar and domestic Atmosphere round the most Important of all Subjects, to connect the visible and the invisible World, without provoking Probability, and to lead the Eye from the milder Light of Time to the Radiations of Eternity.

Such is the Plan and the Moral Part of the Author's Invention; the technic Part, and the Execution of the Artist, though to be examined by other Principles, and addressed to a narrower Circle, equally claim Approbation, sometimes excite our Wonder, and not Seldom our Fears, when we see him play on the very Verge of legitimate Invention; but Wildness so picturesque in itself, so often redeemed by Taste, Simplicity, and Elegance, what Child of Fancy, what Artist would wish to discharge? The Groups and single Figures on their own Basis, abstracted from the general Composition, and considered without Attention to the Plan, frequently exhibit those genuine and unaffected Attitudes, those simple Graces which Nature and the Heart alone can dictate, and only an Eye inspired by both, discover. Every Class of Artists, in every Stage of their Progress or Attainments, from the Student to the finished Master, and from the Contriver of Ornament, to the Painter of History, will find here Materials of Art and Hints of Improvement!'

The Work will be printed by T. Bensley, in Imperial Quarto.

The Price to Subscribers will be Two Guineas; one Guinea to be paid at the Time of subscribing, and the Remainder on Delivery of the Work.— The Price will be considerably advanced to Non-Subscribers.

Subscriptions are received by J. Johnson, St. Paul's Church Yard; T. Payne, Mews' Gate; J. White, Fleet Street; Longman, Hurst, Rees, and Orme, Paternoster Row; Cadell and Davies, Strand; W. Miller,

Albemarle Street; and Mr. Cromek, No. 23, Warren Street, Fitzroy Square, where Specimens may be seen.

London, Nov. 1805.

(d) Perhaps the commission for etching the designs was transferred to Schiavonetti because of a rumour reported years later by the son of Blake's friend Thomas Stothard:

I have heard it stated by my father that Cromek got Blake to make for him a series of drawings from Blair's 'Grave.' Cromek found, and explained to my father, that he had etched one of the subjects, but so indifferently and so carelessly—(see Cumberland's 'Thoughts on Outline,' as an instance in that particular branch of art of his (Blake's) carelessness as an engraver)—that he employed Schrovenetti [*sic*] to engrave them.[1]

(e) Flaxman reported more cheerful news in a letter of 1 December 1805:

Blake is going on gallantly with his drawings from the Grave, which are patronized by a formidable list of R.A's and other distinguished persons—I mentioned before that he has good employment besides, but still I very much fear his abstracted habits are so much at variance with the usual modes of human life, that he will not derive all the advantage to be wished from the present favourable appearances[.]

(f) The transfer of the commission for the engravings naturally strained relations between Blake and Cromek, which culminated in the following letter from Cromek:

64, *Newman Street*
May, 1807

Mr. BLAKE,—Sir, I rec^d, not with^t great surprise, your letter, demanding 4 guineas for the *sketched vignette*, ded^n to the Queen. I have returned the drawing w^h this note, and I will briefly state my reasons for so doing. In the first place I do not think it merits the price you affix to it, *under any circumstances*. In the next place I never had the remotest suspicion that you c^d for a moment entertain the idea of writing *me* to supply money to create an honour in w^h I cannot possibly participate. The Queen allowed *you*, not *me*, to dedicate the work to *her!*[2] The

---

[1] R. T. Stothard, 'Stothard and Blake', *Athenaeum*, no. 1886 (19 December 1863), p. 838; see *Blake Records* (1969), p. 172.

[2] In a letter to James Montgomery of 17 April 1807 (in the Sheffield Public Library), Cromek said that Blake's 'poetic Address to the queen [in Blair's *Grave* is] marked with his usual Characteristics—Sublimity, Simplicity, Elegance and Pathos, his wildness *of course*'.

honour w^d have been yours exclus^y, but that you might not be deprived of any advantage likely to contribute to your reputation, I was willing to pay Mr. Schiavonetti *ten* guineas for etching a plate from the drawing in question.

Another reason for returning the sketch is that *I can do without it*, having already engaged to give a greater number of etchings than the price of the book will warrant; and I neither have nor ever had any encouragement from *you* to place you before the public in a more favourable point of view than that which I have already chosen. You charge me w^h *imposing upon you*. Upon my honour I have no recollection of anything of the kind. If the world and I were to settle accounts tomorrow, I do assure you the balance w^d be considerably in my favour. In this respect '*I am more sinned against than sinning*.' But, if I cannot recollect any instances wherein I have imposed upon *you*, several present themselves in w^h I have imposed upon *myself*. Take two or three that press upon me.

When I first called on you I found you without reputation; I *imposed* on myself the labour, and an Herculean one it has been, to create and establish a reputation for you. I say the labour was Herculean, because I had not only the public to contend with, but I had to battle with a man who had predetermined not to be served. What public reputation you have, the reputation of eccentricity excepted, I have acquired for you, and I can honestly and conscientiously assert that if you had laboured thro' life for yourself as zealously and as earnestly as I have done for you your reputation as an artist w^d not only have been enviable but it would have placed you on an eminence that w^d have put it out of the power of an individual, as obscure as myself, either to add to it or take from it. *I also imposed on myself* when I believed what you so often have told me, that your works were equal, nay superior, to a Raphael or to a Michael Angelo! Unfortunately for me as a publisher the public awoke me from this state of stupor, this mental delusion. That public is willing to give you credit for what real talent is to be found in your productions, *and for no more*.

I have imposed on myself yet more grossly in believing you to be one altogether abstracted from this world, holding converse w^h the world of spirits!—simple, unoffending, a combination of the *serpent* and the *dove*. I really blush when I reflect how I have been cheated in this respect. The most effectual way of benefiting a designer whose aim is general patronage is to bring his designs before the public through the medium of engraving. Your drawings have had the *good fortune* to be engraved by one of the first artists in Europe, and the specimens already shown have already produced you orders that I verily believe you otherwise w^d not have rec^d. Herein I have been gratified, for I was determined to bring you food as well as reputation, tho' from your late conduct I have some reason to embrace your wild opinion, that to manage genius, and to cause it to produce good things, it is absolutely necessary to starve it; indeed, this opinion is considerably heightened by the recollection that your best work, the illustrations of 'The Grave,' was produced when you and Mrs Blake were reduced so low as to be obliged to live on half-a-guinea a week!

Before I conclude this letter, it will be necessary to remark, when I gave you the order for the drawings from the poem of 'The Grave,' I paid you for them more than I could then afford, more in proportion than you were in the habit of receiving, and what you were perfectly satisfied with, though I must do you the justice to confess much less than I think is their real value. Perhaps you have friends and admirers who can appreciate their merit and worth as much as I do. I am decidedly of opinion that the 12 for 'The Grave' should sell at least for 60 guineas. If you can meet with any gentleman who will give you this sum for them, I will deliver them into his hands on the publication of the poem. I will deduct the 20 guineas I have paid you from that sum, and the remainder 40 d^o shall be at your disposal. . . .

With much respect for your talents

I remain, sir,

Your real friend and well-wisher,

R. H. CROMEK.

Most contacts between the two men must have been broken off after this letter.

(g) The Italian engraver Louis Schiavonetti praised 'the last judgment' design when he sent Cromek his etching of it on 21 July 1807:

As to what degree of plaisure I have found in Engraving it you may easily conseive it from the accuracy of the outline, the truth of the light and shadow, and the magical way with which the effect and [h]armony is contrived in the Drawing[.][1]

(h) The fashionable portrait painter, John Hoppner, was probably referring to the *Grave* designs when he wrote in a letter of about July 1808:

[1] Quoted from the letter in my possession.

Respecting Blake's Poems, will you believe me? The merit was all vanished, in my mind at least, on reading them next morning. I therefore took no copy—but if you wish for them Cromek can now refuse you nothing—so I hope you will be modest in your demands of favours of him.

Puffs and flyers for the book in the summer of 1808 described it as 'A magnificent' edition with 'some of the finest of Blake's designs', a 'splendid' edition.[1] (i) The work itself bore the following

ADVERTISEMENT.

The Proprietor of this Work feels highly gratified that it has afforded him an opportunity of contributing to extend those boundaries of the Art of Design which are in themselves of the greatest beauty and value: he takes no other merit but this to himself, and gratefully acknowledges how much he has been obliged to various gentlemen of refined taste,—artists of high rank, and men of established literary repute,—for the aid they have been kindly pleased to grant.

To the elegant and classical taste of Mr. FUSELI he is indebted for excellent remarks on the moral worth and picturesque dignity of the Designs that accompany this Poem. Mr. PHILLIPS is entitled to his kindest thanks, for the capitally painted Portrait of Mr. WILLIAM BLAKE, which is here presented to the Subscribers; and to Mr. SCHIAVONETTI he is under still greater obligations for a SERIES OF ETCHINGS which, it is not too much praise to say, no other artist could have executed so ably.

That he might know how far he was warranted in calling the attention of the connoisseur to what he himself imagined to be a high and original effort of genius, the Proprietor submitted the Drawings, before they were engraved, to the following gentlemen, members of the Royal Academy of Painting, in London. He would esteem himself culpable if he were to dismiss this Advertisement without publicly acknowledging the honourable and most liberal testimonial they bore to their excellence.

BENJAMIN WEST, ESQ.
PRESIDENT OF THE ROYAL ACADEMY.

SIR WILLIAM BEECHEY.	WILLIAM OWEN, ESQ.
RICHARD COSWAY, ESQ.	THOMAS STOTHARD, ESQ.
JOHN FLAXMAN, ESQ.	MARTIN ARCHER SHEE, ESQ.

1 *Blake Records* (1969), p. 191.

THOMAS LAWRENCE, ESQ. ‖ HENRY THOMSON, ESQ.
JOSEPH NOLLEKENS, ESQ. ‖ HENRY TRESHAM, ESQ.
London, July 1808.   R. H. CROMEK.[1]

Some readers apparently valued the designs for their morality.
(j) Thus W. Walker proposed on 31 August 1808 to William Hayley
that for a posthumous collection of poetry by Thomas Bradford

We take for a Frontispiece Mr Blakes *departure from the Soul* . . . [for]
the moral effect Which Mr Blake's fine subject might, and I am
persuaded wou'd have on the young People to Whom I shd. present
this little Work.

Similar feelings were apparently entertained by Robert Scott when
he subscribed for a copy. (k) Years later his son William Bell Scott
wrote that in his home

the most important of all the illustrated books was perhaps *The Grave*,
with Blake's inventions admirably engraved by Sc[h]iavonetti. (There
was also Young's *Night Thoughts*, engraved as well as designed by
Blake himself; but they were so completely inferior that they had no
attractions.) The much-maligned Cromek had visited Edinburgh, no
doubt at the time he was industriously collecting the Burns and Border
scraps of verse he afterwards published, and my father had become one
of his original subscribers for *The Grave*. These inventions had impressed the paternal mind in the profoundest way: the breath of the
spirit blown through the judgment trump on the title-page seemed to
have roused him as well as the skeleton there represented. The parting
of soul and body after the latter is laid on the bier; the meeting of a
family in heaven—indeed nearly every one of the prints he looked
upon as almost sacred, and we all followed him in this, if in little else.
Would it not be really thus after death? Would not the emancipated
soul look at those remaining behind with new feelings, and hover over
the deserted but still beloved body? To these questions we children,
very young when the book was published, answered with perfect
faith.[2]

(l) In his father's copy of Blair's *Grave* (1808), David Scott wrote in
1844:

---

[1] R. Blair, *The Grave* (1808), pp. xi–xii; see *Blake Records* (1969), pp. 192–3.
[2] *Autobiographical Notes of the Life of William Bell Scott*, ed. W. Minto (1892), vol. 1,
pp. 21–2; see *Blake Records* (1969), pp. 193–4.

These, of any series of designs which art has produced, are the most purely elevated in their relation and sentiment. It would be long to discriminate the position they hold in this respect, and at the same time the disregard in which they may be held by some who judge of them in a material relation; while the great beauty which they possess will at once be apparent to others who can appreciate their style in its immaterial connexion. But the sum of the whole in my mind is this: that these designs reach the intellectual or infinite, in an abstract significance, more entirely unmixed with inferior elements and local conventions than any others; that they are the result of high intelligence of thought, and of a progress of art through many styles and stages of different times, produced through a bright generalizing and transcendental mind.

The errors or defects of Blake's mere science in form, and his proneness to overdo some of its best features into weakness, are less perceptible in these than in others of his works. What was a disappointment to him was a benefit to the work,—that it was etched by another, who was able to render it in a style thoroughly consistent, (but which Blake has the originality of having pointed out in his series from Young, though he did not properly effect it,) and to pass over those solecisms which would have interrupted its impression, in a way that, to the apprehender of these, need scarcely give offence, and hide them from the discovery of others. They are etched with most appropriate and consummate ability.[1]

(m) For others, such as James Montgomery, the figures conveyed chiefly not moral piety but shocking nudity.

When the 'Grave' was long afterwards published, with Blake's splendid illustrations, he became the possessor of a copy; but, as several of the plates were hardly of such a nature as to render the book proper to lie on a parlour table for general inspection, he sold his copy for the subscription price; a circumstance which he often regretted, as the death of the artist soon afterwards rendered the work both scarce and proportionately more valuable. Those persons who have once seen these illustrations will readily recollect the print representing the angel of the 'last trump' descending to awake the dead. The celestial messenger is seen in an almost perpendicular position, head downwards, and with his trumpet close to the ear of a corpse which is just beginning to revive,—the bones of the figure are apparently uniting,

[1] A. Gilchrist, *Life of William Blake* (1863), vol. I, p. 377.

and the flesh and skin slowly creeping over the skeleton! The solemn absurdity of this conception, and the ingenious manner in which it is executed, afforded Montgomery a very amusing topic of conversation on one occasion when we were present.[1]

Reviews

(n) The first two reviews were yet more outspoken. The first, by Robert Hunt in the *Examiner* for 7 August 1808, was entitled:

Blake's Edition of Blair's Grave

The large, elegant type, superfine paper, and masterly execution of the twelve highly finished Etchings by SCHIAVONETTI, present an exterior worthy to embody the original and vigorous thoughts of ROBERT BLAIR. The Portrait of Mr. BLAKE, the inventor of the designs, preserves all the nature and spirit of the admirable original by Mr. PHILLIPS. Rich dotted lines in the half tints, just direction and playfulness of line throughout, diversified touch, and vigorous drawing, rank it among the best Engravings of Portraits in any country. In anatomical precision, Mr. SCHIAVONETTI has done more than justice to Mr. BLAKE's Designs. Of these Mr. FUSELI well remarks, that 'the groups and single figures on their own basis, and considered without attention to the plan, frequently exhibit those simple graces which nature and the heart alone can dictate.' I wish his praise of the *plan itself* was equally just. 'His invention,' says Mr. FUSELI, 'has been chiefly employed to spread a *familiar* and *domestic* atmosphere round the most important of all subjects, to *connect the visible and invisible world* without *provoking probability*, and to lead the eye from the milder light of time to the radiations of eternity.' In other words, to perform impossibilities, to convert the pencil into a magical wand, and with it to work wonders, surpassing any recorded in the Tales of the Genii. How *'the visible and the invisible world'* can be *connected* by the aid of the pencil without *'provoking probability,'* nay even without outraging it, none but such a visionary as Mr. BLAKE, or such a frantic as Mr. FUSELI, could possibly fancy. The attempt has always failed even in poetry, notwithstanding its license of fiction and the wide range of fancy which the indetermination of language gives the reader. The greatest poets have failed in their attempts 'to connect the visible and invisible worlds,' and have conveyed no just idea of the incomprehensible and intellectual faculty, whenever they have tried to embody it. MILTON's Messiah and the

---

[1] J. Holland and J. Everett, *Memoirs of the Life and Writings of James Montgomery* (1854), vol. I, p. 38; see *Blake Records* (1969), p. 194.

Angels must *necessarily* act by the instrumentality of the *five senses*, and others, though denominated *ethereal essences*, are really modifications of *matter* like *men*. The utter impossibility of representing the *Spirit* to the eye is proved by the ill effect it has on the stage. When the spirit *Ariel*, who should be viewless, and always fleeting as the air, appears, it is by means of legs which run no faster than those of many of the audience, while her flapless wings are idly stiff on her shoulders, and though she should sometimes be seen by *Prospero* only, she is equally visible to all around, who must *fancy* her invisible. The effect is equally impracticable in the vain effort of painting to unite to the eye the contrary natures of spirit and body, and it is this which renders allegorical pictures so utterly insipid. Indeed to impose on the spectator fire for water would not be more absurd. They have as close analogy to each other as soul and body. Thus when Mr. BLAKE describes 'the soul exploring the recesses of the grave, by a figure clad in drapery, holding a candle, and looking into a tomb' no other idea is suggested but simply of a human being examining a tomb. The corporeal object not only forbids but absolutely prevents the most distant conception that it is a spirit looking into a grave, and SOLOMON, DANIEL, and all the wise men of the East, would not possibly divine such a thought, if the *small* assistance of the title did not help to explain the enigma. It is by the same help we are enabled to discover that by the face of a figure which is springing out of the grave, coming in contact with the face of another figure descending from an opening cloud, is shadowed 'the re-union of the soul and body.' The mouth of the lower figure is certainly a little open, but if this aperture is to admit the body, I beg pardon, the soul above, it is somewhat too small, as it is no longer than the mouth of the upper figure, or soul!! To be sure, that figure is soul, and can therefore enter without any difficulty or squeezing into ever so small a cranny, just as MILTON describes *his* spirits contracting or enlarging at will. But how are we to find out that the figure in the shape of a body is a soul?

'The soul hovering over the body, reluctantly parting with life', is thus described by BLAIR:—

> 'In that dread moment, how the frantic soul
> Raves round the walls of her clay tenement,
> Runs to each avenue, and shrieks for help,
> But shrieks in vain. How wishfully she looks
> On all she's leaving, now no longer her's.'

This is a very animated and highly poetic figure, but how absurd is its literal representation in a picture, by a female figure suspended over an expiring body, and looking wishfully in its face. The figure would indeed be an exact personation of a female friend of the dying, if it was not for its hovering in the air, but that circumstance is but a poor solution of its spirituality, which is altogether belied by the more substantial testimony of bones, flesh, and drapery of linen manufacture. But a more serious censure attaches to two of these most hetero-geneous and serio-fantastic designs. At the awful day of Judgment, before the throne of God himself, a male and female figure are described in most indecent attitudes. It is the same with the salutation of a man and his wife meeting in the pure mansions of Heaven. This however is as appropriate a display of the chastity of celestial rapture, as solid flesh is of *unseen*, *untangible*, and *incorporeal* spirit. This is the work that Mr. FUSELI says, 'holds the mirror up to life: less indeed to discriminate character, than those situations which shew what all are born for, what all ought to act for, and what all must inevitably come to.' These valuable purposes are certainly attained in some degree in the other prints, but here an appearance of libidinousness intrudes itself upon the holiness of our thoughts, and counteracts their impression. It may be said that 'to the pure all things are pure.' But beside that the pure must, in proportion to their purity, be disgusted with obscenity, lessons of religion and morality, whether inculcated by picture or discourse, should have more for their object the benefit of the licentious than the amusement of the virtuous. 'They that are whole need not a Physician, but they that are sick.' In fine, there is much to admire, but more to censure in these prints. There are some ideas that awaken the warmest and best feelings of the heart, others which cherish the worst. Whatever is simply natural, such as 'the death of a wicked strong man,' is power-fully conceived and expressed; but nearly all the allegory is not only far fetched but absurd, inasmuch as a human body can never be mi[s]taken in a picture for its soul, as the visible can never shadow out the invisible world, 'between which, there is a great gulph fixed' of impenetrable and therefore undescribable obscurity.—The work owes its best popularity to the faithful descriptions and manly poetry of ROBERT BLAIR and to the unrivalled graver of L. SCHIAVONETTI.

R.H.[1]

(o) To the *Examiner* attack Blake replied in his *Descriptive Catalogue:*

[1] R[obert] H[unt], 'Blake's Edition of Blair's Grave', *Examiner*, 7 August 1808, pp. 509–10; see *Blake Records* (1969), pp. 195–7.

The connoisseurs and artists who have made objections to Mr. B.'s mode of representing spirits with real bodies, would do well to consider that the Venus, the Minerva, the Jupiter, the Apollo, which they admire in Greek statues are all of them representations of spiritual existences, of Gods immortal, to the mortal perishing organ of sight; and yet they are embodied and organized in solid marble. Mr. B. requires the same latitude, and all is well. The Prophets describe what they saw in Vision as real and existing men, whom they saw with their imaginative and immortal organs; the Apostles the same; the clearer the organ the more distinct the object. A Spirit and a Vision are not, as the modern philosophy supposes, a cloudy vapour, or a nothing: they are organized and minutely articulated beyond all that the mortal and perishing nature can produce. He who does not imagine in stronger and better lineaments, and in stronger and better light than his perishing and mortal eye can see, does not imagine at all. The painter of this work asserts that all his imaginations appear to him infinitely more perfect and more minutely organized than any thing seen by his mortal eye. Spirits are organized men. Moderns wish to draw figures without lines, and with great and heavy shadows; are not shadows more unmeaning than lines, and more heavy? O who can doubt this!

(p) An even more extensive attack appeared in the *Antijacobin Review* for November 1808:

The Grave, a Poem, illustrated by Twelve Etchings, executed by Louis Schiavonetti, from the Original Inventions of William Blake. 4to. pp. 50. £2. 12s. 6d. 1808, Cromek. Cadell and Davis.

A Work that has been so frequently re-printed as *Blair's Grave*, and has so long maintained a distinguished rank in public estimation, would not demand any attention from us but through peculiar circumstances. The poem itself, indeed, we do not intend to criticise any further than by remarking, that its most exquisite beauties are occasionally shaded by too colloquial a phraseology, and a too frequent choice of metaphorical illustrations from low and common objects; possibly however, its enlarged celebrity has been the result of these very defects, and the moral tendency of the whole been increased by its being thus brought within the comprehension and scope of common understandings. What we have now to do is to examine into the presumed merits of the *Original Inventions* with which this edition is embellished; we say presumed merits, because the designs have been trumpeted forth in a way that might lead many to suppose them in possession of all the principles that unite in the perfection of art.

Mr. Blake was formerly an engraver, but his talents in that line scarcely advancing to mediocrity, he was induced as we have been informed, to direct his attention to the art of design; and aided as his friends report, by visionary communications with the spirits of the Raffaeles, the Titians, the Caraccis, the Corregios, and the Michael-Angelos of past ages, he succeeded in producing the 'Inventions' before us; as well as some others on similar principles, which though submitted to public inspection at the Royal Academy, have not yet been subjected to the operations of the *Burin*. Were we to act on the assumption of the above statement being an absolute fact, we should be justified in grounding our opinion of Mr. Blake's productions on much severer laws of criticism than we really mean to be guided by; we should have a right to expect the intire union and concentrated strength of all the above great masters in the designs for the Grave; and to inquire wherefore the graces of the Caracci were not blended with the sweetness of Corregio, and the full and flowing pencil of Titian combined with the majesty of Raffaele, and the grandeur, sublimity, and energy of Michael Angelo? But waving all considerations of supposed spiritual agency and inspiration, we shall judge only of Mr. Blake's designs from the plain principles of taste and common sense, yet not without reference to the high station in the ranks of art which the proprietor (Mr. Cromek,) claims for them. We must here quote some passages from the advertisement prefixed to this publication.

'The proprietor of this work feels highly gratified that it has afforded him *an opportunity of contributing to extend those boundaries of the Art of Design* which are in themselves of *the greatest beauty and value:* he takes no other merit but this to himself, and *gratefully acknowledges how much he has been obliged to various gentlemen of refined taste, artists of high rank, and men of established literary repute*, for the aid they have been kindly pleased to grant. To the elegant and classical taste of Mr. Fuseli he is indebted for *excellent remarks* on the *moral worth and picturesque dignity* of *the designs* that accompany this poem: and to Mr. SCHIA-VONETTI he is under *still greater obligations* for a SERIES of ETCHINGS which, *it is not too much praise* to say, *no other artist* could *have executed so ably.* That he might know how far he was warranted in calling the attention of the connoisseur to what he himself imagined to be *a high and original effort of genius*, the proprietor submitted the drawings *before they were engraved,* to the following gentlemen, members of the Royal Academy of Painting in London. He would *esteem himself culpable* if he were to *dismiss this advertisement without publicly acknowledging* the *honourable* and *most liberal testimony they bore to their excellence.'* The names recorded are those of 'Benjamin West, Esq. P.R.A. Sir William Beachey, Richard Cosway, Esq. John Flaxman, Esq. Thomas Lawrence, Esq. Joseph Nollekens, Esq. William Owen, Esq. Thomas Stothard, Esq. Martin Archer Shee, Esq. Henry Thomson, Esq. and Henry Tresham, Esq.'

There is quackery in more things than medicine; yet we think that Mr. Cromek's *address* (as will occasionally occur in real life,) is somewhat *too broad* to effect his purpose; nor is the recommendatory preface of Fuseli, though far more laboured than 'classical taste' would allow, without its full share of what we should denominate the empiric art. Not however, that we have the least intention of imputing to the *historical professor* [i.e., Fuseli], any idea of profiting by the sale of this work; but that we conceive he has hazarded assertions for the benefit of others, which under circumstances wherein his own interest only was concerned, his better judgment must have utterly disclaimed. We must substantiate our opinion by an extract.

—'Conscious that *affectation of originality* and *trite repetition* would equally impede his success, the author of the Moral Series [of designs] [*sic*] before us, has endeavoured to wake sensibility by touching our sympathies with *nearer, less ambiguous,* and *less ludicrous imagery!* than what mythology, gothic superstition, or symbols as far-fetched as inadequate, could supply. His *invention* has been chiefly employed to spread a *familiar and domestic atmosphere* round the *most important of all subjects, to connect the visible* and the *invisible world without provoking probability, and to lead the eye from the milder light of time to the radiations of eternity.* Such is the plan and the moral part of the author's invention; the technic part and the execution of the artist, though to be examined by other principles, and addressed to a narrower circle, equally claim approbation, sometimes *excite our wonder,* and *not seldom our fears* when *we see him play* on *the very verge of legitimate invention*: but *wildness so picturesque in itself,* so often *redeemed by taste, simplicity and elegance,* what *child of fancy,* what *artist* would *wish to discharge?* The *groups* and *single figures* on their *own basis, abstracted* from the *general composition,* and considered without attention to the plan, *frequently exhibit* those *genuine and unaffected attitudes* those *simple graces* which *nature and the heart alone can dictate,* and *only an eye inspired by both, discover.* EVERY CLASS of

ARTISTS, in EVERY STAGE of *their progress or attainments*, from the STUDENT to the FINISHED MASTER, and from the CONTRIVER of ORNAMENT to the PAINTER of HISTORY, will here find'—What? '*materials of art and hints of improvement.*'

Oh! 'lame and impotent conclusion!' why so they might, Mr. Fuseli, even in the rude scrawls that decorate the whig-whams of an untutored Indian. *Materials* of *art*, and *hints* of *improvement*! What a falling off is this, after all the florid commendations implied by the previous members of the paragraph! Did the honourable Professor *feel* that he had said too much, and eloquent though he be in literary composition, prefer descending to the bathos, to the disgrace of rendering his judgement more questionable by continuing an undeserved panegyric? But it is now time to examine the Designs themselves; some of which we must premise, have very little, if any, connection with the Poem they are avowedly published to illustrate. We should not indeed, have been able to discover what all the subjects meant, were it not for an explanatory supplement of four pages; yet that supplement we trust, for the honor of the Republic of Letters, was not written by any of the gentlemen of '*refined taste*, and *established literary repute*,' referred to in Mr. Cromek's advertisement,. In the description, the Designs are arranged very differently to their situations in the book itself; and for this the following reason is given. 'By the arrangement here made, the regular progression of man, from his *first* descent into the vale of death, to his *last* admission into life eternal is exhibited. These designs, detached from the work they embellish, *form of themselves* a *most interesting Poem!!*'

The figure of 'Christ descending into the Grave' which is the subject of the first print, is deficient in dignity; and 'expression does not lend its finished glow,' to give the semblance of divinity to the countenance. There is in fact, a prettiness about the face, which were it not for the beard would better consort with the graceful character of a young female, than with the majesty of the

> 'ETERNAL KING whose *potent arm* sustains
> The Keys of Hell and Death.'

The 'Descent of Man into the Vale of Death', has hardly any closer connection with Blair's poem than the words

> 'Tis here all meet!'

yet to make up the deficiency we have the following full description.

'The pious daughter weeping and conducting her sire onward; age, creeping carefully on hands and knees; an elder, without friend or kindred; a miser; a batchelor, blindly proceeding no one knows where, ready to drop into the dark abyss; frantic youth rashly devoted to vice and passion, rushing past the diseased and old, who totters on crutches; the wan declining virgin; the miserable distracted widow; the hale country youth; and the mother and her numerous progeny, are *among the groups* which speak irresistibly to the feelings.' In this enumeration of *groups*, almost every *single* figure in the piece is included and yet have we sought in vain for the 'elder, without friend or kindred,' unless it be him who is bearing a child and pressing it with parental tenderness to his bosom. The figures are tolerably well drawn; but there is nothing particularly masterly either in the attitudes or expression; nothing that requires more than common abilities either in the composition or grouping. The scene represents a rocky and winding path, leading downward from the entrance of a cavern.

The print of 'Death's Door,' illustrative of the lines,

> 'Tis but a night, a long and moonless night
> We make the grave our bed, and then are gone!'

is thus described—'The door opening, *that* seems to make utter darkness visible; age, on crutehes [*sic*], hurried by a tempest into it. Above is the renovated man seated in light and glory.' Death's door is delineated as a square aperture opening into a rocky recess, into which an aged man, his hair and garment blown forward by the wind, is represented as entering. In this figure the feebleness of age is well depicted, and there is a chasteness and simplicity in it which we vainly seek for in the 'renovated man seated in light and glory.' The latter excites the idea of pain, and his posture is that of a naked madman rather than that of an inhabitant of the realms of bliss.

The 'Death of the Strong Wicked Man' is conceived with greater energy of mind, and more happily expressed than any other design in the whole work. Where indeed, could be found the artist so dull of thought, as not to have every faculty of his soul animated to exertion by the powerful imagery of Blair.

> '*Strength* too! thou surly and less gentle boast
> Of those that loud laugh at the village ring!
> A fit of common sickness pulls thee down
> With greater ease than e'er thou didst the stripling
> That rashly dar'd thee to the unequal fight.
> What groan was that I heard? Deep groan indeed,

With anguish heavy laden! Let me trace it:
From yonder bed it comes, where the strong man,
By stronger arm belaboured, gasps for breath
Like a hard hunted beast. How his great heart
Beats thick! his roomy chest by far to[o] scant
To give the lungs full play! What now avail
The strong-built sinewy limbs, and well spread shoulders?
See how he tugs for life, and lays about him,
Mad with his pain! eager he catches hold
Of what comes next to hand, and grasps it hard,
Just like a creature drowning! Hideous sight!
O how his eyes stand out, and stare full ghastly,
While the distemper'd rank and deadly venom
Shoots like a burning arrow 'cross his bowels,
And drinks his marrow up! Heard you that groan?
It was his last. See how the great Goliath,
Just like a child that brawled itself to rest
Lies still!—

Had Mr. Blake contented himself with pourtraying the death-bed
of the strong man, the frantic sorrows of the despairing wife, and the
mute yet expressive woes of the afflicted daughter, his picture would
have deserved a very enlarged portion of commendation. The extremities convulsed with agony, the expanded chest heaving with inexpres-
sible pain, the swelling muscle, and the breadth of limb, are well
adapted to give the idea of strength laid low; but when to all this is
superadded a perfectly *corporeal* representation of 'the masculine Soul'
of the dying man 'hurried through the casement in flame,' the mind is
shocked at the outrage done to nature and probability; and notwithstanding the opinion of Mr. Fuseli, we hesitate not to characterize the
imagination of the artist, as carried far, very far, beyond the 'verge of
legitimate invention.'

The 'Death of the good Old Man,' is yet more objectionable. If it
were really Mr. Blake's intention 'to connect the visible and the
invisible world without provoking probability,' he should have done
it with threads of silk and not with bars of iron. The beings of another
world when depicted on the same canvas as earthly bodies, should be
sufficiently immaterial to be veiled by the gossamer, and not, as they
are here designed, with all the fullness and rotundity of mortal flesh.
What is yet more absurd, is to see the spirit of the good man borne

aloft between two angels, and clothed in the *same habiliments* as the body that lies on the pallet below! Mr. Blake should have recollected, that when the Prophet Elijah was taken up to heaven in a chariot of fire, his mantle 'fell from him.' The other parts of this design are good, and the humility and Christian resignation of the figures are strikingly accordant with the peaceful end of the Good Man, whose hand extended upon the gospels, at once displays his faith, and his confidence.

> 'How calm his exit!
> Night dews fall not more gently on the ground,
> Nor weary worn-out winds expire so soft.
> Behold him in the ev'ning tide of life,
> A life well spent, whose early care it was
> His riper years should not upbraid his green:
> By unperceiv'd degrees he wears away,
> Yet, like the sun, seems larger at his setting.'

'The Soul hovering over the Body,' illustrative of the passage

> 'How wishfully she looks
> On all she's leaving, now no longer her's!'

has the same defect of giving *substantial* form to incorporeal substance, and arraying it in earthly habiliments, as the former picture. Neither do we like the position of the soul, which is bending over the body, in a strained and awkward manner.

'The Soul exploring the recesses of the Grave,' has no prototype, we believe, in Blair's Grave: it is however thus described. 'The soul prior to the dissolution of the body, exploring through and beyond the tomb, and there discovering the emblems of mortality and immortality.' All this is represented by a female figure bearing a torch, and entering into a cavern, at the extremity of which lies a mouldering body partly surrounded by flames. Upon the top of the cavern stands a fear-struck maniac—we know not what else it can represent,— and in the back-ground are the summits of mountains, some buildings, and the waning moon. What these things mean, we are at a loss to discover, even with the assistance of the explanation. Certainly the *invention* is *original*; yet if this be a specimen of the 'picturesque wildness,' so 'often redeemed by taste, simplicity, and elegance,' we assuredly 'would wish to discharge' it altogether. Besides, in this design, the artist has departed from his own principles, as far as those principles are exemplified in the deaths of the Good and of the Bad Man; in both which pieces we see the spirit taking its flight to the realms of eternity immediately on the extinction of the mortal breath: in this the soul is made to wait on 'the dissolution of the body.' These inconsistencies must not be tolerated, even in the absurd effusions which we are here so strongly called upon to commend.

'The Councellor, King, Warrior, Mother and Child, in the Tomb,' is conceived in a much better taste; though considered as 'a high and original effort of genius,' we find but little to commend in it. Imagine a recessed Gothic tomb in a church wall, with the sculptured effigies of a departed family of 'the great deceased,' lying within it, and you have a complete idea of this design. *Invention* is here unnecessary; any Cathedral will furnish the prototypes.

'The Skeleton re-animated,' (which is the subject of the Vignette Title) is intended to illustrate this passage:

> 'When the dread trumpet sounds, the slumb'ring dust,
> Not unattentive to the call, shall wake;
> And every joint possess its proper place.'

In the design, we behold a naked figure, in nearly a perpendicular attitude, with the head downwards, as if descending from Heaven, sounding a trumpet over the face of the skeleton, which is throwing aside the winding sheet, and slowly rising from the tomb. The latter being partially environed by a few flames and a cloud of smoke, has been magnified by the ingenious writer of the supplementary description into 'the world in flames,' typifying 'the renovation of all things, the end of time, and the beginning of eternity!' The full expression of nudity, even in moral works, is not wholly desirable; and we think, that the descending angel, if angel he be who is coming headlong from on high, but without the least vestige of the angelic character than what mortal man precisely exhibits, might have been furnished with wings to infold his nakedness. To see a corporeal figure 'upborne upon nothing,' and blowing a trumpet in a constrained and ungraceful position, has something in it so repugnant to our feelings, as well as to 'legitimate invention' in art, that were Mr. Fuseli himself 'trumpet-tongued,' and should tell us that such a design merited 'approbation,' we should protest against the soundness of his judgment.

'The Re-union of the Soul and Body,' offers equal violence to true taste, as most of the subjects we have noticed; and there is a *seeming* incongruity in making the one masculine, and the other feminine: we say seeming, because it is difficult to determine whether the body was intended for that of the male or not.[1] Both are equally *substantial* in form and appearance, and were we not told that their action represented the re-union of the soul and body, we should on a first glance suppose, that the body was meant for a young man extending his arms to prevent a youthful female from falling headlong down to the earth.

'The Meeting of a Family in Heaven' is another subject for which we may look in vain through the Poem of Blair: we shall therefore insert the description as it stands, in plain prose.

'The sweet felicity, the endearing tenderness, the ineffable affection, that are here depicted, are sufficiently obvious. The husband clasps his wife; the children embrace; the boy recognizes, and eagerly springs to his father.'

It is omitted, that the above is performed under the wings of two angels, who, buoyant in the clouds, extend their pinions till, like the longer sides of an Isosceles triangle, they meet in a point at the top, and diverge outwardly. This gives a pyramidical formality to the whole design, which catches and detains the eye. The positions of the principal figures are also ill chosen; for however expressive they may be of conjugal love, it is of conjugal love *on earth*, and possesses little of that exalted character, which we may conceive to be displayed in the realms of heaven.

We are at length come to the last of these designs, 'The Day of Judgment;' a production in which there is much to commend, and much to censure. There is an impressive vigour in the general manage-ment and plan of the composition that demands approbation, but the figure of the SAVIOUR, who is seated on the throne of judgment, with the book of life open upon his knees, is deficient both in dignity and power; and the action of some of the groups is much too familiar. Mr. Blake's knowledge of drawing, and of the human figure, is better displayed by this, than any other of his designs; and he has executed some very difficult foreshortnings with great success.

We shall here close our remarks upon these designs. Though occasionally invigorated by an imagination chastened by good taste, we regard them in general as the offspring of a morbid fancy; and we think, that this attempt 'to connect the visible with the invisible world, by a familiar and domestic atmosphere,' has totally failed. The curtain that separates these worlds is still undrawn by mortal hands; and so we augur it will continue till that great day, when 'Heaven's portals shall be opened,' and the millions that now lie captive in the grave shall spring

[1] The body seems to be fairly clearly male.

—— 'into life,
Day-light, and liberty.' ——

Though all the prints bear the denomination of etchings, we discover the marks of the dry-point in most of them; but in some more than others. They are executed with much spirit and truth, yet we doubt whether Mr. Schiavonetti has done complete justice to the original drawings. A considerable time has elapsed since we had an opportunity of seeing them, but if our memory fails not, the defect of giving strong corporeal semblance to spiritual forms was much less glaring in them, than in the prints. The figures were more shadowy and insubstantial; and consequently, the effect of the whole was greatly improved.

One engraving we have yet to mention, and that is the *Portrait of Mr. Blake*, from a picture by T. Phillips, Esq. R.A. The bold and vigorous manner in which this is executed would alone confer a lasting fame on the talents of Schiavonetti, were all his other works destroyed. It represents a man about the middle period of life, with an open, expressive countenance, but accompanied by a wildness in the eye, by no means inconsistent with the ideas we might form of Mr. Blake, from what has been said above. The portrait itself, which the artist, with a most praiseworthy liberality, has presented to Mr. Cromek, is a very fine and well painted picture; and will doubtless descend with admiration to posterity. We hail the abilities of Mr. Phillips, as fully calculated to support, and even to improve the rising character of the *English School*; for by that honourable term the concentrated productions of English artists ought now to be distinguished.

The dedication of this edition of the Grave to the Queen, written by Mr. Blake, is one of the most abortive attempts to form a wreath of poetical flowers that we have ever seen. Should he again essay to climb the Parnassian heights, his friends would do well to restrain his wanderings by the strait waistcoat. Whatever licence we may allow him as a painter, to tolerate him as a poet would be insufferable. The subscribers to this work amount to about six hundred.

(q) The last known review of Blake's *Grave* designs appeared in the *Monthly Magazine* for 1 December 1808:

The Grave; a Poem by Blair, illustrated by Twelve Etchings, executed by Louis Schiavonetti, from the original Inventions of William Blake. 1808.

The series of engravings which is given under this title, in illustration

131

of the well known poem of *The Grave*, forms one of the most singular works ever published in England. In respect to the executive merits of the designs, there is considerable correctness and knowledge of form in the drawing of the various figures; the grouping is frequently pleasing, and the composition well arranged; some of them have even an air of ancient art, which would not have disgraced the Roman school. In the *ideal* part, or that which is supposed to connect them with the poem, there is a wildness of fancy and eccentricity, that leave the poet at a very considerable distance. Some are, perhaps, exceptionable; such as, *The Soul exploring the Recesses of the Grave*, represented by a female figure bearing a small light in her hand; and the *Soul rejoining the Body*, under the same appearance of a female rushing downwards to meet the embraces of the body which she had left. It is almost needless to say, these are images, or conceptions rather, which admit of no just graphic representations. *Death's Door* is the best of the series.

The author of these designs is an engraver of no mean talents in his art, and is said to receive the conceptions of them from 'Visions bright,' which, like the Muse of Milton—

> 'Visit his slumbers nightly, or when morn
> Purples the East.'

A portrait of Mr. Blake is prefixed to the publication, etched with spirit, from a picture by *Philips*. The head is finished with the graver, and is an excellent specimen of art, in the utmost degree creditable to Schiavonetti, by whose hand it is executed. The engraving indeed is, throughout the whole series, highly commendable. The work is accompanied by a warm and eloquent panegyric from the pen of Fuseli, the learned keeper of the Royal Academy.[1]

General comments, 1810–26

(r) One of the most enthusiastic critics of Blake's *Grave* designs was William Paulet Carey, who wrote in 1817:

The superior moral influence of paintings from *Sacred* history over those from *profane*, is great indeed. . . . If Blake had designed a series of subjects from heathen story, his genius could not have made so deep and lasting an impression upon the public, as it has done, by his solemn and affecting series of designs, for *Blair's* poem of The Grave, engraved by that lamented artist, Schiavonetti. . . .

[1] Anon., 'The Grave . . .', *Monthly Review*, vol. XXVI (1808), p. 458; see *Blake Records* (1969), pp. 209–10.

FUSELI in his just and forcible introduction to BLAKE's noble series of designs for CROMEK's edition of Blair's poem of the Grave, remarks that, through frequent repetition,—'The serpent, with its tail in its mouth, from a type of eternity, has become a *child's bauble*; even the nobler idea of Hercules passing between Virtue and Vice, or the *varied imagery of Death leading his patients to the grave*, owe their effect upon us more to *technical excellence*, than allegoric utility.' The contexts and the prints may warrant a conclusion that it was, from this conviction, BLAKE, in those imperishable designs, did not attempt to give any defined form of Death the Destroyer, to whom almost any other artist would have assigned a most conspicuous place. The skeleton rising out of the shroud, laid beside the grave, over which an angel sounds the last trumpet, is an emblem of the resurrection of the Dead, not a personification of Death, the insatiate Devourer.

Having mentioned these drawings, by BLAKE, I feel their strong hold upon me: and must obey the impulse. It would be impossible to enumerate, in a restricted space, the succession of beauties, in these affecting groups; yet I cannot, without self-reproach, and an abandonment of a public duty, pass them in silence. They abound in images of domestic gentleness and pathos; in varied grace, and unadorned elegance of form. Their primitive simplicity of disposition and character, is united with bold and successful novelty, and a devotional grandeur of conception. Although obliged to derive almost the entire of his materials from the Sepulchre, there is not an image capable of exciting disgust, or offence in the whole. Even when representing the dread unknown beyond the grave, he still contrives to keep the Fancy within the sphere of human sympathy. His agents, in general, after having shaken off the grosser substance of flesh, still retain the unaltered form. They appear to move round us upon solid earth; like ourselves, enjoy the light of day, and are canopied by an unclouded sky. With a few unimportant exceptions, his style is uniformly chaste. His energy is devoid of extravagance or distortion; his anatomical learning of pedantry; his grandeur free from wildness, and his beauty from affectation. His Spiritual forms are truly 'Angels and Ministers of grace.' His gloom has nothing depressing or sullen; its soothing spell charms the attention and fills the mind with serenity, hope and elevation. His solemn religious fervor, without deeply wounding our self-love, abates the angry passions; whispers an eternal lesson of admonition, and inspires us with *what ought to be the aim of all religious instruction, a love of our Fellow-Travellers in the vale of mortality*. The heart follows the rapt Enthusiast with pleasing sadness, and shares in the mournful delight of his journey, while his placid but melancholy fancy bids the bloom of Beauty triumph over the shadows of Death; breathes a nameless loveliness on things unearthly; and sheds a mild and holy illumination on the night of the grave.

I have applied the term 'placid' to the finely tempered spirit of this Artist's genius, as it appears in those affecting compositions, and in the deep serenity expressed in his portrait, by the masculine graver of the elder *Schiavonetti*, from the painting by *Phillips*. I never had the good fortune to see him; and so entire is the uncertainty, in which he is involved, that after many inquiries, I meet with some in doubt whether he is still in existence. But I have accidentally learned, from a Lady, since I commenced these remarks, that he is, certainly, now a resident in London. I have, however, heard enough to warrant my belief that his professional encouragement has been very limited, compared with his powers.

One fact is clear, that the purchaser of his drawings for the 'Grave,' was not a person of *rank* and *independent fortune*. The world is indebted to the superior taste and liberal spirit of that ingenious engraver, CROMEK, as a printseller and publisher, for the engravings of those designs. Beyond the circle of artists, I anxiously look round for the Designer's *Patrons*. In an Engraver, now no more, he found a purchaser, and in the Royal Academy, a recommendation to his country. *Posterity will inquire the rest.* . . .

I would fail in my sense of duty, were I not here to notice a fact, which does honour to the Royal Academy. If my information be not erroneous, and I think it is not, BLAKE is one of those highly gifted men, who owe the vantage ground of their fame, solely to their own powers. I have heard that he was, originally, an engraver of book plates. Yet, far from endeavouring to keep him in the back-ground, or question his merits, in 1808, when he executed the drawings for the 'Grave,' eleven Members of the Royal Academy, bore testimony, in a public advertisement, to their extraordinary excellence. The name of the Venerable President, WEST, appeared at the head of the list; followed by Sir WILLIAM BEECHEY, RICHARD COSWAY, JOHN FLAXMAN, THOMAS LAWRENCE, JOSEPH NOLLEKENS, WILLIAM OWEN, THOMAS STOTHARD, MARTIN ARCHER SHEE, HENRY THOMSON AND HENRY TRESHAM, Esquires. In addition to this powerful recommendation, FUSELI, the Lecturer of that Body, wrote for publication, his high opinion of the series. The truth and eloquence of his remarks, would alone, confer permanent distinction on the designs, even if they had not been consecrated to Posterity, by the inspiration, which they breathe. PHILLIPS, whose best portraits unite a *correct definition of details*, and an admirable truth of resemblance, with grace, spirit, and a noble breadth and harmony of effect, bore testimony to the merits of BLAKE's drawings, by painting his head for CROMEK, the intended publisher of the plates. The vigorous character of nature, in this masterly picture, is a fine lesson for the florid and flimsy *Mannerists* of the day. The countenance, expresses the deep calm of a spirit, lifted above the little concerns of this world, and, already in imagination, winging its way beyond the skies. In this honourable effort of the Royal Academicians to draw the attention of the public to the highest department of invention, portrait painters, sculptors and historical designers, liberally co-operated.[1]

(s) Blake was unexpectedly praised with great generosity in the fashionable *Repository of Arts* for June 1810 in connection with his *Grave* designs:

Blake's plates from Blair's *Grave*, lately engraved, are excellent studies for a young artist. Blake has lately received much deserved commendation from Fuseli. Perhaps, this engraver has more genius than any one in his profession in this country. If he would study the ornamental requisites more, he would probably attain much higher celebrity than he has already acquired.[2]

(t) Another of Blake's admirers, at least for a time, was C. H. B. Ker, who wrote to George Cumberland on 20 August 1810:

Blake's Grave—What a very fine work it is, and how much justice

---

[1] W. P. Carey, *Critical Description and Analytical Review of 'Death on the Pale Horse'*, *Painted by Benjamin West* (1817), pp. 9, 128–36; the first paragraph only was reprinted in the Philadelphia edition (1836), p. 20; paragraphs 2–5 are reprinted with minor stylistic changes but without comment in 'Remarks on Blake's Designs Illustrative of Blair's Grave' (From '*Critical Description of* West's *Death on the Pale Horse*), By Mr. William Carey, *Repository of Arts, Literature, Fashions, Manufactures, &c.*, 2nd S., vol. v (1 May 1818), pp. 278–80; see *Blake Records* (1969), pp. 245–8.

Elsewhere (in his *Critical Description of the Procession of Chaucer's Pilgrims to Canterbury, Painted by Thomas Stothard*, [1808], pp. 10–11), Carey noted 'that we are indebted to Mr. Cromek for . . . the idea of employing that extraordinary Artist, *Blake*, to compose his *grand designs* for Blair's *Grave*'. And in his *Desultory Exposition of an Anti-British System of Incendiary Publication, &c* (1819), pp. 22, 32, he cited his account of Blake's 'imperishable series of designs for the Grave' given in his *Pale Horse* book.

[2] Juninus, 'On Splendour of Colours, &c.', *Repository of Arts, Literature, Commerce, Manufactures, Fashions, and Politics*, II (June 1810 Supplement), pp. 408–9.

Schiavonetti has done it[; it is] with¹ excepti[on] the best thing of the sort which has appear[ed] this Century.

(u) The reviewer of another book in the *Quarterly Review* for March 1826 paused to remark:

Among Blake's strange designs for Blair's poem of the Grave, is one representing the reunion of the body and the soul; the highest genius alone could have conceived it, and only madness have dared to attempt the execution.[1]

(v) A yet stranger context in which Blake's *Grave* designs appeared was as illustrations for a series of poems written for them by José Joaquin de Mora and published, with Schiavonetti's etchings, in London in 1826, and with the following introduction (here translated):

The compositions in this volume are included solely as illustrations of the engravings. They concern the true poetry of the work, which is not more admirable for the correctness of the drawing and for the merit of the execution than for the achievement of the design and for the sublime intelligence which reigns in the allegories.

Two celebrated artists have contributed to the completion of these engravings: William Black [*sic*], the designer, whose portrait adorns the frontispiece, and Louis Schiavonetti, the engraver, whose graver has served to interpret so many master-works. Anyone may follow the hackneyed paths of artistic execution: they are true poets who can recognize the secret of inspiration, and who in their productions aspire to a higher sphere than that contained in the mere exterior representation of objects.

The author of these verses has not done more than to indicate the subjects of the prints, attempting to imitate the convention and the style which was employed in sacred poetry by eminent men in Spain in the sixteenth-century; however, he has given more latitude to the philosophical part than to the mystical, so that the appearance is bold, severe, and sublime in order to enter into the circle of ideas which form the dominion of literature. Moreover, although religion in our epoch has not lost its august dignity, the progress of reason has brought it [religion] to men, if it may be said, and the works of many writers, as learned as they are virtuous, have shown us that rationality can be applied,

---

[1] Anon., 'Art. V.—*Vie des Révélations de la Soeur Nativité . . .*', *Quarterly Review*, vol. XXXIII (March 1826), p. 390; see *Blake Records* (1969), p. 326.

without violence and without profanation, to eternal truths as to moral precepts.[1]

(w) And finally, Edward Denny wrote to Blake on 4 November 1826, asking for

a copy of Blair's Grave, with your illustrations. . . . I am very much interested in it, I was shewn the work a day or two ago, & I think it one of the most beautiful & interesting things I have seen of yours.

30. *The Prologue and Characters of Chaucer's Pilgrims* (1812)

1812

The Prologue and Characters of Chaucer's Pilgrims, Selected from his Canterbury Tales; intended to illustrate a particular design of Mr. William Blake, which is engraved by himself. And may be seen at Mr. Colnaghi's, Cockspur Street; at Mr. [James] Blake's, No. 28, Broad Street, Golden Square; and at the Publisher's, Mr. Harris, Bookseller, St. Paul's Church Yard. Price two shillings and sixpence. (1812.)

(a) According to the anonymous Introduction,

To the genius and fancy of that celebrated Artist, Mr. Blake, it occurred, that tho' the names and habits of men altered by time, yet their characters remained the same; and as Chaucer had drawn them Four Hundred years past, he might as justly delineate them at the present period, and by a pleasant picture, bring to our imagination the merry company setting out upon their journey.

[1] José Joaquin de Mora, *Meditaciones Poeticas* (London, 1826), pp. ii–iii; see *Blake Records* (1969), pp. 333–5.

As the Canterbury Tales may be too long a story for modern amusement, I have selected the Prologue and the Characters, that the heads, as represented by Mr. Blake, may be compared with the lineaments drawn by Chaucer, and I think the merit of the artist will be generally acknowledged.

(b) The only public reference to the work is in a letter by 'P.' to the *Gentleman's Magazine*, Vol. LXXXII (September 1812), p. 217, about the Talbot (formerly Tabarde) Inn: 'A well-painted Sign [i.e. design?] by Mr. Blake represents Chaucer and his merry Company setting out [from it] on their journey.' This could alternatively refer to the separate master-engraving of the subject.

31. Virgil, *Pastorals* (1821)

1821–63

The Pastorals of Virgil, with a Course of English Reading, Adapted for Schools: in which all The Proper Facilities are given, enabling youth to acquire The Latin Language, in the Shortest Period of Time. Illustrated by 230 Engravings. By Robert John Thornton, M.D. Member of the University of Cambridge, &c. &c. Third Edition [2 vols] (London, stereotyped edition, 1821).

(a) Blake's only woodcuts, the twenty-six he made for Thornton's Virgil, appeared in difficult circumstances:

When Blake had produced his cuts, which were, however, printed with an *apology*, a shout of derision was raised by the wood-engravers. 'This will never do,' said they; 'we will show what it ought to be'— that is, what the public taste would like—

and three of the plates were badly re-engraved from Blake's designs by another hand.[1] (b) They might all have been so ruined, but

it fortunately happened that [Thornton] meeting one day several artists at Mr. Aders' table,—Lawrence, James Ward, Linnell, and others,—conversation fell on the Virgil. All present expressed warm admiration of Blake's art, and of those designs and woodcuts in particular. By such competent authority reassured, if also puzzled, the good Doctor began to think there must be more in them than he and his publishers could discern. The contemplated sacrifice of the [seventeen] blocks already cut was averted. The three other designs, however, had been engraved by another, nameless hand. . . .[2]

(c) The 'apology' with which Blake's plates were printed said:

The Illustrations of this English Pastoral are by the famous BLAKE, the illustrator of Young's Night Thoughts, and Blair's Grave; who designed and engraved them himself. This is mentioned, as they display less of art than genius, and are much admired by some eminent painters.

Blake's young disciples, who afterwards became eminent, were almost reverential about the Virgil designs. (d) Years later Edward Calvert wrote to his son:

Some small woodcuts of Blake are in your possession, they are only illustrations of a little pastoral poem by Phillips. They are done as if by a child; several of them careless and incorrect, yet there is a spirit in them, humble enough and of force enough to move simple souls to tears.[3]

(e) Samuel Palmer's description was similar:

I sat down with Mr. Blake's Thornton's Virgil woodcuts before me, thinking to give to their merits my feeble testimony. I happened first to think of their sentiment. They are visions of little dells, and nooks, and corners of Paradise; models of the exquisitest pitch of intense poetry. I thought of their light and shade, and looking upon them I found no word to describe it. Intense depth, solemnity, and vivid brilliancy only coldly and partially describe them. There is in all such a

[1] [Henry Cole,] 'Fine Arts. The Vicar of Wakefield, With thirty-two Illustrations. By W. Mulready', Athenaeum, 21 January 1843, p. 165, a review of Mulready's plates; see Blake Records (1969), p. 267.

[2] A. Gilchrist, Life of William Blake (1863), vol. I, p. 273; see Blake Records (1969), pp. 267–8.

[3] [Samuel Calvert,] A Memoir of Edward Calvert Artist (1893), p. 19; see Blake Records (1969), p. 271.

mystic and dreamy glimmer as penetrates and kindles the inmost soul, and gives complete and unreserved delight, unlike the gaudy daylight of this world. They are like all that wonderful artist's works the drawing aside of the fleshly curtain, and the glimpse which all the most holy, studious saints and sages have enjoyed, of that rest which remaineth to the people of God. The figures of Mr. Blake have that intense, soul-evidencing attitude and action, and that elastic, nervous spring which belongs to uncaged immortal spirits.[1]

32. *Remember Me!* (1825, 1826)

1825

Remember Me! A New Years Gift or Christmas Present, 1825 [1826] (1825, 1826).

Blake's engraving of his own design of 'The Hiding of Moses' is introduced with the words:

This is that precise point where the power of the painter would be called upon to exert the utmost stretch of his talents. He would have to paint the heart-rending solicitude of the fond mother, about to leave the babe in such a perilous situation, amongst the rushes, and her first-born child to the mercy of the waves, and if not a prey to the devouring crocodile, at the disposal of the family of that monarch, 'who knew not Joseph;' and his power was absolute. None but an artist possessing the imagination and abilities of Mr. Blake could possibly accomplish a task so replete with difficulty that made a painter, when he was trying to represent a father sacrificing his daughter, cover his head in his mantle, feeling that the subject was beyond his power of depicting it.[2]

---

1 A. H. Palmer, *The Life and Letters of Samuel Palmer* (1892), pp. 15–16; see *Blake Records* (1969), pp. 271–2.
2 *Remember Me!* (1825), pp. 33–4; see *Blake Records* (1969), p. 296.

33. *Illustrations of The Book of Job* (1826)

1826–45

ספר איוב

Illustrations of The Book of Job Invented & Engraved by William Blake 1825 London Published as the Act directs March 8: 1825 by William Blake Nº 3 Fountain Court Strand [1826].

Though Blake's *Job* designs are today perhaps his best-known engravings, when they were first published by John Linnell in April 1826 they appealed primarily to a very limited circle, chiefly artist-friends of Linnell. (a) A copy was presented to the Royal Academy,

upon the merits of which he received the highest congratulations from the following Royal Academicians: Sir Thomas Lawrence, Mr. Baily, Mr. Philips, Mr. Chantrey, Mr. James Ward, Mr. Arnald, Mr. Collins, Mr. Westmacott, and many other artists of eminence.[1]

(b) On 11 April 1826 an Oxford undergraduate named E. T. Daniell wrote to Linnell:

since I saw you [I] have fallen into a violent fit about them and am becoming a speedy convert to your opinion on the subject. If the sort of thing could once become the taste here our Authorities would soon follow one another but the difficulty is to set one off.

(c) The first known complaint about the book came from Blake's friend the connoisseur Robert Balmanno:

22 April 1826
Dear Sir I have received Mr Blakes Illustrations to the Book of Job & perused the work with great attention & much interest.
    You will not be offended if I say, your binder has put you to great

---

[1] J. T. Smith, *Nollekens and his Times* (1828); see *Blake Records* (1969), p. 468. The connection between this praise and the Royal Academy copy is my inference, not Smith's. For the buyers of *Job*, see *Blake Records* (1969), pp. 586–605.

expense in doing them up, & has thereby *to me* very greatly lessened the pleasure I should have taken in them. The back is so squeezed & pinched, the prints crack & wrinkle[?] every time they are turned over, & *must* in a short time be much damaged.

I cannot handle the book without pain. With your permission therefore I will return it, and ask you for a set on plain paper *loose* & without any fly leaves between.

Balmanno was so indignant with Linnell's reply to this letter that he decided to 'see Mr Blake himself & arrange with him' rather than deal with Linnell.

(d) One of the most enthusiastic critics was Sir Edward Denny, who wrote to Linnell on 20 November:

What shall I say, what *can* I say of the Book of Job[?] I can only say that it is a *great work*—and though I cannot venture to pass my humble comments upon any thing so truly sublime—I do indeed feel its exquisite beauty & marvellous grandeur. It is a privelege to possess such a work & still greater to be able to feel it.—it is I think the most perfect thing I have ever seen from the hands of Mr Blake, & if his Dante is superior, he will, I may almost say, outdo himself—

(e) Linnell seems to have asked acquaintances to sell copies for him; one of them, H. S. C. Shorts, reported from Salisbury on 5 January 1827:

I have returned the Illustrations of Job. . . . I have been unable to find a customer for it[;] in fact Salisbury being a place in which the Arts are but little cultivated It is difficult to find any person to appreciate much less purchase a work of this description[.] My Father admired one or two of the designs but as I expected it is not at all the style which pleases him.

(f) After Blake's death, his old friend George Cumberland wrote a letter of condolence to Catherine Blake, on 25 November 1829, in which he said of *Job*:

That elaborate work, I have not only shewn to all our amateurs and artists here without success but am now pushing it through Clifton [near Bristol], by means of *Mr Lane* the Bookseller there, having previously placed it with Mr *Tyson*, Mr *Trimlet*, and another of our Print Sellers here without success—and as that is the case, and that even those who desired me to write to my friend for a List of his works and prices (among whom were his great admirers from having seen what I possessed—viz. Dr King of Clifton & Mr Rippengale the Artist.) declined giving him any orders, on account, as they said, of the prices—I should not recommend you to send any more here—but rather to fix a place in London where all his works may be disposed of offering a complete set for Sale to the British Museum Print room, as that will make them best known.—better even than their independant author who for his many virtues most deserved to be so—a Man who has stocked the english school with fine ideas,—above trick, fraud, or servility.

On 3 December Cumberland wrote to his son George (Jr),

as to the Job . . . I have tried all shops & acquaintance in vain hitherto— it is a Sad work yet full of Imagination.

He wrote to his son again on 26 December about his *Job* commission and Mrs Blake:

I never could consider it as equal to his other performances . . . let her know that I have always taken every measure to promote the sale of Mr B works among my friends here without the smallest Success, the prices having always been a hindrance—That I heartily wish her every success, and shall still do all I can to serve her, but take no more Prints of any one to sell here by the Booksellers, as nothing does here[.]

(g) On 11 March 1828 H. Dumaresq wrote to Linnell:

I have shewn the Illustrations of the Book of Job to many of my friends, but I have not yet found them in general impressed with any sense of their beauty nor inclined to purchase the work. It will be valued only by Artists, I suspect altho the encomium of those distinguished persons named in your former note would induce one to hope for the credit of the public taste that designs so highly thought of by them might find abundance of purchasers.

(h) In April 1830 Linnell lent a copy of *Job* to the Quaker poet Bernard Barton, and on the 22nd Barton replied that he was too poor to buy it himself and that he had been unable to sell it:

There is a dryness and hardness in Blake's manner of engraving which is very apt to be repulsive to print-collectors in general—to any, indeed, who have not taste enough to appreciate the force and originality of his conceptions, in spite of the manner in which he has embodied them. I candidly own I am not surprised at this; his style is little calculated to take with admirers of modern engraving. It puts me in mind of some old prints I have seen, and seems to combine somewhat of old Albert Durer with Bolswert. I cannot but wish he could have clothed his imaginative creations in a garb more attractive to ordinary mortals, or else given simple outlines of them. The extreme beauty, elegance, and grace of several of his marginal accompaniments induce me to think that they would have pleased more generally in that state. But his was not a mind to dictate to; and what he has done is quite enough to stamp him as a genius of the highest order. A still prouder and more enduring meed of praise is due to the excellence and sterling worth of the man: his child-like simplicity, his manly independence, his noble aspirations after the purest and loftiest of all fame, appear to me to form a singular union of those virtues which distinguished the better citizens of Greece and Rome with the milder graces which adorned the primitive Apostles. To have been the friend of such a man is a proud and enviable distinction.

Eight years later, on 8 August 1838, Barton wrote to Linnell again about Blake's

too besetting faults, extravagance and distortion, as well as that hardness which too frequently mars some of his most graceful idealities.[1]

There are no known reviews of *Job*.

(i) F. T. Palgrave wrote from Balliol College to his mother in February 1845 about an evening with Mr Jowett, who

showed me a book which I dare say papa knows—W. Blake's 'Illustrations of the Book of Job.' They are a number of little etchings, drawn and etched by Blake; and certainly they show immense power and originality. Though often quite out of drawing and grotesque, they are most interesting—far more than Flaxman, for instance. Schiavonetti's etchings in the 'Grave,' though far more correct, give but a faint idea of the force and vigour of these. If you can possibly borrow them, I am sure you will be exceedingly interested by them—I have seen nothing so extraordinary for a long time. Some, as of Job in misery, and of the Morning Stars singing for joy, are beautiful; some, as of a man tormented by dreams and the Vision of the Night, are most awful;

---

[1] *Blake Records* (1969), p. 401.

and what adds much to the pleasure of seeing them, is that every stroke seems to do its utmost in expression, and to show that one mind both planned and executed them.[1]

34. *Blake's Illustrations of Dante* (?1838)

1824–?32

Blake's Illustrations of Dante, Seven Plates, designed and engraved by W. Blake, Author of 'Illustrations of the Book of Job,' &c. &c. Price £2 2s. India Paper . . . (London, ?1838).

Blake's last great work, never completed and indeed not published in his lifetime, was his drawings (102 of them) and engravings (seven) in illustration of Dante's *Divine Comedy.* (a) Samuel Palmer, then nineteen years old, wrote:

On Saturday, 9th October, 1824, Mr. Linnell called and went with me to Mr. Blake. We found him lame in bed, of a scalded foot (or leg). There, not inactive, though [almost] sixty-seven years old, but hard-working on a bed covered with books sat he up like one of the Antique patriarchs, or a dying Michael Angelo. Thus and there was he making in the leaves of a great book (folio) the sublimest design from his (not superior) Dante. He said he began them with fear and trembling. I said 'O! I have enough of fear and trembling.' 'Then,' said he, 'you'll do.' He designed them (100 I think) during a fortnight's illness in bed! And there, first, with fearfulness (which had been more, but that his designs from Dante had wound me up to forget myself), did I show him some of my first essays in design; and the sweet encouragement he gave me (for Christ blessed little children) did not tend basely to presumption and idleness, but made me work harder and better that afternoon and night.

[1] G. F. Palgrave, *Francis Turner Palgrave* (1899), p. 27.

(b) Blake's friend, the dilettante (and later the poisoner) Thomas Griffiths Wainewright, wrote to Linnell in February 1827: 'His Dante is the most wonderful emanation of imagination that I ever heard of.'

(c) Crabb Robinson reported in his diary for 2 February 1827:

Gotzenberg[er] the young painter from Germany called on me and I accompanied him to Blake[.] We looked over Blakes Dante—Gotzenberger seemed highly gratif.^{d} by the designs and Mrs Aders says G. considers[?] B as the first & Flaxman as the second man he has seen in England—[1]

(d) On 15 June 1830 Bernard Barton wrote to Linnell:

I thank thee very cordially for Blake's illustration of a scene in Dante, and feel myself equally, if not more, thy debtor for the pretty little pastoral etching of thy own. At the risk of being thought to possess a tame and insipid taste, I must confess I prefer it to Blake's. I admire the imaginative genius displayed in the latter, but I love the simple feeling and truth to Nature evinced in the former.

(e) Perhaps the last word should be Frederick Tatham's, who wrote in his 'Life of Blake':

He read Dante when he was past 60, altho' before he never knew a word of Italian & he drew from it a hundred such designs, as have never been done by any Englishman at any period or by any foreigner since the 15th Century, & then his only competitor was Michael Angelo.[2]

---

[1] Crabb Robinson was influenced by Gotzenberger's judgment to suppress his own; his diary for 17 December 1825 records that Blake 'shewed me his designs, of which I have nothing to say but that they evince a power of grouping & of throw^g grace & interest over conceptions most monstrous & disgusting which I sho^d not have anticipated.' But in his reminiscences for the same visit (*Blake Records* [1969], p. 543) he said only: 'He was making designs or engraving, I forget which[.]—Cary's Dante was before [him.] —He shewed me some of his Designs from Dante, of which I do not presume to speak[.]— They were too much above me[.]—But Götzenberger, whom I afterwards took to see them, expressed the highest admiration of them.'

[2] *Blake Records* (1969), p. 527.

PART V   GENERAL ESSAYS
ON BLAKE

35. B. H. Malkin, *A Father's Memoirs of his Child*

1806

Benjamin Heath Malkin wrote the earliest essay on Blake and incorporated it in the introductory letter (addressed to Thomas
Johnes) in his *A Father's Memoirs of his Child* (1806), pp. xvii–xli. He
associated Blake with his prodigious son, who died at the age of six,
and this of course affected the reactions to Blake of his readers and
critics.

Malkin's biographical information is good and appears to have
come from Blake himself. He gives 'How Sweet I Roamed' and 'I
Love the Jocund Dance' from *Poetical Sketches,* 'Laughing Song',
'Holy Thursday', and 'The Divine Image' from *Songs of Innocence*
and 'The Tyger' from *Songs of Experience* (all the poems from the
Songs being given here in conventional typography for the first
time) and thus introduced these works to readers who otherwise
would have ignored them. The book was published at Malkin's
expense, and, though reviewed several times, had a rather limited
circulation; of 1,000 copies printed, Malkin gave away over 40, and
450 were pulped in 1811. Nevertheless, Malkin's sympathetic and
judicious account of Blake was the means of introducing a wide
contemporary audience to Blake's poetry (his art is largely ignored),
through circulation of the book itself,[1] through reviews, and
through accounts by Crabb Robinson, J. T. Smith, and Allan
Cunningham derived from it.[2]

---

[1] In the spring of 1807 Wordsworth and his sister copied out from Malkin 'Holy
Thursday', 'Laughing Song', 'The Tyger', and 'I Love the Jocund Dance' into a commonplace book (see *Blake Records* [1969], p. 430, n. 1).
[2] Six biographical paragraphs about Blake are omitted at the beginning.

Mr. Blake has long been known to the order of men among whom he ranks; and is highly esteemed by those, who can distinguish excellence under the disguise of singularity. Enthusiastic and high flown notions on the subject of religion have hitherto, as they usually do, prevented his general reception, as a son of taste and of the muses. The sceptic and the rational believer, uniting their forces against the visionary, pursue and scare a warm and brilliant imagination, with the hue and cry of madness. Not contented with bringing down the reasonings of the mystical philosopher, as they well may, to this degraded level, they apply the test of cold calculation and mathematical proof to departments of the mind, which are privileged to appeal from so narrow and rigorous a tribunal. They criticise the representations of corporeal beauty, and the allegoric emblems of mental perfections; the image of the visible world, which appeals to the senses for a testimony to its truth, or the type of futurity and the immortal soul, which identifies itself with our hopes and with our hearts, as if they were syllogisms or theorems, demonstrable propositions or consecutive corollaries. By them have the higher powers of this artist been kept from public notice, and his genius tied down, as far as possible, to the mechanical department of his profession. By them, in short, has he been stigmatised as an engraver, who might do tolerably well, if he was not mad. But men, whose names will bear them out, in what they affirm, have now taken up his cause. On occasion of Mr. Blake engaging to illustrate the poem of The Grave, some of the first artists in this country have stept forward, and liberally given the sanction of ardent and encomiastic applause. Mr. Fuseli, with a mind far superior to that jealousy above described, has written some introductory remarks in the Prospectus of the work. To these he has lent all the penetration of his understanding, with all the energy and descriptive power characteristic of his style. Mr. Hope and Mr. Locke have pledged their character as connoisseurs, by approving and patronising these designs. Had I been furnished with an opportunity of shewing them to you, I should, on Mr. Blake's behalf, have requested your concurring testimony, which you would not have refused me, had you viewed them in the same light.

Neither is the capacity of this untutored proficient limited to his professional occupation. He has made several irregular and unfinished attempts at poetry. He has dared to venture on the ancient simplicity; and feeling it in his own character and manners, has succeeded better than those, who have only seen it through a glass. His genius in this line assimilates more with the bold and careless freedom, peculiar to our writers at the latter end of the sixteenth, and former part of the seventeenth century, than with the polished phraseology, and just, but subdued thought of the eighteenth. As the public have hitherto had no opportunity of passing sentence on his poetical powers, I shall trespass on your patience, while I introduce a few specimens from a collection, circulated only among the author's friends, and richly embellished by his pencil.

LAUGHING SONG.

When the green woods laugh with the voice of joy,
And the dimpling stream runs laughing by,
When the air does laugh with our merry wit,
And the green hill laughs with the noise of it,

When the meadows laugh with lively green,
And the grasshopper laughs in this merry scene,
When Mary and Susan and Emily,
With their sweet round mouths, sing Ha, ha, he!

When the painted birds laugh in the shade,
Where our table with cherries and nuts is spread,
Come live and be merry and join with me,
To sing the sweet chorus of Ha, ha, he!

The Fairy Glee of Oberon, which [John Samuel] Stevens's exquisite music has familiarised to modern ears, will immediately occur to the reader of these laughing stanzas. We may also trace another less obvious resemblance to Jonson, in an ode gratulatory to the Right Honourable Hierome, Lord Weston, for his return from his embassy, in the year 1632. The accord is to be found, not in the words nor in the subject; for either would betray imitation: but in the style of thought, and, if I may so term it, the date of the expression.

Such pleasure as the teeming earth
Doth take in easy nature's birth,
When she puts forth the life of every thing:
And in a dew of sweetest rain,
She lies delivered without pain,
Of the prime beauty of the year, the spring.

The rivers in their shores do run,
The clouds rack clear before the sun,
The rudest winds obey the calmest air:

Rare plants from every bank do rise,
And every plant the sense surprise,
Because the order of the whole is fair!

The very verdure of her nest,
Wherein she sits so richly drest,
As all the wealth of season there was spread;
Doth show the graces and the hours
Have multiplied their arts and powers,
In making soft her aromatic bed.

Such joys, such sweets, doth your return
Bring all your friends, fair lord, that burn
With love, to hear your modesty relate
The bus'ness of your blooming wit,
With all the fruit shall follow it,
Both to the honour of the king and state.

The following poem of Blake is in a different character. It expresses with majesty and pathos, the feelings of a benevolent mind, on being present at a sublime display of national munificence and charity.

HOLY THURSDAY.

'Twas on a Holy Thursday, their innocent faces clean,
The children walking two and two, in red and blue and green;
Grey-headed beadles walked before, with wands as white as snow,
Till into the high dome of Paul's, they, like Thames' waters, flow.

Oh! What a multitude they seemed, these flowers of London town!
Seated in companies they sit, with radiance all their own!
The hum of multitudes was there, but multitudes of lambs;
Thousands of little boys and girls, raising their innocent hands.

Now like a mighty wind they raise to heaven the voice of song,
Or like harmonious thunderings, the seats of heaven among!
Beneath them sit the aged men, wise guardians of the poor:
Then cherish pity, lest you drive an angel from your door.

The book of Revelation, which may well be supposed to engross much of Mr. Blake's study, seems to have directed him, in common with Milton, to some of the foregoing images. 'And I heard as it were the voice of a great multitude, and as the voice of many waters, and as the voice of mighty thunderings, saying, Alleluia: for the Lord God omnipotent reigneth.' [Revelation 19:6] Milton comprises the mighty thunderings in the epithet 'loud,' and adopts the comparison of many waters, which image our poet, having in the first stanza appropriated differently, to their flow rather than to their sound, exchanges in the last for that of a mighty wind.

> He ended; and the heav'nly audience loud
> Sung hallelujah, as the sound of seas,
> Through multitude that sung.
>
> PARADISE LOST, Book x. 641.

It may be worth a moment's consideration, whether Dr. Johnson's remarks on devotional poetry, though strictly just where he applies them, to the artificial compositions of Waller and Watts, are universally and necessarily true. Watts seldom rose above the level of a mere versifier. Waller, though entitled to the higher appellation of poet, had formed himself rather to elegance and delicacy, than to passionate emotions or a lofty and dignified deportment. The devotional pieces of the Hebrew bards are clothed in that simple language, to which Johnson with justice ascribes the character of sublimity. There is no reason therefore, why the poets of other nations should not be equally successful, if they think with the same purity, and express themselves in the same unaffected terms. He says indeed with truth, that 'Repentance trembling in the presence of the judge, is not at leisure for cadences and epithets.' But though we should exclude the severer topics from our catalogue, mercy and benevolence may be treated poetically, because they are in unison with the mild spirit of poetry. They are seldom treated successfully; but the fault is not in the subject. The mind of the poet is too often at leisure for the mechanical prettinesses of cadence and epithet, when it ought to be engrossed by higher thoughts. Words and numbers present themselves unbidden, when the soul is inspired by sentiment, elevated by enthusiasm, or ravished by devotion. I leave it to the reader to determine, whether the following stanzas have any tendency to vindicate this species of poetry; and whether their simplicity and sentiment at all make amends for their inartificial and unassuming construction.

THE DIVINE IMAGE.

> To Mercy, Pity, Peace, and Love,
> All pray in their distress,
> And to these virtues of delight
> Return their thankfulness.

For Mercy, Pity, Peace, and Love,
Is God our Father dear:
And Mercy, Pity, Peace, and Love,
Is man, his child and care.

For Mercy has a human heart;
Pity, a human face;
And Love, the human form divine,
And Peace, the human dress.

Then every man, of every clime,
That prays in his distress,
Prays to the human form divine,
Love, Mercy, Pity, Peace.

And all must love the human form,
In Heathen, Turk, or Jew!
Where Mercy, Love, and Pity dwell,
There God is dwelling too.

Shakspeare's Venus and Adonis, Tarquin and Lucrece, and his Sonnets, occasioned it to be said by a contemporary, that, 'As the soul of Euphorbus was thought to live in Pythagoras, so the sweet witty soul of Ovid lives in mellifluous honey-tongued Shakspeare.'[1] These poems, now little read, were favourite studies of Mr. Blake's early days. So were Jonson's Underwoods and Miscellanies, and he seems to me to have caught his manner, more than that of Shakspeare in his trifles. The following song is a good deal in the spirit of the Hue and Cry after Cupid, in the Masque on Lord Haddington's marriage. It was written before the age of fourteen, in the heat of youthful fancy, unchastised by judgment. The poet, as such, takes the very strong liberty of equipping himself with wings, and thus appropriates his metaphorical costume to his corporeal fashion and seeming. The conceit is not unclassical; but Pindar and the ancient lyrics arrogated to themselves the bodies of swans for their august residence. Our Gothic songster is content to be encaged by Cupid; and submits, like a young lady's favourite, to all the vagaries of giddy curiosity and tormenting fondness.

How sweet I roamed from field to field,
And tasted all the summer's pride,

[1] This quotation comes originally from Francis Meres, *Palladis Tamia*, London, 1598 (Gerald Eades Bentley, *Shakespeare, A Biographical Handbook*, New Haven, 1961, pp. 153, 226).

Till I the prince of love beheld,
    Who in the sunny beams did glide!

He shewed me lilies for my hair,
    And blushing roses for my brow;
He led me through his gardens fair,
    Where all his golden pleasures grow.

With sweet May dews my wings were wet,
    And Phoebus fired my vocal rage;
He caught me in his silken net,
    And shut me in his golden cage.

He loves to sit and hear me sing,
    Then, laughing, sports and plays with me;
Then stretches out my golden wing,
    And mocks my loss of liberty.

The playful character ascribed to the prince of love, and especially his wanton and fantastic action while sporting with his captive, in the two last stanzas, render it probable that the author had read the Hue and Cry after Cupid. If so, it had made its impression; but the lines could scarcely have been remembered at the time of writing, or the resemblance would have been closer. The stanzas, to which I especially allude, are these.

Wings he hath, which though ye clip,
    He will leap from lip to lip,
    Over liver, lights, and heart,
    But not stay in any part;
    And, if by chance his arrow misses,
    He will shoot himself, in kisses.

Idle minutes are his reign;
    Then the straggler makes his gain,
    By presenting maids with toys,
    And would have ye think 'em joys:
    'Tis th'ambition of the elf,
    To have all childish as himself.

The two following little pieces are added, as well by way of contrast, as for the sake of their respective merits. In the first, there is a simple and pastoral gaiety, which the poets of a refined age have generally found much more difficult of attainment, than the glitter of wit, or the affectation of antithesis. The second rises with the subject. It wears that garb of grandeur, which the idea of creation communicates to a mind of the higher order. Our bard, having brought the topic he descants on from warmer latitudes than his own, is justified in adopting an imagery, of almost oriental feature and complection.

SONG.

I love the jocund dance,
The softly breathing song,
Where innocent eyes do glance,
    And where lisps the maiden's tongue.

I love the laughing gale,
I love the echoing hill,
Where mirth does never fail,
    And the jolly swain laughs his fill.

I love the peasant cot,
I love the innocent bower,
Where white and brown is our lot,
    Or fruit in the mid-day hour.

I love the oaken seat,
Beneath the oaken tree,
Where all the old villagers meet,
    And laugh our sports to see.

I love our neighbours all,
But, Kitty, I better love thee;
And love them I ever shall;
    But thou art all to me.

THE TIGER.

Tiger, Tiger, burning bright,
In the forest of the night!
What immortal hand or eye
Could frame thy fearful symmetry?

In what distant deeps or skies,
Burnt the fire of thine eyes?
On what wings dare he aspire?
What the hand dare seize the fire?

And what shoulder, and what art,
Could twist the sinews of thy heart?
When thy heart began to beat,
What dread hand forged thy dread feet?[1]

What the hammer? What the chain?
In what furnace was thy brain?
What the anvil? What dread grasp
Dared its deadly terrors clasp?

When the stars threw down their spears,
And watered heaven with their tears,
Did he smile his work to see?
Did he, who made the lamb, make thee?

Tiger, tiger, burning bright,
In the forests of the night;
What immortal hand or eye
Dare frame thy fearful symmetry?[2]

Besides these lyric compositions, Mr. Blake has given several specimens of blank verse. Here, as might be expected, his personifications are bold, his thoughts original, and his style of writing altogether epic in its structure. The unrestrained measure, however, which should warn the poet to restrain himself, has not unfrequently betrayed him into so wild a pursuit of fancy, as to leave harmony unregarded, and to pass the line prescribed by criticism to the career of imagination. . . .

---

[1] Normally this line is 'What dread hand? & what dread feet?'. In copy P, however, it is altered as in Malkin, except that the verb is 'Formd'. In his copy of Malkin, Beckford wrote: 'Some splendid specimens from that treasury of Nonsense. Mr. Blake the mad draughtsman's poetical compositions: "Tiger, Tiger burning bright, In the forest of the night, etc." Surely the receiver and disseminator of such trash is as bad as the thief who seems to have stolen them from the walls of Bedlam.' (F. Rosebery, 'Books from Beckford's Library now at Barnbougle', *Book Collector*, vol. XIV [1965], p. 327.)

[2] At this point 'Jabez Legg 1809' wrote in his copy of the book (now in Columbia University Library), 'This is a little too much about Mr. Blake' (D. V. Erdman, 'Every thing has its vermin', *Blake Newsletter*, vol. II [1969], p. 68).

36. H. C. Robinson, 'William Blake, artist, poet, and religious mystic'

1811

[H. C. Robinson,] 'William Blake, Künstler, Dichter, und Religiöser Schwärmer', *Vaterländisches Museum*, vol. I (January 1811), pp. 107–31.

Henry Crabb Robinson described the genesis of his anonymous essay on Blake in his Reminiscences:

I was amusing myself this Spring [of 1810] by writing an account of the insane poet painter & engraver *Blake*—Perthes of Hamburg had written to me asking me to send him an article for a new German magazine entitled Vaterlandische Annalen [i.e., *Vaterländisches Museum*] which he was about to set up and Dr *Malkin* having, in the memoirs of his Son given an account of this extraordinary genius with Specimens of his poems I resolved out of these to compose a paper And this I did and the paper was translated by D^r [W. H.] Julius . . . before I drew up this paper I went to see a Gallery of Blakes paintings—which were exhibited by his brother a hosier in Carnaby Market—[1]

The biographical information in Robinson's essay is good, though mostly derived from Malkin. He quotes *'To the Muses' from *Poetical Sketches*, *'Introduction' and 'Holy Thursday' from *Innocence*, 'The Tyger' and *'The Garden of Love' from *Experience*, and passages from *America* and *Europe*, those marked with an asterisk (*) for the first time in conventional typography. Robinson's account of Blake seems to have had little direct effect on the public.

---

1 *Blake Records* (1969), pp. 223, 225. On receiving the first number of *Vaterländisches Museum* with a translation of his essay in it, Robinson wrote in his diary for 28 April 1811: 'In most respects [it is] well done, but in one or two instances the Sense of the verse was mistaken.' The translation back into English below is adapted from that of K. A. Esdaile, 'An early appreciation of William Blake', *Library*, 3rd S., vol. V (1914), pp. 236–56.

[Modern translation]

WILLIAM BLAKE,

ARTIST, POET, AND RELIGIOUS MYSTIC

The lunatic, the lover, and the poet
Are of imagination all compact.
                    SHAKESPEARE.

Of all the conditions which arouse the interest of the psychologist, none assuredly is more attractive than the union of genius and madness in single remarkable minds, which, while on the one hand they compel our admiration by their great mental powers, yet on the other move our pity by their claims to supernatural gifts. Of such is the whole race of ecstatics, mystics, seers of visions, and dreamers of dreams, and to their list we have now to add another name, that of William Blake.

This extraordinary man, who is at this moment living in London, although more than fifty years of age, is only now beginning to emerge from the obscurity in which the singular bent of his talents and the eccentricity of his personal character have confined him. We know too little of his history to claim to give a complete account of his life, and can do no more than claim to have our information on very recent authority. It must suffice to know by way of introduction that he was born in London of parents of moderate means, and early gave himself up to his own guidance, or rather, misguidance. In his tenth year he went to a drawing school, in his fourteenth (as apprentice) to an engraver of the name of Basire, well known by his plates to Stuart's *Athens* and his engraving of West's 'Orestes and Pylades'. Even as a boy, Blake was distinguished by the singularity of his taste. Possessed with a veritable passion for Gothic architecture, he passed whole days in drawing the monuments in Westminster Abbey. In addition he collected engravings, especially after Raphael and Michael Angelo, and idolised Albert Dürer and Heemskerk.

Although he afterwards worked as a student at the Royal Academy, he had already shown his bent to an art so original that, isolated from his fellow-students, he was far removed from all regular or ordinary occupation. His name is nevertheless to be found under some very commonplace plates to children's books; but while he cherished artistic visions utterly opposed to the taste of connoisseurs, and regarded more recent methods in drawing and engraving as sins against art, he preferred, in his phrase, to be a martyr for his religion—i.e., his art—to debasing his talents by a weak submission to the prevailing fashion of art in an age of artistic degradation. Moreover, as his religious convictions had brought on him the credit of being an absolute lunatic, it is hardly to be wondered at that, while professional connoisseurs know nothing of him, his very well-wishers cannot forbear betraying their compassion, even while they show their admiration. One attempt at introducing him to the great British public has indeed succeeded, his illustrations to Blair's *Grave*, a religious poem very popular among the serious, which connoisseurs find remarkable alike for its beauties and defects, blaming its want of taste and delicacy, while admiring the imaginative powers of the poet. Blake, although properly speaking an engraver, was not commissioned to engrave his own drawings, the execution being entrusted, for reasons which we shall soon hear, to Schiavonetti, who executed his task with great neatness, but with such an admixture of dots and lines as must have aroused the indignation of the artist. This work, which besides the twelve drawings contains an excellent portrait of Blake and the original text, costs two and a half guineas. It is preceded by some remarks of Fuseli's, which we insert as a proof of the merits of our artist, since we cannot give an actual reproduction of his work. After mentioning the utility of such a series of moral designs in an age so frivolous as ours, before which the allegories of antiquity faint and fail, Fuseli continues, 'the author of the moral series before us . . . [see No. 29c].' One can see this is no 'damning with feigned praise', for the faults indicated by Fuseli are only too apparent. In fact, of all the artists who ever lived, even of those perverted spirits described by Goethe in his entertaining 'Sammler und die Seinigen' (*Propyläen*, vol. ii, part 2) under the title of poetisers, phantom-hunters, and the like, none so completely betrays himself as our artist.

We shall return to these drawings later, and will now proceed to speak of the little book on which we have specially drawn, a book, besides, which is one of the most curious ever published.

The illustrations to the *Grave*, though only perhaps admired by the few, were by these few loudly and extravagantly praised. Blake, who had become known by their praises, now resolved to come forward. Only last year he opened an exhibition of his frescoes, proclaiming that he had rediscovered the lost art of fresco. He demanded of those who had considered his works the slovenly daubs of a madman, destitute alike of technical skill and harmony of proportion, to examine them now with greater attention. 'They will find,' he adds, 'that if Italy is

enriched and made great by Rafael, if Michael Angelo is its supreme
glory, if Art is the glory of a Nation, if Genius and Inspiration are the
great Origin and Bond of Society, the distinction my Works have
obtained from those who best understand such things calls for my
Exhibition as the greatest of Duties to my Country.'

At the same time he published a *Descriptive Catalogue* of these fresco
pictures, out of which we propose to give only a few unconnected
passages. The original consists of a veritable folio of fragmentary
utterances on art and religion, without plan or arrangement, and the
artist's idiosyncrasies will in this way be most clearly shown.

The vehemence with which, throughout the book, he declaims
against oil painting and the artists of the Venetian and Flemish schools is
part of the fixed ideas of the author. His preface begins with the following words: 'The eye that can prefer the Colouring of Titian and Rubens
to that of Michael Angelo and Rafael, ought to be modest and doubt its
own powers,' but, as he proceeds with his descriptions, his wrath against
false schools of painting waxes, and in holy zeal he proclaims that the
hated artists are evil spirits, and later art the offspring of hell. Chiaro-
scuro he plainly calls 'an infernal machine in the hands of Venetian and
Flemish Demons.' The following will make it appear that these expressions are not merely theoretical phrases. Correggio he calls 'a soft
and effeminate, and consequently a most cruel demon.' Rubens is 'a
most outrageous demon.' . . . He does not conceal the ground of this
preference [for Raphael and Michael Angelo], and the following passage,
while it reveals the artist's views on the technique of his art, contains
a truth which cannot be denied, and which underlies his whole doctrine.
'The great and golden rule of art, as well as of life, is this: That the
more distinct, sharp, and wiry the bounding line, the more perfect the
work of art. . . .' This passage is sufficient to explain why our artist was
not permitted to engrave his own designs. In the same spirit he proclaims the guilt of the recent distinction between a painting and a
drawing. 'If losing and obliterating the outline constitutes a Picture,
Mr. B. will never be so foolish as to do one.—There is no difference
between Rafael's Cartoons and his Frescos, or Pictures, except that the
Frescos, or Pictures, are more finished.' He denies Titian, Rubens and
Correggio all merit in colouring, and says, 'their men are like leather,
and their women like chalk.' In his own principal picture his naked
forms are almost crimson. They are Ancient Britons, of whom he says,
'The flush of health in flesh exposed to the open air, nourished by the
spirits of forests and floods in that ancient happy period, which history

has recorded, cannot be like the sickly daubs of Titian or Rubens. As to a modern Man, stripped from his load of cloathing, he is like a dead corpse.'

We now pass from the technique of his art to the meaning and poetical portions in which the peculiarities of our artist are still more clearly seen. His greatest enjoyment consists in giving bodily form to spiritual beings. Thus in the *Grave* he has represented the re-union of soul and body, and to both he has given equal clearness of form and outline. In one of his best drawings, the 'Death of the Strong Wicked Man,' the body lies in the death agony, and a broken vessel, whose contents are escaping, indicates the moment of death, while the soul, veiled in flame, rises from the pillow. The soul is a copy of the body, yet in altered guise, and flies from the window with a well-rendered expression of horror. In other engravings the soul appears hovering over the body, which it leaves unwillingly; in others we have the Re-union of both at the Resurrection and so forth. These are about the most offensive of his inventions.

In his Catalogue we find still further vindication of the reproaches brought against his earlier work. 'Shall Painting be confined to the sordid drudgery of fac-simile representations of merely mortal and perishing substances, and not be as poetry and music are, elevated into its own proper sphere of invention and visionary conception?' He then alleges that the statues of the Greek gods are so many bodily representations of spiritual beings. 'A Spirit and a Vision are not, as the modern philosophy supposes, a cloudy vapour, or a nothing: they are organized and minutely articulated beyond all that the mortal and perishing nature can produce. Spirits are organized men.'

In a certain sense every imaginative artist must maintain the same, but it will always remain doubtful in what sense our artist uses these expressions. For in his own description of his allegorical picture of Pitt guiding Behemoth, and Nelson Leviathan (pictures which the present writer, although he has seen them, dares not describe) he says, ['] these pictures are similar to those Apotheoses of Persian, Hindoo, and Egyptian antiquity, which are still preserved on rude monuments.['] . . . As this belief of our artist's in the intercourse which, like Swedenborg, he enjoys with the spiritual world has more than anything else injured his reputation, we subjoin another remarkable passage from his *Catalogue*. His greatest and most perfect work is entitled 'The Ancient Britons.' It is founded on that strange survival of Welsh bardic lore which Owen gives thus under the name of Triads:

In the last battle that Arthur fought, the most Beautiful was one
That return'd, and the most Strong another: with them also return'd
The most Ugly, and no other beside return'd from the bloody Field.

The most Beautiful, the Roman Warriors trembled before and
    worshipped:
The most Strong, they melted before him and dissolved in his
    presence:
The most Ugly they fled with outcries and contortions of their
    Limbs.

The dark words are explained by a yet darker commentary. 'The
Strong Man represents the human sublime. . . .' The picture represents
these three beings fighting with the Romans; but we prefer to let the
artist speak of his own works. 'It has been said to the Artist, "take the
Apollo for the model of your beautiful Man. . . ." '
Elsewhere he says that Adam and Noah were Druids, and that he
himself is an inhabitant of Eden. Blake's religious convictions appear
to be those of an orthodox Christian; nevertheless, passages concerning
earlier mythologies occur which might cast a doubt on it. These
passages are to be found in his account of this picture of Chaucer's
Pilgrims, certainly the most detailed and accurate of his works since,
kept within limits by his subject, he could not run riot in his imagination. . . . These passages could be explained as the diatribes of a fervid
monotheist against polytheism; yet, as our author elsewhere says, 'The
antiquities of every nation under Heaven, is no less sacred than those
of the Jews,' his system remains more allied to the stoical endurance of
Antiquity than to the essential austerity of Christianity.

These are the wildest and most extravagant passages of the book,
which lead to the consideration with which we begin this account. No
one can deny that, as even amid these aberrations gleams of reason and
intelligence shine out, so a host of expressions occur among them which
one would expect from a German rather than an Englishman. The
Protestant author of *Herzensergiessungen eines kunstliebenden Kloster-
bruders* [W. H. Rackenroder] created the character of a Catholic in whom
Religion and love of Art were perfectly united, and this identical person,
singularly enough, has turned up in Protestant England. Yet Blake does
not belong by birth to the established church, but to a dissenting sect;
although we do not believe that he goes regularly to any Christian
church. He was invited to join the Swedenborgians under Proud, but
declined, notwithstanding his high opinion of Swedenborg, of whom he

says: 'The works of this visionary are well worthy the attention of Painters and Poets; they are foundations for grand things; the reason they have not been more attended to is because corporeal demons have gained a predominance.' Our author lives, like Swedenborg, in communion with the angels. He told a friend, from whose mouth we have the story, that once when he was carrying home a picture which he had done for a lady of rank, and was wanting to rest in an inn, the angel Gabriel touched him on the shoulder and said, Blake, wherefore art thou here? Go to, thou shouldst not be tired. He arose and went on unwearied. This very conviction of supernatural suggestion makes him deaf to the voice of the connoisseur, since to any reproach directed against his works he makes answer, why it cannot in the nature of things be a failure. 'I know that it is as it should be, since it adequately reproduces what I saw in a vision and must therefore be beautiful.'

It is needless to enumerate all Blake's performances. The most famous we have already mentioned, and the rest are either allegorical or works of the pen. We must, however, mention one other of his works before ceasing to discuss him as an artist. This is a most remarkable edition of the first four books of Young's *Night Thoughts*, which appeared in 1797, and is no longer to be bought, so excessively rare has it become. In this edition the text is in the middle of the page; above and below it are engravings by Blake after his own drawings. They are of very unequal merit; sometimes the inventions of the artist rival those of the poet, but often they are only preposterous translations of them, by reason of the unfortunate idea peculiar to Blake, that whatsoever the fancy of the spiritual eye may discern must also be as clearly penetrable to the bodily eye. So Young is literally translated, and his thought turned into a picture. Thus for example the artist represents in a drawing Death treading crowns under foot, the sun reaching down his hand, and the like. Yet these drawings are frequently exquisite. We hear that the publisher has not yet issued a quarter of the drawings delivered to him by the artist and has refused to sell the drawings, although a handsome sum was offered him for them.

We have now to introduce our artist as poet, so as to be able to give some examples of his work in this branch of art, since he himself has published nothing in the proper sense of the word. The poems breathe the same spirit and are distinguished by the same peculiarities as his drawings and prose criticisms. As early as 1783 a little volume was printed with the title of *Poetical Sketches* by W. B. No printer's name is given on the title-page, and in the preface it states that the poems were composed between his thirteenth and twentieth years. They are of very unequal merit. The metre is usually so loose and careless as to betray a total ignorance of the art, whereby the larger part of the poems are rendered singularly rough and unattractive. On the other hand, there is a wildness and loftiness of imagination in certain dramatic fragments which testifies to genuine poetical feeling. An example may serve as a measure of the inspiration of the poet at this period.

To the Muses. . . .

A still more remarkable little book of poems by our author exists, which is only to be met with in the hands of collectors. It is a duodecimo entitled 'Songs of Innocence and Experience, shewing the two contrary states of the human soul. The Author and Printer W. Blake.' The letters appear to be etched, and the book is printed in yellow. Round and between the lines are all sorts of engravings; sometimes they resemble the monstrous hieroglyphs of the Egyptians, sometimes they represent not ungraceful arabesques. Wherever an empty space is left after the printing a picture is inserted. These miniature pictures are of the most vivid colours, and often grotesque, so that the book presents a most singular appearance. It is not easy to form a comprehensive opinion of the text, since the poems deserve the highest praise and the gravest censure. Some are childlike songs of great beauty and simplicity; these are the *Songs of Innocence*, many of which, nevertheless, are excessively childish. The *Songs of Experience*, on the other hand, are metaphysical riddles and mystical allegories. Among them are poetic pictures of the highest beauty and sublimity; and again there are poetical fancies which can scarcely be understood even by the initiated.

As we wish to make the knowledge of our author as complete as possible, we will give an example of either kind. The book has an 'Introduction' from which we here insert the first and the two last stanzas (the fourth and fifth). . . .

We can only give one more example of these joyous and delicious songs, that called 'Holy Thursday,' which describes the procession of children from all the charity schools to St. Paul's Cathedral which always takes place on this day. . . .

We cannot better set forth the many-sided gifts of our poet than by following up this singularly delicate and simple poem with this truly inspired and original description of 'The Tyger'. . . .

Of the allegorical poems we prefer to give one which we think we understand, rather than one which is to us wholly incomprehensible.

The following *Song of Experience* probably represents man after the loss of his innocence, as, bound by the commandment and the priests its servants, he looks back in longing to his earlier state, where before was no commandment, no duty, and nought save love and voluntary sacrifice.

The Garden of Love. . . .

Besides these songs two other works of Blake's poetry and painting have come under our notice, of which, however, we must confess our inability to give a sufficient account. These are two quarto volumes which appeared in 1794, printed and adorned like the *Songs*, under the titles of *Europe*, a Prophecy, and *America*, a Prophecy. The very 'Prophecies of Bakis' are not obscurer. *America* appears in part to give a poetical account of the Revolution, since it contains the names of several party leaders. The actors in it are a species of guardian angels. We give only a short example, nor can we decide whether it is intended to be in prose or verse [*America*, pl. 10]. . . .

The obscurity of these lines in such a poem by such a man will be willingly overlooked.

Europe is a similar mysterious and incomprehensible rhapsody, which probably contains the artist's political visions of the future, but is wholly inexplicable. It appears to be in verse, and these are the first four lines [*Europe*, 1, pl. 4]. . . .

These Prophecies, like the *Songs*, appear never to have come within the ken of the wider public.

We have now given an account of all the works of this extraordinary man that have come under our notice. We have been lengthy, but our object is to draw the attention of Germany to a man in whom all the elements of greatness are unquestionably to be found, even though those elements are disproportionately mingled. Closer research than was permitted us would perhaps shew that as an artist Blake will never produce consummate and immortal work, as a poet flawless poems; but this assuredly cannot lessen the interest which all men, Germans in a higher degree even than Englishmen, must take in the contemplation of such a character. We will only recall the phrase of a thoughtful writer, that those faces are the most attractive in which nature has set something of greatness which she has yet left unfinished; the same may hold good of the soul.

37. Obituary in *Literacy Gazette*

1827

The first obituary of Blake was an elegant one in the *Literary Gazette*, which generated a number of others.[1]

William Blake;
The Illustrator of the Grave, &c.

To those few who have sympathies for the ideal and (comparatively speaking) the intellectual in art, the following notice is addressed. Few persons of taste are unacquainted with the designs by Blake, appended as illustrations to a 4to edition of Blair's Grave. It was borne forth into the world on the warmest praises of all our prominent artists, Hoppner, Phillips, Stothard, Flaxman, Opie, Tresham, Westmacott, Beechey, Lawrence, West, Nollekins, Shee, Owen, Rossi, Thomson, Cosway, and Soane; and doubly assured with a preface by the learned and severe Fuseli, the latter part of which we transcribe:—'The author of the moral series before us [has given us] . . . materials of art and hints of improvement'!

When it is stated, that the pure-minded Flaxman pointed out to an eminent literary man the obscurity of Blake as a melancholy proof of English apathy towards the grand, the philosophic, or the enthusiastically devotional painter; and that he, Blake, has been several times employed for that truly admirable judge of art Sir T. Lawrence, any further testimony to his extraordinary powers is unnecessary. Yet has Blake been allowed to exist in a penury which most artists,*—beings

---

[1] Anon., 'William Blake: the illustrator of The Grave, &c.', *Literary Gazette*, 18 August 1827, pp. 540–1. The author may be Blake's admirer 'William Carey [who] was the chief contributor' to the early numbers of the *Literary Gazette* (William Jerdan, *Autobiography* [1852], vol. II, p. 176).

The obituary was repeated, with minor variants (often erroneous) in the *Gentleman's Magazine*, vol. XCVIII (October 1827), pp. 377–8 (listing some of Blake's works), the *Monthly Magazine*, n.s., vol. IV (October 1827), p. 435, the *New Monthly Magazine*, vol. XXI (1 December 1827), pp. 535–6, the *Annual Register* vol. LXIX (1828), pp. 253–4, and the *Annual Biography and Obituary*, vol. XII (1828), pp. 416–18; see *Blake Records* (1969), pp. 248–9, 354–7, 359, 361–2.

* The term is employed in its generic and comprehensive sense.

necessarily of a sensitive temperament,—would deem intolerable. Pent, with his affectionate wife, in a close back-room in one of the Strand courts, his bed in one corner, his meagre dinner in another, a ricketty table holding his copper-plates, his colours, books (among them his Bible, a Sessi Velatello's Dante, and Mr. Carey's translation, were at the top), his large drawings, sketches and MSS.;—his ancles frightfully swelled, his chest disordered, old age striding on, his wants increased, but not his miserable means and appliances: even yet was his eye undimmed, the fire of his imagination unquenched, and the preternatural, never-resting activity of his mind unflagging. He had not merely a calmly resigned, but a cheerful and mirthful countenance; in short, he was a living commentary on Jeremy Taylor's beautiful chapter on Contentedness. He took no thought for his life, what he should eat, or what he should drink; nor yet for his body, what he should put on; but had a fearless confidence in that Providence which had given him the vast range of the world for his recreation and delight.

Blake died last Monday! Died as he lived! piously cheerful! talking calmly, and finally resigning himself to his eternal rest, like an infant to its sleep. He has left *nothing* except some pictures, copper-plates, and his principal work, a Series of a hundred large Designs from Dante.

William Blake was brought up under Basire, the eminent engraver. He was active in mind and body, passing from one occupation to another, without an intervening minute of repose. Of an ardent, affectionate, and grateful temper, he was simple in manner and address, and displayed an inbred courteousness of the most agreeable character. Next November he would have been *sixty-nine* [i.e., seventy]. At the age of sixty-six he commenced the study of Italian, for the sake of reading Dante in the original, which he accomplished!

His widow is left (we fear, from the accounts which have reached us) in a very forlorn condition, Mr. Blake himself having latterly been much indebted for succour and consolation to his friend Mr. Linnell, the painter. We have no doubt but her cause will be taken up by the distributors of those funds which are raised for the relief of distressed artists, and also by the benevolence of private individuals.

When further time has been allowed us for inquiry, we shall probably resume this matter; at present, (owing the above information to the kindness of a correspondent,) we can only record the death of a singular and very able man.[1]

---

[1] The promise to resume this matter was never fulfilled in the *Literary Gazette*.

38. Obituary in *Literary Chronicle*

1827

The obituary in the *Literary Chronicle* was also full and informed. It refers at the close to Blake's inscription in Upcott's autograph album, which begins: 'William Blake[,] one who is very much delighted with being in good Company[.] Born 28 Novr 1757 in London & has died Several times since[.]'[1]

William Blake

The late Mr. William Blake, whose recent decease has been publicly notified, may be instanced as one of those ingenious persons which every age has produced, whose eccentricities were still more remarkable than their professional abilities, the memory of which extra circumstances have largely contributed to the perpetuation of their fame.

Mr. Blake, celebrated for his graphic illustrations of Blair's poem of the Grave, however ingenious that series of designs, was still more remarkable, as before observed, for the singularity of his opinions, and for his pretended knowledge of the world of spirits.

It is not our intention to speak of the aberrations of men of genius with levity, but would rather advert [to] them, with commiseration and pity. Yet, to dwell upon the pursuits, or to relate the opinions of such visionaries as the late Mr. Blake with seriousness, would be an attempt beyond the extremest limits of our editorial gravity.

That he *believed* to have *seen* and *conversed* with those with whom he pretended acquaintance, we no more doubt than that he is now incorporated with those incorporeal beings with whom he was so familiar. But still more strange, perhaps, is that which is no less true—that there are those, men of sense and of quick perception too, who actually believe what he believed to have seen to be true!

Mr. Blake, in our hearing, with, apparently, the powers of reasoning

---

[1] Anon, 'William Blake', *Literary Chronicle and Weekly Review*, 1 September 1827, pp. 557–8; see *Blake Records* (1969), pp. 351–3.

on the objects before him, as clearly, distinctly, and rationally as the most sane logician, has declared, that he had frequently seen and conversed with the ancient kings and prophets. With David, Saul, Hezekiah and other great personages mentioned in Holy Writ; nay, that he drew their portraits in his sketch-book, which portraits we have seen. 'Seeing is believing,' saith the adage. We have seen these—ergo, we believe, as aforesaid, that Mr. Blake thought that he had seen, and confirmed the fact by sketching their portraits.

In illustration of which, it may be worth relating here, that which he related to us, namely—

That the first time he saw King Saul, he was clad in armour. That his helmet was of a form and structure unlike any that he had seen before, though he had been in the armories of all nations since the flood. Moreover, that King Saul stood in that position which offered only a view in part of the said helmet, and that he could not *decently* go round to view the whole.

Thus the sketch of the helmet,—for artists have a rule not to touch at home upon that which they have sketched abroad, neither from nature or the life; this rule, Mr. Blake invariably maintained, wherein the material of his art was exercised upon those of his sitters, who were immaterial. This sketch of the helmet then remained as he first sketched it—incomplete.

'Some months after' (the first sitting,) said Mr. Blake, 'King Saul appeared to me again (when he took a second sitting,) and then I had an opportunity of seeing the other part of the helmet.'

We saw the said helmet when completed, and, in sober truth can assert, that the helmet and the armour are most extraordinary!

The MAN FLEA.—Mr. Blake had a conversation with a *flea*, which, on being related to us, naturally enough reminded us of the saying of the great Napoleon, 'that from the sublime to the ridiculous—was but a step.'

The flea communicated to Mr. Blake what passed, as related to himself, at the *Creation*. 'It was first intended,' said he (the flea) 'to make me as big as a bullock; but then when it was considered from my construction, so armed—and so powerful withal, that in proportion to my bulk, (mischievous as I now am) that I should have been a too mighty destroyer; it was determined to make me—no bigger than I am.'

It must, in justice to the genius and professional renown of Mr. Blake, be added, that he made a drawing, composed in a poetic mood, of this little pernicious *vampire*, enlarging it to the figure of a man, encased in armour, folded somewhat analogously to the rhinoceros-like coat of the flea, and denominated it—*The Man Flea*; and, to speak without *hyperbole*, it is indubitably the most ingenious, and able personi-fication of a *devil*, or a malignant and powerful *fiend*, that ever emanated from the inventive pencil of a painter.

Apropos—In a book of autographs, in the possession of the librarian of the London Institution, is the autograph of this artist, who has added to a very clever drawing, 'William Blake, born in 1765, has died several times since ! ! !'

39. Allan Cunningham *Lives of . . .*
British Painters

1830

Allan Cunningham's skilful anecdotal biography of Blake in his *Lives of the Most Eminent British Painters, Sculptors, and Architects*, vol. II (1830), pp. 140–79 (expanded in the second edition, vol. II [1830], pp. 143–88), was probably the most important factor in keeping Blake's name alive from 1830 until Gilchrist's epochal *Life* in 1863. He had good information, for he not only inquired among Blake's friends and borrowed extensively from the essays by B. H. Malkin and J. T. Smith, but, he said, 'I know Blake's character, for I knew the man.'[1]

The series in general was very popular from the first; within months of publication, the 12,000 copies of vol. III were 'already out of print',[2] and a new edition of vol. II appeared in the same year as the first. The Blake life was widely reviewed[3] and quoted, and it was the basis of most of the casual accounts of Blake until the 1860s. In particular, the works by Blake which Cunningham quoted (usually inaccurately) were probably the primary channel through which most readers of the time approached his works directly.

The first edition of Cunningham's life stressed a schizophrenic interpretation of Blake: 'The day was given to the graver' and

[1] *Blake Records* (1969), p. 375, a letter of 29 July 1829.

[2] D. Hogg, *Life of Allan Cunningham* (1875), p. 300, quoting a letter of 29 May 1830.

[3] There were reviews in (1) the *Athenaeum*, 6 February 1830, pp. 66–8 (quoting ¶ 9–11, 47–8); (2) all but the first paragraph of this review were silently reprinted in the *Literary Port Folio*, vol. I ([Philadelphia] 13 May 1830), p. 150; (3) *Zeitgenossen*, vol. III ([Leipzig], 1830), pp. 170–8 (scarcely more than a translation of ¶ 8–10, 23–4, 36–9, 41–4, 47–9); (4) *London Literary Gazette*, 8 February 1830, pp. 85–6 (quoting ¶ 8–10, 23–4, 36–44, 47–9); *Gentleman's Magazine*, vol. L (February 1830), pp. 141–3 (quoting ¶ 39); (6) *Monthly Review*, vol. XIII (March 1830), pp. 453–4 (quoting ¶ 34); (7) *London University Magazine*, vol. II (March 1830) begins as a review (see pp. 199–205); (8) *Fraser's Magazine*, vol. II (March 1830) is a kind of review (quoting ¶ 2–12, 14–34, 36–9, 41, 46–7); (9) *Casket*, vol. V ([Philadelphia] May 1830), pp. 231–2 (quoting ¶ 36–9, 41); (10) this review is largely reprinted in the *New England Weekly Review*, 3 May 1830, p.1 (quoting ¶ 36–7); (11) *American Monthly Magazine*, vol. III (June 1831), pp. 164–71 (quoting ¶ 1–2, 9–12, 14, 19–24, 38–9, 41, 48); (12) *Edinburgh Review*, vol. LIX (April 1834), p. 53; see *Blake Records* (1969), pp. 377–93, 398, 400, 626.

sanity, 'and he bestowed his evenings upon painting and poetry' of a mad kind (¶8). This strain survives in the enlarged second edition (printed below), but here he added ¶13, 35, 40, 53–8, including six new poems and considerably greater praise, and he made a few trifling changes in the earlier text (which are ignored below). For example, in the first edition he found 'no meaning' in the prose of *Poetical Sketches* (¶7), but he altered this in the second edition to 'little or no meaning'. The first edition was reprinted in 1831, 1837, 1839, 1842, 1844, 1846, 1907; the second and considerably superior edition was reprinted in 1880, 1886, 1893, 1969, and 1970. Paragraph numbers inserted by the editor.

WILLIAM BLAKE

1 Painting, like poetry, has followers, the body of whose genius is light compared to the length of its wings, and who, rising above the ordinary sympathies of our nature, are, like Napoleon, betrayed by a star which no eye can see save their own. To this rare class belonged William Blake.

2 He was the second son of James Blake and Catharine his wife, and born on the 28th of November, 1757, in 28, Broad Street, Carnaby Market, London. His father, a respectable hosier, caused him to be educated for his own business, but the love of art came early upon the boy; he neglected the figures of arithmetic for those of Raphael and Reynolds; and his worthy parents often wondered how a child of theirs should have conceived a love for such unsubstantial vanities. The boy, it seems, was privately encouraged by his mother. The love of designing and sketching grew upon him, and he desired anxiously to be an artist. His father began to be pleased with the notice which his son obtained— and to fancy that a painter's study might after all be a fitter place than a hosier's shop for one who drew designs on the backs of all the shop bills, and made sketches on the counter. He consulted an eminent artist, who asked so large a sum for instruction, that the prudent shopkeeper hesitated, and young Blake declared he would prefer being an engraver —a profession which would bring bread at least, and through which he would be connected with painting. It was indeed time to dispose of him. In addition to his attachment to art, he had displayed poetic symptoms—scraps of paper and the blank leaves of books were found covered with groups and stanzas. When his father saw sketches at the top of the sheet and verses at the bottom, he took him away to Basire,

the engraver, in Green Street [i.e., Great Queen Street], Lincoln's Inn Fields, and bound him apprentice for seven years. He was then fourteen years old.

3   It is told of Blake that at ten years of age he became an artist, and at twelve a poet. Of his boyish pencillings I can find no traces—but of his early intercourse with the Muse the proof lies before me in seventy pages of verse, written, he says, between his twelfth and his twentieth year, and published, by the advice of friends, when he was thirty [i.e., twenty-six]. There are songs, ballads, and a dramatic poem; rude sometimes and unmelodious, but full of fine thought and deep and peculiar feeling. To those who love poetry for the music of its bells, these seventy pages will sound harsh and dissonant; but by others they will be more kindly looked upon. John Flaxman, a judge in all things of a poetic nature, was so touched with many passages, that he not only counselled their publication, but joined with a gentleman of the name of Matthews in the expense, and presented the printed sheets to the artist to dispose of for his own advantage. One of these productions is an address to the Muses—a common theme, but sung in no common manner. . . .

4   The little poem called 'The Tiger' has been admired for the force and vigour of its thoughts by poets of high name. Many could weave smoother lines—few could stamp such living images. . . .

5   In the dramatic poem of King Edward the Third there are many nervous lines, and even whole passages of high merit. The structure of the verse is often defective, and the arrangement inharmonious; but before the ear is thoroughly offended, it is soothed by some touch of deep melody and poetic thought. The princes and earls of England are conferring together on the eve of the battle of Cressy—the Black Prince takes Chandos aside, and says—

> 'Now we're alone, John Chandos, I'll unburthen
> And breathe my hopes into the burning air—
> Where thousand Deaths are posting up and down,
> Commissioned to this fatal field of Cressy:
> Methinks I see them arm my gallant soldiers,
> And gird the sword upon each thigh, and fit
> The shining helm, and string each stubborn bow,
> And dancing to the neighing of the steeds;—
> Methinks the shout begins—the battle burns;—
> Methinks I see them perch on English crests,
> And breathe the wild flame of fierce war upon
> The thronged enemy.'

6   In the same high poetic spirit Sir Walter Manny converses with a
genuine old English warrior, Sir Thomas Dagworth.

> 'O, Dagworth!—France is sick—the very sky
> Though sunshine light, it seems to me as pale
> As is the fainting man on his death-bed,
> Whose face is shown by light of one weak taper—
> It makes me sad and sick unto the heart;
> Thousands must fall to-day.'

Sir Thomas answers.

> 'Thousands of souls must leave this prison-house
> To be exalted to those heavenly fields
> Where songs of triumph, psalms of victory,
> Where peace, and joy, and love, and calm content,
> Sit singing on the azure clouds, and strew
> The flowers of heaven upon the banquet table.
> Bind ardent hope upon your feet, like shoes,
> And put the robe of preparation on.
> The table, it is spread in shining heaven.
> Let those who fight, fight in good steadfastness;
> And those who fall shall rise in victory.'

7   I might transcribe from these modest and unnoticed pages many
such passages. It would be unfair not to mention that the same volume
contains some wild and incoherent prose, in which we may trace more
than the dawning of those strange, mystical, and mysterious fancies on
which Blake subsequently misemployed his pencil. There is much that
is weak, and something that is strong, and a great deal that is wild and
mad, and all so strangely mingled, that little or no meaning can be
assigned to it; it seems like a lamentation over the disasters which came
on England during the reign of King John.

8   Though Blake lost himself sometimes in the enchanted region of
song, he seems not to have neglected to make himself master of the
graver, or to have forgotten his love of designs and sketches. He was
a dutiful servant to Basire, and he studied occasionally under Flaxman
and Fuseli; but it was his chief delight to retire to the solitude of his
room, and there make drawings, and illustrate these with verses, to
be hung up together in his mother's chamber. He was always at work;
he called amusement idleness, sight-seeing vanity, and money-making
the ruin of all high aspirations. 'Were I to love money,' he said, 'I

should lose all power of thought; desire of gain deadens the genius of man. I might roll in wealth and ride in a golden chariot, were I to listen to the voice of parsimony. My business is not to gather gold, but to make glorious shapes, expressing god-like sentiments.' The day was given to the graver, by which he earned enough to maintain himself respectably; and he bestowed his evenings upon painting and poetry, and intertwined these so closely in his compositions, that they cannot well be separated.

9   When he was six-and-twenty years old [i.e., twenty-four], he married Katharine Boutcher, a young woman of humble connexions—the dark-eyed Kate of several of his lyric poems. She lived near his father's house, and was noticed by Blake for the whiteness of her hand, the brightness of her eyes, and a slim and handsome shape, corresponding with his own notions of sylphs and naïads. As he was an original in all things, it would have been out of character to fall in love like an ordinary mortal; he was describing one evening in company the pains he had suffered from some capricious lady or another, when Katharine Boutcher said, 'I pity you from my heart.' 'Do you pity me?' said Blake, 'then I love you for that.' 'And I love you,' said the frank-hearted lass, and so the courtship began. He tried how well she looked in a drawing, then how her charms became verse; and finding moreover that she had good domestic qualities, he married her. They lived together long and happily.

10   She seemed to have been created on purpose for Blake:—she believed him to be the finest genius on earth; she believed in his verse—she believed in his designs; and to the wildest flights of his imagination she bowed the knee, and was a worshipper. She set his house in good order, prepared his frugal meal, learned to think as he thought, and, indulging him in his harmless absurdities, became, as it were, bone of his bone, and flesh of his flesh. She learned—what a young and handsome woman is seldom apt to learn—to despise gaudy dresses, costly meals, pleasant company, and agreeable invitations—she found out the way of being happy at home, living on the simplest of food, and contented in the homeliest of clothing. It was no ordinary mind which could do all this; and she whom Blake emphatically called his 'beloved', was no ordinary woman. She wrought off in the press the impressions of his plates—she coloured them with a light and neat hand—made drawings much in the spirit of her husband's compositions, and almost rivalled him in all things save in the power which he possessed of seeing visions of any individual living or dead, whenever he chose to see them.

11   His marriage, I have heard, was not agreeable to his father; and he then left his roof and resided with his wife in Green Street, Leicester Fields. He returned to Broad Street, on the death of his father, a devout man, and an honest shopkeeper, of fifty years' standing, took a first floor and a shop, and in company with one Parker, who had been his fellow-apprentice, commenced printseller. His wife attended to the business, and Blake continued to engrave, and took Robert, his favourite brother, for a pupil. This speculation did not succeed—his brother too sickened and died; he had a dispute with Parker—the shop was relinquished, and he removed to 28, Poland Street. Here he commenced that series of works which give him a right to be numbered among the men of genius of his country. In sketching designs, engraving plates, writing songs, and composing music, he employed his time, with his wife sitting at his side, encouraging him in all his undertakings. As he drew the figure he meditated the song which was to accompany it, and the music to which the verse was to be sung, was the offspring too of the same moment. Of his music there are no specimens—he wanted the art of noting it down—if it equalled many of his drawings, and some of his songs, we have lost melodies of real value.

12   The first fruits were the 'Songs of Innocence and Experience,' a work original and natural, and of high merit, both in poetry and in painting. It consists of some sixty-five or seventy scenes, presenting images of youth and manhood—of domestic sadness, and fireside joy—of the gaiety, and innocence, and happiness of childhood. Every scene has its poetical accompaniment, curiously interwoven with the group or the landscape, and forming, from the beauty of the colour and the prettiness of the pencilling, a very fair picture of itself. Those designs are in general highly poetical; more allied, however, to heaven than to earth—a kind of spiritual abstractions, and indicating a better world and fuller happiness than mortals enjoy. The picture of Innocence is introduced with the following sweet verses.

'Piping down the valleys wild,
    Piping songs of pleasant glee,
On a cloud I saw a child,
    And he laughing said to me—

Pipe a song about a lamb;
    So I piped with merry cheer.
Piper, pipe that song again—
    So I piped—he wept to hear.

Drop thy pipe, thy happy pipe,
　　Sing thy songs of happy cheer—
So I sung the same again,
　　While he wept with joy to hear.

Piper, sit thee down and write
　　In a book that all may read—
So he vanished from my sight:
　　And I plucked a hollow reed,

And I made a rural pen,
　　And I stained the water clear,
And I wrote my happy songs,
　　Every child may joy to hear.'

13　　Another song, called 'The Chimney Sweeper', is rude enough truly, but yet not without pathos.

'When my mother died I was very young,
And my father sold me while yet my tongue
Could scarcely cry—weep! weep! weep! [weep]
So your chimneys I clean and in soot I sleep.

There's little Tom Dacre, who cried when his head,
That curl'd like a lamb's back, was shaved; so I said,
Hush, Tom, never mind it, for when your head's bare,
You know that the soot cannot spoil your white hair.

And so he was quiet—and on that very night,
As Tommy was sleeping, he had such a sight;
There thousands of sweepers, Dick, Joe, Ned, and Jack,
Were all of them locked up in coffins of black;

And by came an Angel, who had a bright key,
He opened the coffins and set them all free;
Then down a green vale, leaping, laughing they run,
And wash in a river, and shine like the sun.

Then, naked and white, all their bags left behind,
They rise up on pure clouds and sport in the wind:
And the Angel told Tom, if he'd be a good boy,
He'd have God for his father and never want joy.

And so Tommy awoke and we rose in the dark,
And got with our bags and our brushes to work;
Though the morning was cold, he was happy and warm,
So, if all do their duty, they need not fear harm.'

14   In a higher and better spirit he wrought with his pencil. But then he imagined himself under spiritual influences; he saw the forms and listened to the voices of the worthies of other days; the past and the future were before him, and he heard, in imagination, even that awful voice which called on Adam amongst the trees of the garden. In this kind of dreaming abstraction, he lived much of his life; all his works are stamped with it; and though they owe much of their mysticism and obscurity to the circumstance, there can be no doubt that they also owe to it much of their singular loveliness and beauty. It was wonderful that he could thus, month after month, and year after year, lay down his graver after it had won him his daily wages, and retire from the battle for bread, to disport his fancy amid scenes of more than earthly splendour, and creatures pure as unfallen dew.

15   In this lay the weakness and the strength of Blake, and those who desire to feel the character of his compositions, must be familiar with his history and the peculiarities of his mind. He was by nature a poet, a dreamer, and an enthusiast. The eminence which it had been the first ambition of his youth to climb, was visible before him, and he saw on its ascent or on its summit those who had started earlier in the race of fame. He felt conscious of his own merit, but was not aware of the thousand obstacles which were ready to interpose. He thought that he had but to sing songs and draw designs, and become great and famous. The crosses which genius is heir to had been wholly unforeseen—and they befel him early; he wanted too the skill of hand, and fine tact of fancy and taste, to impress upon the offspring of his thoughts that popular shape, which gives such productions immediate circulation. His works were therefore looked coldly on by the world, and were only esteemed by men of poetic minds, or those who were fond of things out of the common way. He earned a little fame, but no money by these speculations, and had to depend for bread on the labours of the graver.

16   All this neither crushed his spirit, nor induced him to work more in the way of the world; but it had a visible influence upon his mind. He became more seriously thoughtful, avoided the company of men, and lived in the manner of a hermit, in that vast wilderness, London. Necessity made him frugal, and honesty and independence

prescribed plain clothes, homely fare, and a cheap habitation. He was thus compelled more than ever to retire to worlds of his own creating, and seek solace in visions of paradise for the joys which the earth denied him. By frequent indulgence in these imaginings, he gradually began to believe in the reality of what dreaming fancy painted—the pictured forms which swarmed before his eyes assumed, in his apprehension, the stability of positive revelations, and he mistook the vivid figures, which his professional imagination shaped, for the poets, and heroes, and princes of old. Amongst his friends, he at length ventured to intimate that the designs on which he was engaged, were not from his own mind, but copied from grand works revealed to him in visions; and those who believed that, would readily lend an ear to the assurance that he was commanded to execute his performances by a celestial tongue!

17   Of these imaginary visitations he made good use, when he invented his truly original and beautiful mode of engraving and tinting his plates. He had made the designs of his Days [i.e., *Songs*] of Innocence, and was meditating, he said, on the best means of multiplying their resemblance in form and in hue; he felt sorely perplexed. At last he was made aware that the spirit of his favourite brother Robert was in the room, and to this celestial visitor he applied for counsel. The spirit advised him at once: 'write,' he said, 'the poetry, and draw the designs upon the copper with a certain liquid (which he named, and which Blake ever kept a secret); then cut the plain parts of the plate down with aquafortis, and this will give the whole, both poetry and figures, in the manner of stereotype.' The plan recommended by this gracious spirit was adopted; the plates were engraved, and the work printed off. The artist then added a peculiar beauty of his own. He tinted both the figures and the verse with a variety of colours, amongst which, while yellow prevails, the whole has a rich and lustrous beauty, to which I know little that can be compared. The size of these prints is four inches and an half high by three inches wide. The original genius of Blake was always confined, through poverty, to small dimensions. Sixty-five plates of copper were an object to him who had little money. The Gates of Paradise, a work of sixteen designs, and those exceedingly small, was his next undertaking. The meaning of the artist is not a little obscure; it seems to have been his object to represent the innocence, the happiness, and the upward aspirations of man. They bespeak one intimately acquainted with the looks and the feelings of children. Over them there is shed a kind of mysterious halo which raises feelings of

devotion. The Songs of Innocence, and the Gates of Paradise, became popular among the collectors of prints. To the sketch-book and the cabinet the works of Blake are unfortunately confined.

18   If there be mystery in the meaning of the Gates of Paradise, his succeeding performance, by name URIZEN, has the merit or the fault of surpassing all human comprehension. The spirit which dictated this strange work was undoubtedly a dark one; nor does the strange kind of prose which is intermingled with the figures serve to enlighten us. There are in all twenty-seven designs, representing beings human, demoniac, and divine, in situations of pain and sorrow and suffering. One character—evidently an evil spirit—appears in most of the plates; the horrors of hell, and the terrors of darkness and divine wrath, seem his sort portion. He swims in gulphs of fire—descends in cataracts of flame—holds combats with scaly serpents, or writhes in anguish without any visible cause. One of his exploits is to chase a female soul through a narrow gate and hurl her headlong down into a darksome pit. The wild verses, which are scattered here and there, talk of the sons and the daughters of Urizen. He seems to have extracted these twenty-seven scenes out of many visions—what he meant by them even his wife declared she could not tell, though she was sure they had a meaning, and a fine one. Something like the fall of Lucifer and the creation of Man is dimly visible in this extravagant work; it is not a little fearful to look upon; a powerful, dark, terrible, though undefined and indescribable, impression is left on the mind—and it is in no haste to be gone. The size of the designs is four inches by six; they bear date, 'Lambeth, 1794.' He had left Poland Street, and was residing in Hercules Buildings.

19   The name of Blake now began to be known a little, and Edwards, the bookseller, employed him to illustrate Young's Night Thoughts. The reward in money was small, but the temptation in fame was great: the work was performed something in the manner of old books with illuminated margins. Along the ample margins which the poetry left on the page the artist sketched his fanciful creations; contracting or expanding them according to the space. Some of those designs were in keeping with the poems, but there were others which alarmed fastidious people: the serious and the pious were not prepared to admire shapes trembling in nudity round the verses of a grave divine. In the exuberance of Young there are many fine figures; but they are figures of speech only, on which art should waste none of its skill. This work was so much, in many parts, to the satisfaction of Flaxman, that

he introduced Blake to Hayley the poet, who, in 1800, persuaded him to remove to Felpham in Sussex, to make engravings for the Life of Cowper. To that place he accordingly went with his wife and sister, and was welcomed by Hayley with much affection. Of his journey and his feelings he gives the following account to Flaxman, whom he usually addressed thus, 'Dear Sculptor of Eternity.'

20   'We are arrived safe at our cottage, which is more beautiful than I thought it, and more convenient. It is a perfect model for cottages, and I think for palaces of magnificence, only enlarging and not altering its proportions, and adding ornaments and not principals. Nothing can be more grand than its simplicity and usefulness. Felpham is a sweet place for study, because it is more spiritual than London. Heaven opens here on all sides her golden gates; her windows are not obstructed by vapours; voices of celestial inhabitants are more distinctly heard, and their forms more distinctly seen, and my cottage is also a shadow of their houses. My wife and sister are both well, and are courting Neptune for an embrace.'

21   Thus far had he written in the language and feelings of a person of upper air; though some of the expressions are tinctured with the peculiar enthusiasm of the man, they might find shelter under the license of figurative speech, and pass muster as the poetic language of new-found happiness. Blake thus continues:—

22   'And now begins a new life, because another covering of earth is shaken off. I am more famed in heaven for my works than I could well conceive. In my brain are studies and chambers filled with books and pictures of old, which I wrote and painted in ages of eternity before my mortal life, and those works are the delight and study of archangels. Why then should I be anxious about the riches or fame of mortality? You, O dear Flaxman, are a sublime archangel, my friend and companion from eternity. Farewell, my dear friend, remember me and my wife in love and friendship to Mrs. Flaxman, whom we ardently desire to entertain beneath our thatched roof of russet gold.'

23   This letter, written in the year 1800, gives the true two-fold image of the author's mind. During the day he was a man of sagacity and sense, who handled his graver wisely, and conversed in a wholesome and pleasant manner: in the evening, when he had done his prescribed task, he gave a loose to his imagination. While employed on those engravings which accompany the works of Cowper, he saw such company as the country where he resided afforded, and talked with Hayley about poetry with a feeling to which the author of the Triumphs

of Temper was an utter stranger; but at the close of day away went
Blake to the sea shore to indulge in his own thoughts and

'High converse with the dead to hold.'

Here he forgot the present moment and lived in the past; he conceived,
verily, that he had lived in other days, and had formed friendships with
Homer and Moses; with Pindar and Virgil; with Dante and Milton.
These great men, he asserted, appeared to him in visions, and even
entered into conversation. Milton, in a moment of confidence, entrusted
him with a whole poem of his, which the world had never seen; but
unfortunately the communication was oral, and the poetry seemed to
have lost much of its brightness in Blake's recitation. When asked
about the looks of those visions, he answered, 'They are all majestic
shadows, gray but luminous, and superior to the common height of
men.' It was evident that the solitude of the country gave him a larger
swing in imaginary matters. His wife often accompanied him to these
strange interviews; she saw nothing and heard as little, but she was
certain that her husband both heard and saw.

24   Blake's mind at all times resembled that first page in the
magician's book of gramoury, which made

'The cobweb on the dungeon wall,
Seem tapestry in lordly hall.'

His mind could convert the most ordinary occurrence into something
mystical and supernatural. He often saw less majestic shapes than those
of the poets of old. 'Did you ever see a fairy's funeral, madam?' he once
said to a lady, who happened to sit by him in company. 'Never, sir!'
was the answer. 'I have,' said Blake, 'but not before last night. I was
walking alone in my garden, there was great stillness among the
branches and flowers and more than common sweetness in the air; I
heard a low and pleasant sound, and I knew not whence it came. At
last I saw the broad leaf of a flower move, and underneath I saw a
procession of creatures of the size and colour of green and gray grass-
hoppers, bearing a body laid out on a rose leaf, which they buried
with songs, and then disappeared. It was a fairy funeral.' It would,
perhaps, have been better for his fame had he connected it more with
the superstitious beliefs of his country—amongst the elves and fairies
his fancy might have wandered at will—their popular character would
perhaps have kept him within the bounds of traditionary belief, and
the sea of his imagination might have had a shore.

25   After a residence of three years in his cottage at Felpham, he removed to 17, South Molton Street, London, where he lived seventeen years. He came back to town with a fancy not a little exalted by the solitude of the country, and in this mood designed and engraved an extensive and strange work which he entitled 'Jerusalem.' A production so exclusively wild was not allowed to make its appearance in an ordinary way: he thus announced it. 'After my three years' slumber on the banks of the ocean, I again display my giant forms to the public.' Of these designs there are no less than an hundred; what their meaning is the artist has left unexplained. It seems of a religious, political, and spiritual kind, and wanders from hell to heaven, and from heaven to earth; now glancing into the distractions of our own days, and then making a transition to the antediluvians. The crowning defect is obscurity; meaning seems now and then about to dawn; you turn plate after plate, and read motto after motto, in the hope of escaping from darkness into light. But the first might as well be looked at last; the whole seems a riddle which no ingenuity can solve. Yet, if the work be looked at for form and effect rather than for meaning, many figures may be pronounced worthy of Michael Angelo. There is wonderful freedom of attitude and position; men, spirits, gods, and angels, move with an ease which makes one lament that we know not wherefore they are put in motion. Well might Hayley call him his 'gentle visionary Blake.' He considered the Jerusalem to be his greatest work, and for a set of the tinted engravings charged twenty-five guineas. Few joined the artist in his admiration. The Jerusalem, with all its giant forms, failed to force its way into circulation.

26   His next work was the illustrations of Blair's Grave, which came to the world with the following commendation by Fuseli. 'The author of the moral series before us, has endeavoured to awaken sensibility by touching our sympathies with nearer, less ambiguous, and less ludicrous imagery, than what mythology, gothic superstition, or symbols, as far fetched as inadequate could supply. His avocation has been chiefly employed to spread a familiar and domestic atmosphere round the most important of all subjects, to connect the visible and the invisible world without provoking probability, and to lead the eye from the milder light of time to the radiations of eternity.' For these twelve 'Inventions,' as he called them, Blake received twenty guineas from Cromek, the engraver—a man of skill in art and taste in literature. The price was little, but nevertheless it was more than what he usually received for such productions; he also undertook to engrave them. But Blake's

mode of engraving was as peculiar as his style of designing; it had little of that grace of execution about it which attracts customers, and the Inventions, after an experiment or two, were placed under the fashionable graver of Louis Schiavonetti. Blake was deeply incensed—he complained that he was deprived of the profit of engraving his own designs, and, with even less justice, that Schiavonetti was unfit for the task.

27   Some of these twelve *Inventions* are natural and poetic, others exhibit laborious attempts at the terrific and the sublime. The old Man at Death's Door is one of the best—in the Last Day there are fine groups and admirable single figures—the Wise Ones of the Earth pleading before the inexorable Throne, and the Descent of the Condemned, are creations of a high order. The Death of the Strong Wicked Man is fearful and extravagant, and the flames in which the soul departs from the body have no warrant in the poem or in belief. The Descent of Christ into the Grave is formal and tame; and the hoary old Soul, in the Death of the Good Man, travelling heavenward between two orderly Angels, required little outlay of fancy. The frontispiece—a naked Angel descending headlong and rousing the Dead with the Sound of the last Trumpet—alarmed the devout people of the north, and made maids and matrons retire behind their fans.

28   If the tranquility of Blake's life was a little disturbed by the dispute about the twelve 'Inventions,' it was completely shaken by the controversy which now arose between him and Cromek respecting his Canterbury Pilgrimage, and the famous one by Stothard. That two artists at one and the same time should choose the same subject for the pencil, seems scarcely credible—especially when such subject was not of a temporary interest. The coincidence here was so close, that Blake accused Stothard of obtaining knowledge of his design through Cromek, while Stothard with equal warmth asserted that Blake had commenced his picture in rivalry of himself. Blake declared that Cromek had actually commissioned him to paint the Pilgrimage before Stothard thought of his; to which Cromek replied, that the order had been given in a vision, for he never gave it. Stothard, a man as little likely to be led aside from truth by love of gain as by visions, added to Cromek's denial the startling testimony that Blake visited him during the early progress of his picture, and expressed his approbation of it in such terms, that he proposed to introduce Blake's portrait in the procession, as a mark of esteem. It is probable that Blake obeyed some imaginary revelation in this matter, and mistook it for the order of an earthly employer; but whether commissioned by a vision or by mortal lips, his

Canterbury Pilgrimage made its appearance in an exhibition of his principal works in the house of his brother, in Broad Street, during the summer of 1809.

29   Of original designs, this singular exhibition contained sixteen—they were announced as chiefly 'of a spiritual and political nature'—but then the spiritual works and political feelings of Blake were unlike those of any other man. One piece represented 'The Spiritual Form of Nelson guiding Leviathan.' Another, 'The Spiritual Form of Pitt guiding Behemoth.' This, probably, confounded both divines and politicians; there is no doubt that plain men went wondering away. The chief attraction was the Canterbury Pilgrimage, not indeed from its excellence, but from the circumstance of its origin, which was well known about town, and pointedly alluded to in the catalogue. The picture is a failure. Blake was too great a visionary for dealing with such literal wantons as the Wife of Bath and her jolly companions. The natural flesh and blood of Chaucer prevailed against him. He gives grossness of body for grossness of mind,—tries to be merry and wicked—and in vain.

30   Those who missed instruction in his pictures, found entertainment in his catalogue, a wild performance, overflowing with the oddities and dreams of the author—which may be considered as a kind of public declaration of his faith concerning art and artists. His first anxiety is about his colours. 'Colouring,' says this new lecturer on the *Chiaro-Scuro*, 'does not depend on where the colours are put, but on where the lights and darks are put, and all depends on form or outline. Where that is wrong the colouring can never be right, and it is always wrong in Titian and Correggio, Rubens and Rembrandt; till we get rid of them we shall never equal Raphael and Albert Durer, Michael Angelo and Julio Romano. Clearness and precision have been my chief objects in painting these pictures—clear colours and firm determinate lineaments, unbroken by shadows—which ought to display and not hide form, as is the practice of the later schools of Italy and Flanders. The picture of the Spiritual Form of Pitt, is a proof of the power of colours unsullied with oil or with any cloggy vehicle. Oil has been falsely supposed to give strength to colours, but a little consideration must show the fallacy of this opinion. Oil will not drink or absorb colour enough to stand the test of any little time and of the air. Let the works of artists since Rubens' time witness to the villainy of those who first brought oil painting into general opinion and practice, since which we have never had a picture painted that would show itself by the side of an earlier composition. This is an awful thing to say to oil painters; they may

call it madness, but it is true. All the genuine old little pictures are in fresco and not in oil.'

31   Having settled the true principles and proper materials of colour, he proceeds to open up the mystery of his own productions. Those who failed to comprehend the pictures on looking at them, had only to turn to the following account of the Pitt and the Nelson. 'These two pictures,' he says, 'are compositions of a mythological cast, similar to those apotheoses of Persian, Hindoo, and Egyptian antiquity, which are still preserved in rude monuments, being copies from some stupendous originals now lost, or perhaps buried to some happier age. The Artist, having been taken, in vision, to the ancient republics, monarchies, and patriarchates of Asia, has seen those wonderful originals, called in the sacred Scriptures the cherubim, which were painted and sculptured on the walls of temples, towns, cities, palaces, and erected in the highly cultivated states of Egypt, Moab, and Edom, among the rivers of Paradise, being originals from which the Greeks and Hetrurians copied Hercules, Venus, Apollo, and all the ground-works of ancient art. They were executed in a very superior style to those justly admired copies, being with their accompaniments terrific and grand in the highest degree. The artist has endeavoured to emulate the grandeur of those seen in his vision, and to apply it to modern times on a smaller scale. The Greek Muses are daughters of Memory, and not of Inspiration or Imagination, and therefore not authors of such sublime conceptions: some of these wonderful originals were one hundred feet in height; some were painted as pictures, some were carved as bass-relievos, and some as groups of statues, all containing mythological and recondite meaning. The artist wishes it was now the fashion to make such monuments, and then he should not doubt of having a national commission to execute those pictures of Nelson and Pitt on a scale suitable to the grandeur of the nation who is the parent of his heroes, in highly finished fresco, where the colours would be as permanent as precious stones.'

32   The man who could not only write down, but deliberately correct the printer's sheets which recorded, matter so utterly wild and mad, was at the same time perfectly sensible to the exquisite nature of Chaucer's delineations, and felt rightly what sort of skill his inimitable Pilgrims required at the hand of an artist. He who saw visions in Cœle-Syria and statues an hundred feet high, wrote thus concerning Chaucer: 'The characters of his pilgrims are the characters which compose all ages and nations: as one age falls another rises, different

to mortal sight, but to immortals only the same: for we see the same characters repeated again and again, in animals, in vegetables, and in men; nothing new occurs in identical existence. Accident ever varies; substance can never suffer change nor decay. Of Chaucer's characters, some of the names or titles are altered by time, but the characters themselves for ever remain unaltered, and consequently they are the physiognomies of universal human life, beyond which nature never steps. Names alter—things never alter; I have known multitudes of those who would have been monks in the age of monkery, who in this deistical age are deists. As Linnæus numbered the plants, so Chaucer numbered the classes of men.'

33   His own notions and much of his peculiar practice in art are scattered at random over the pages of this curious production. His love of a distinct outline made him use close and clinging dresses; they are frequently very graceful—at other times they are constrained, and deform the figures which they so scantily cover. 'The great and golden rule of art, (says he,) is this:—that the more distinct and sharp and wiry the bounding line, the more perfect the work of art; and the less keen and sharp this external line, the greater is the evidence of weak imitative plagiarism and bungling: Protogenes and Apelles knew each other by this line. How do we distinguish the oak from the beech, the horse from the ox; but by the bounding outline? How do we distinguish one face or countenance from another, but by the bounding line and its infinite inflexions and movements? Leave out this line and you leave out life itself: all is chaos again, and the line of the Almighty must be drawn out upon it before man or beast can exist.'

34   These abominations—concealed outline and tricks of colour—now bring on one of those visionary fits to which Blake was so liable, and he narrates with the most amusing wildness sundry revelations made to him concerning them. He informs us that certain painters were *demons*—let loose on earth to confound the 'sharp wiry outline,' and fill men's minds with fears and perturbations. He signifies that he himself was for some time a miserable instrument in the hands of Chiaro-Scuro demons, who employed him in making 'experiment pictures in oil.' 'These pictures,' says he, 'were the result of temptations and perturbations labouring to destroy imaginative power by means of that infernal machine called Chiaro-Scuro, in the hands of Venetian and Flemish demons, who hate the Roman and Florentine schools. They cause that every thing in art shall become a machine; they cause that the execution shall be all blocked up with brown

shadows; they put the artist in fear and doubt of his own original conception. The spirit of Titian was particularly active in raising doubts concerning the possibility of executing without a model. Rubens is a most outrageous demon, and by infusing the remembrances of his pictures, and style of execution, hinders all power of individual thought. Correggio is a soft and effeminate, consequently a most cruel demon, whose whole delight is to cause endless labour to whoever suffers him to enter his mind.' When all this is translated into the language of sublunary life, it only means that Blake was haunted with the excellencies of other men's works, and, finding himself unequal to the task of rivalling the soft and glowing colours and singular effects of light and shade of certain great masters, betook himself to the study of others not less eminent, who happened to have laid out their strength in outline.

35   The impression which the talents and oddities of Blake made on men of taste and genius, is well described by one whose judgment in whatever is poetical no one will question. Charles Lamb had communicated to James Montgomery's book on chimney sweepers the little song by Blake, which I have already quoted; it touched the feelings of Bernard Barton so deeply, that he made inquiries of his friend about the author, upon which he received the following letter in explanation, written some six years ago.—'Blake is a real name I assure you,' says Lamb; 'and a most extraordinary man he is if he be still living. He is the Blake whose wild designs accompany a splendid edition of Blair's Grave, which you may perhaps have seen or heard of; in one of which he pictures the parting of soul and body by a solid mass of human form floating off God knows how, from a lumpish mass—fac-simile to itself —left behind on the death-bed. He paints in water-colours marvellous strange pictures—visions of his brain which he asserts that he has seen. They have great merit. He has seen the old Welch bards on Snowdon. He has seen the beautifullest, the strongest and the ugliest man left alive from the massacre of the Britons by the Romans, and has painted them from memory, (I have seen these paintings,) and asserts them to be as good as the figures of Raphael and Angelo, but not better, as they had precisely the same retro-visions and prophetic visions with himself. The painters in oil (which he will have it that neither of these great masters ever practiced) he affirms to have been the ruin of art: and asserts, that all the while he was engaged on his water paintings, Titian was disturbing him—Titian, the evil genius of oil painting! His pictures—one in particular—the Canterbury Pilgrims, have wonderful power and

spirit, but hard and dry, yet with grace. He has written a catalogue of them, with a most spirited criticism on Chaucer, but mystical and full of vision. I have heard of his poems, but never seen them. There is one to a tiger, which I have heard recited, beginning

"Tiger, tiger, burning bright,
Through the deserts of the night,"

which is glorious. But, alas! I have not the book, and the man is flown, whither I know not—to Hades, or a mad-house—but I must look on him as one of the most extraordinary persons of the age.'

36   To describe the conversations which Blake held in prose with demons and in verse with angels, would fill volumes, and an ordinary gallery could not contain all the heads which he drew of his visionary visitants. That all this was real, he himself most sincerely believed; nay, so infectious was his enthusiasm, that some acute and sensible persons who heard him expatiate, shook their heads, and hinted that he was an extraordinary man, and that there might be something in the matter. One of his brethren, an artist of some note, employed him frequently in drawing the portraits of those who appeared to him in visions. The most propitious time for those 'angel-visits' was from nine at night till five in the morning; and so docile were his spiritual sitters, that they appeared at the wish of his friends. Sometimes, however, the shape which he desired to draw was long in appearing, and he sat with his pencil and paper ready and his eyes idly roaming in vacancy; all at once the vision came upon him, and he began to work like one possest.

37   He was requested to draw the likeness of Sir William Wallace— the eye of Blake sparkled, for he admired heroes. 'William Wallace!' he exclaimed, 'I see him now—there, there, how noble he looks—reach me my things!' Having drawn for some time, with the same care of hand and steadiness of eye, as if a living sitter had been before him, Blake stopt suddenly, and said, 'I cannot finish him—Edward the First has stept in between him and me.' 'That's lucky,' said his friend, 'for I want the portrait of Edward too.' Blake took another sheet of paper, and sketched the features of Plantagenet; upon which his majesty politely vanished, and the artist finished the head of Wallace. 'And pray, Sir,' said a gentleman, who heard Blake's friend tell his story— 'was Sir William Wallace an heroic-looking man? And what sort of personage was Edward?' The answer was: 'there they are, Sir, both framed and hanging on the wall behind you, judge for yourself.' 'I

looked (says my informant) and saw two warlike heads of the size of common life. That of Wallace was noble and heroic, that of Edward stern and bloody. The first had the front of a god, the latter the aspect of a demon.'

38   The friend who obliged me with these anecdotes on observing the interest which I took in the subject, said, 'I know much about Blake—I was his companion for nine years. I have sat beside him from ten at night till three in the morning, sometimes slumbering and some-times waking, but Blake never slept; he sat with a pencil and paper drawing portraits of those whom I most desired to see. I will show you, Sir, some of these works.' He took out a large book filled with drawings, opened it, and continued, 'Observe the poetic fervour of that face—it is Pindar as he stood a conqueror in the Olympic games. And this lovely creature is Corinna, who conquered in poetry in the same place. That lady is Lais, the courtesan—with the impudence which is part of her profession, she stept in between Blake and Corinna, and he was obliged to paint her to get her away. There! that is a face of a different stamp—can you conjecture who he is?' 'Some scoundrel, I should think, Sir.' 'There now—that is a strong proof of the accuracy of Blake—he is a scoundrel indeed! The very individual task-master whom Moses slew in Egypt. And who is this now—only imagine who this is?' 'Other than a good one, I doubt, Sir.' 'You are right, it is a fiend—he resembles, and this is remarkable, two men who shall be nameless; one is a great lawyer, and the other—I wish I durst name him—is a suborner of false witnesses. This other head now?—this speaks for itself—it is the head of Herod; how like an eminent officer in the army!'

39   He closed the book, and taking out a small panel from a private drawer, said, 'this is the last which I shall show you; but it is the greatest curiosity of all. Only look at the splendour of the colouring and the original character of the thing!' 'I see,' said I, 'a naked figure with a strong body and a short neck—with burning eyes which long for moisture, and a face worthy of a murderer, holding a bloody cup in his clawed hands, out of which it seems eager to drink. I never saw any shape so strange, nor did I ever see any colouring so curiously splendid—a kind of glistening green and dusky gold, beautifully varnished. But what in the world is it?' 'It is a ghost, Sir—the ghost of a flea—a spiritualization of the thing!' 'He saw this in a vision then,' I said. 'I'll tell you all about it, Sir. I called on him one evening, and found Blake more than usually excited. He told me he had seen a

wonderful thing—the ghost of a flea! And did you make a drawing of
him? I inquired. No, indeed, said he, I wish I had, but I shall, if he
appears again! He looked earnestly into a corner of the room, and then
said, here he is—reach me my things—I shall keep my eye on him.
There he comes! his eager tongue whisking out of his mouth, a cup in
his hand to hold blood, and covered with a scaly skin of gold and
green;—as he described him so he drew him.'

40   Visions, such as are said to arise in the sight of those who indulge
in opium, were frequently present to Blake, nevertheless he sometimes
desired to see a spirit in vain. 'For many years,' said he, 'I longed to
see Satan—I never could believe that he was the vulgar fiend which
our legends represent him—I imagined him a classic spirit, such as he
appeared to him of Uz [i.e., Job], with some of his original splendour
about him. At last I saw him. I was going up stairs in the dark, when
suddenly a light came streaming amongst my feet, I turned round, and
there he was looking fiercely at me through the iron grating of my
staircase window. I called for my things—Katherine thought the fit of
song was on me, and brought me pen and ink—I said, hush!—never
mind—this will do—as he appeared so I drew him—there he is.' Upon
this, Blake took out a piece of paper with a grated window sketched on
it, while through the bars glared the most frightful phantom that ever
man imagined. Its eyes were large and like live coals—its teeth as
long as those of a harrow, and the claws seemed such as might appear
in the distempered dream of a clerk in the Herald's office. 'It is the
gothic fiends of our legends, said Blake—the true devil—all else are
apocryphal.'

41   These stories are scarcely credible, yet there can be no doubt of
their accuracy. Another friend, on whose veracity I have the fullest
dependence, called one evening on Blake, and found him sitting with
a pencil and a panel, drawing a portrait with all the seeming anxiety
of a man who is conscious that he has got a fastidious sitter; he looked
and drew, and drew and looked, yet no living soul was visible. 'Disturb
me not,' said he, in a whisper, 'I have one sitting to me.' 'Sitting to
you!' exclaimed his astonished visitor, 'where is he, and what is he?—
I see no one.' 'But I see him, Sir,' answered Blake haughtily, 'there he is,
his name is Lot—you may read of him in the Scripture. *He* is sitting for
his portrait.'

42   Had he always thought so idly, and wrought on such visionary
matters, this memoir would have been the story of a madman, instead
of the life of a man of genius, some of whose works are worthy of any

age or nation. Even while he was indulging in these laughable fancies, and seeing visions at the request of his friends, he conceived, and drew, and engraved, one of the noblest of all his productions—the Inventions for the Book of Job. He accomplished this series in a small room, which served him for kitchen, bedchamber, and study, where he had no other companion but his faithful Katherine, and no larger income than some seventeen or eighteen shillings a week. Of these Inventions, as the artist loved to call them, there are twenty-one, representing the Man of Uz sustaining his dignity amidst the inflictions of Satan, the reproaches of his friends, and the insults of his wife. It was in such things that Blake shone; the Scripture overawed his imagination, and he was too devout to attempt aught beyond a literal embodying of the majestic scene. He goes step by step with the narrative; always simple, and often sublime—never wandering from the subject, nor overlaying the text with the weight of his own exuberant fancy.

43   The passages, embodied, will show with what lofty themes he presumed to grapple. 1. Thus did Job continually. 2. The Almighty watches the good man's household. 3. Satan receiving power over Job. 4. The wind from the wilderness destroying Job's children. 5. And I alone am escaped to tell thee. 6. Satan smiting Job with sore boils. 7. Job's friends comforting him. 8. Let the day perish wherein I was born. 9. Then a spirit passed before my face. 10. Job laughed to scorn by his friends. 11. With dreams upon my bed thou scarest me— thou affrightest me with visions. 12. I am young and ye are old, wherefore I was afraid. 13. Then the Lord answered Job out of the whirlwind. 14. When the morning stars sang together, and the sons of God shouted for joy. 15. Behold now Behemoth, which I made with thee. 16. Thou hast fulfilled the judgment of the wicked. 17. I have heard thee with the hearing of my ear, but now my eye rejoiceth in thee. 18. Also the Lord accepted Job. 19. Every one also gave him a piece of money. 20. There were not found women fairer than the daughters of Job. 21. So the Lord blessed the latter end of Job more than the beginning.

44   While employed on these remarkable productions, he was made sensible that the little approbation which the world had ever bestowed on him was fast leaving him. The waywardness of his fancy, and the peculiar execution of his compositions, were alike unadapted for popularity; the demand for his works lessened yearly from the time that he exhibited his Canterbury Pilgrimage; and he could hardly procure sufficient to sustain life, when old age was creeping upon him.

Yet, poverty-stricken as he was, his cheerfulness never forsook him—he uttered no complaint—he contracted no debt, and continued to the last manly and independent. It is the fashion to praise genius when it is gone to the grave—the fashion is cheap and convenient. Of the existence of Blake few men of taste could be ignorant—of his great merits multitudes knew, nor was his extreme poverty any secret. Yet he was reduced—one of the ornaments of the age—to a miserable garret and a crust of bread, and would have perished from want, had not some friends, neither wealthy nor powerful, averted this disgrace from coming upon our country. One of these gentlemen, Mr. Linnel, employed Blake to engrave his Inventions of the Book of Job; by this he earned money enough to keep him living—for the good old man still laboured with all the ardour of the days of his youth, and with skill equal to his enthusiasm. These engravings are very rare, very beautiful, and very peculiar. They are in the earlier fashion of workmanship, and bear no resemblance whatever to the polished and graceful style which now prevails. I have never seen a tinted copy, nor am I sure that tinting would accord with the extreme simplicity of the designs, and the mode in which they are handled. The Songs of Innocence, and these Inventions for Job, are the happiest of Blake's works, and ought to be in the portfolios of all who are lovers of nature and imagination.

45   Two extensive works, bearing the ominous names of Prophecies, one concerning America, the other Europe, next made their appearance from his pencil and graver. The first contains eighteen, and the other seventeen plates, and both are plentifully seasoned with verse, without the incumbrance of rhyme. It is impossible to give a satisfactory description of these works; the frontispiece of the latter, representing the Ancient of Days, in an orb of light, stooping into chaos, to measure out the world, has been admired less for its meaning than for the grandeur of its outline. A head and a tail-piece in the other have been much noticed—one exhibits the bottom of the sea, with enormous fishes preying on a dead body—the other, the surface, with a dead body floating, on which an eagle with outstretched wings is feeding. The two angels pouring out the spotted plague upon Britain—an angel standing in the sun, attended by three furies—and several other Inventions in these wild works, exhibit wonderful strength of drawing and splendour of colouring. Of loose prints—but which were meant doubtless to form part of some extensive work—one of the most remarkable is the Great Sea Serpent; and a figure, sinking in a stormy

sea at sunset—the glow of which, with the foam upon the dark waves, produces a magical effect.

46   After a residence of seventeen years in South Molton Street, Blake removed (not in consequence, alas! of any increase of fortune,) to No. 3, Fountain Court, Strand. This was in the year 1823 [i.e., 1821]. Here he engraved by day and saw visions by night, and occasionally employed himself in making Inventions for Dante; and such was his application that he designed in all one hundred and two, and engraved seven. It was publicly known that he was in a declining state of health; that old age had come upon him, and that he was in want. Several friends, and artists among the number, aided him a little, in a delicate way, by purchasing his works, of which he had many copies. He sold many of his 'Songs of Innocence,' and also of 'Urizen,' and he wrought incessantly upon what he counted his masterpiece, the 'Jerusalem,' tinting and adorning it, with the hope that his favourite would find a purchaser. No one, however, was found ready to lay out twenty-five guineas on a work which no one could have any hope of comprehending, and this disappointment sank to the old man's heart.

47   He had now reached his seventy-first [i.e., seventieth] year, and the strength of nature was fast yielding. Yet he was to the last cheerful and contented. 'I glory,' he said, 'in dying, and have no grief but in leaving you, Katherine; we have lived happy, and we have lived long; we have been ever together, but we shall be divided soon. Why should I fear death? Nor do I fear it. I have endeavoured to live as Christ commands, and have sought to worship God truly—in my own house, when I was not seen of men.' He grew weaker and weaker—he could no longer sit upright; and was laid in his bed, with no one to watch over him, save his wife, who, feeble and old herself, required help in such a touching duty.

48   The Ancient of Days was such a favourite with Blake, that three days before his death, he sat bolstered up in bed, and tinted it with his choicest colours and in his happiest style. He touched and retouched it—held it at arm's length, and then threw it from him, exclaiming, 'There! that will do! I cannot mend it.' He saw his wife in tears—she felt this was to be the last of his works—'Stay, Kate (cried Blake) keep just as you are—I will draw your portrait—for you have ever been an angel to me'—she obeyed, and the dying artist made a fine likeness.

49   The very joyfulness with which this singular man welcomed the coming of death, made his dying moments intensely mournful. He lay

chaunting songs, and the verses and the music were both the offspring of the moment. He lamented that he could no longer commit those inspirations, as he called them, to paper [.] 'Kate,' he said, 'I am a changing man—I always rose and wrote down my thoughts, whether it rained, snowed, or shone, and you arose too and sat beside me—this can be no longer.' He died on the 12th of August, 1828 [i.e., 1827], without any visible pain—his wife, who sat watching him, did not perceive when he ceased breathing.

50   William Blake was of low stature and slender make, with a high pallid forehead, and eyes large, dark, and expressive. His temper was touchy, and when moved, he spoke with an indignant eloquence, which commanded respect. His voice, in general, was low and musical, his manners gentle and unassuming, his conversation a singular mixture of knowledge and enthusiasm. His whole life was one of labour and privation,—he had never tasted the luxury of that independence, which comes from professional profit. This untoward fortune he endured with unshaken equanimity—offering himself, in imagination, as a martyr in the great cause of poetic art;—*pitying* some of his more fortunate brethren for their inordinate love of gain; and not doubting that whatever he might have won in gold by adopting other methods, would have been a poor compensation for the ultimate loss of fame. Under this agreeable delusion, he lived all his life—he was satisfied when his graver gained him a guinea a week—the greater the present denial, the surer the glory hereafter.

51   Though he was the companion of Flaxman and Fuseli, and sometimes their pupil, he never attained that professional skill, without which all genius is bestowed in vain. He was his own teacher chiefly; and self-instruction, the parent occasionally of great beauties, seldom fails to produce great deformities. He was a most splendid tinter, but no colourist, and his works were all of small dimensions, and therefore confined to the cabinet and the portfolio. His happiest flights, as well as his wildest, are thus likely to remain shut up from the world. If we look at the man through his best and most intelligible works, we shall find that he who could produce the Songs of Innocence and Experience, the Gates of Paradise, and the Inventions for Job, was the possessor of very lofty faculties, with no common skill in art, and moreover that, both in thought and mode of treatment, he was a decided original. But should we, shutting our eyes to the merits of those works, determine to weigh his worth by his Urizen, his Prophecies of Europe and America, and his Jerusalem, our conclusion would be very unfavourable; we

would say that, with much freedom of composition and boldness of posture, he was unmeaning, mystical, and extravagant, and that his original mode of working out his conceptions was little better than a brilliant way of animating absurdity. An overflow of imagination is a failing uncommon in this age, and has generally received of late little quarter from the critical portion of mankind. Yet imagination is the life and spirit of all great works of genius and taste; and, indeed, without it, the head thinks and the hand labours in vain. Ten thousand authors and artists rise to the proper, the graceful, and the beautiful, for ten who ascend into 'the heaven of invention.' A work—whether from poet or painter—conceived in the fiery extasy of imagination, lives through every limb; while one elaborated out by skill and taste only will look, in comparison, like a withered and sapless tree beside one green and flourishing. Blake's misfortune was that of possessing this precious gift in excess. His fancy overmastered him—until he at length confounded 'the mind's eye' with the corporeal organ, and dreamed himself out of the sympathies of actual life.

52   His method of colouring was a secret which he kept to himself, or confided only to his wife; he believed that it was revealed in a vision, and that he was bound in honour to conceal it from the world. 'His modes of preparing his grounds,' says Smith, in his Supplement to the Life of Nollekens, 'and laying them over his panels for printing, mixing his colours, and manner of working, were those which he considered to have been practised by the early fresco painters, whose productions still remain in many instances vividly and permanently fresh. His ground was a mixture of whiting and carpenters' glue, which he passed over several times in the coatings; his colours he ground himself, and also united with them the same sort of glue, but in a much weaker state. He would, in the course of painting a picture, pass a very thin transparent wash of glue-water over the whole of the parts he had worked upon, and then proceed with his finishing. He had many secret modes of working, both as a colourist and an engraver. His method of eating away the plain copper, and leaving the lines of his subjects and his words as stereotype, is, in my mind, perfectly original. Mrs. Blake is in possession of the secret, and she ought to receive something considerable for its communication, as I am quite certain it may be used to advantage, both to artists and literary characters in general.' The affection and fortitude of this woman entitle her to much respect. She shared her husband's lot without a murmur, set her heart solely upon his fame, and soothed him in those hours of misgiving

and despondency which are not unknown to the strongest intellects. She still lives to lament the loss of Blake—and *feel* it.

53   Of Blake's merits as a poet I have already spoken—but something more may be said—for there is a simplicity and a pathos in many of his snatches of verse worthy of the olden muse. On all his works there is an impress of poetic thought, and what is still better a gentle humanity and charitable feeling towards the meanest work of God, such as few bards have indulged in. On the orphan children going to church on Holy Thursday, the following touching verses were composed—they are inserted between the procession of girls and the procession of boys in one of his singular engravings. . . .

54   Under the influence of gayer feelings, he wrote what he called the Laughing Song—his pencil drew young men and maidens merry round a table, and a youth, with a plumed cap in one hand and a wine-cup in the other, chaunts these gladsome verses. . . .

55   In the Song of the Lamb, there is a simplicity which seems easily attained till it is tried, and a religious tenderness of sentiment in perfect keeping with the poetry. A naked child is pencilled standing beside a group of lambs, and these verses are written underneath.

> 'Little lamb, who made thee?
> Little lamb, who made thee?
> Gave thee life, and bade thee feed,
> By the stream and o'er the mead;
> Gave thee clothing of delight,
> Softest clothing—woolly bright;
> Gave thee such a tender voice,
> Making all the vales rejoice?
>   Little lamb, who made thee?
>   Dost thou know who made thee?
>
> Little lamb, I'll tell thee;
> Little lamb, I'll tell thee;
> He is called by thy name,
> For he calls himself a lamb;
> He is meek, and he is mild,
> He became a little child;
> I a child, and thou a lamb,
> We are called by his name.
>   Little lamb, God bless thee;
>   Little lamb, God bless thee.'

56   It would be unjust to the memory of the painter and poet to omit a song which he composed in honour of that wife who repaid with such sincere affection the regard which he had for her. It has other merits. . . . ['I love the jocund dance']

57   Images of a sterner nature than those of domestic love were, however, at all times, familiar to his fancy; I have shown him softened down to the mood of babes and sucklings; I shall exhibit him in a more martial temper. In a ballad, which he calls Gwinn, King of Norway, there are many vigorous verses—the fierce Norwegian has invaded England with all his eager warriors.

> 'Like reared stones around a grave
> They stand around their king.'

But the intrepid islanders are nothing dismayed; they gather to the charge; these are the words of Blake forty-six years ago;—and this man's poetry obtained no notice, while Darwin and Hayley were gorged with adulation.

> 'The husbandman now leaves his plough,
>   To wade through fields of gore,
> The merchant binds his brows in steel,
>   And leaves the trading shore.
>
> The shepherd leaves his mellow pipe,
>   And sounds the trumpet shrill,
> The workman throws his hammer down,
>   To heave the bloody bill.
>
> Like the tall ghost of Barraton,
>   Who sports in stormy sky,
> Gwinn leads his host, as black as night
>   When pestilence doth fly.
>
> With horses and with chariots,
>   There all his spearmen bold
> March to the sound of mournful song,
>   Like clouds around him rolled.
>
> The armies stand like balances
>   Held in the Almighty's hand,
> Gwinn, thou hast filled thy measure up,
>   Thou'rt swept from English land.

197

Earth smokes with blood, and groans and shakes
   To drink her children's gore,
A sea of blood! nor can the eye
   See to the trembling shore.

And on the verge of this wild sea
   Famine and Death do cry,
The shrieks of women and of babes
   Around the field do fly.'

58   As Blake united poetry and painting in all his compositions, I have endeavoured to show that his claims to the distinction of a poet were not slight. He wrought much and slept little, and has left volumes of verse, amounting, it is said, to nearly an hundred, prepared for the press. If they are as wild and mystical as the poetry of his Urizen, they are as well in manuscript—if they are as natural and touching as many of his songs of Innocence, a judicious selection might be safely published.

40. Anon., 'The inventions of William Blake, painter and poet'

1830

London University Magazine, vol. II (March 1830), pp. 318–23.

The anonymous essay on Blake in the *London University Magazine* is one of the most perceptive and critically original to appear for many years. The quotation of *Thel*, 'A Cradle Song' from *Innocence*, and the 'Introduction' and 'A Poison Tree' from *Experience* appearing for the first time in conventional typography, the references to 'Albion' and *Jerusalem*, and the tantalizing allusion to 'Blake and Coleridge, when in company', demonstrate that the author had remarkably good information and good taste.

[The author complains]

first, of the insertion [by Cunningham] of stories which are falsely coloured; then of the stealing, borrowing, or copying a considerable portion of the life from Nolleken's Own Times; and, last of all, of a smile of contempt when speaking of Blake's private sentiments and feelings, which certainly is not becoming or respectful in a fellow artist. In our opinion, it was rather foolish of Mr. Cunningham to attempt the life of so extraordinary a man as Blake, the peculiar character of whose mind he could no more comprehend, than he could produce rival works in either poetry or painting. Thus far with Mr. Allan; we will now proceed to a subject far more agreable than a mere review of the Lives of the Painters. The public have only had a slight glimpse of the noble Songs of Innocence and Experience, by William Blake, but even that has laid open great beauties to its view. It is a curious circumstance, and well worthy the attention of all persons, that in this age of reason, Englishmen should have allowed two such men as Flaxman and Blake, to pass from this life without evincing the smallest regard for them. Perhaps 'reason stumbles all night over bones of the dead,' as Blake has elegantly expressed it, and pays but small attention to real genius; or it may be partly accounted for through the want of a good philosophy, which, Mad. De Stael says, has not as yet been taught in England. These, perhaps, are a few of the many reasons why Blake and Flaxman have been buried in obscurity; but we have a confident hope that Coleridge, Blake, and Flaxman are the forerunners of a more elevated and purer system, which has even now begun to take root in the breast of the English nation; they have laid a foundation for future minds—Coleridge, for the development of a more internal philosophy—Blake and Flaxman, for a purer and more ennobling sentiment in works of art.

After having preluded in this manner, let us direct our eyes to the beauties of Blake's poems.

THE INTRODUCTION TO THE SONGS OF EXPERIENCE.

> Hear the voice of the Bard,
> Who present, past, and future sees,
> Whose ears have heard
> The holy word
> That walked among the ancient trees,
>
> Calling the lapsed soul,
> And weeping in the evening dew,
> That might control
> The starry pole,
> And fallen, fallen light renew.
>
> O Earth, O Earth, return!
> Arise from out the dewy grass!
> Night is worn,
> And the morn
> Rises from the slumberous mass.
>
> Turn away no more!
> Why wilt thou turn away?
> The starry floor,
> The watry shore,
> Is given thee till break of day.

Around these lines the stars are rolling their resplendent orbs, and in the cloud on which the song floats, a human form is lying, anxiously surveying their courses: these are a few wild notes struck forth by the hand of a master. But let us continue to look over his notes, bright both with poetry and forms divine, which demonstrate an intimate knowledge of the passions and feelings of the human breast.

THE POISON TREE.

I was angry with my friend,
I told my wrath, my wrath did end;
I was angry with my foe,
I told it not, my wrath did grow.

Then I wat'red it in fears,
Night and morning, with my tears,
And I sunned it with smiles,
And with soft, deceitful wiles.

And it grew both day and night,
Till it bore an apple bright;
And my foe beheld it shine,
And he knew that it was mine.

And he into my garden stole,
When the night had veiled the pole;
In the morning, glad, I see
My foe outstretch'd beneath the tree.

If Blake had lived in Germany, by this time he would have had commentators of the highest order upon every one of his effusions; but here, so little attention is paid to works of the mind, and so much to natural knowledge, that England, in the eyes of the thinking world, seems fast sinking into a lethargy, appearing as if the *Poison Tree* had poured the soporific distillation over its body, which now lies under it almost dead and lifeless. . . . The powers, then, of both mind and body having been freely exercised, the result is a genius, who stands forth as a representative of his race; and thus we may say, Blake in his single person united all the grand combination of art and mind, poetry, music, and painting; and we may carry the simile still further, and say, that as England is the least fettered by the minds of other nations, so Blake poured forth his effusions in his own grand style, copying no one, (nolumes leges Angliae mutari,) but breathing spirit and life into his works; and though shaping forms from the world of his creative and sportive imagination, yet he still remembered he was a moral as well as intellectual citizen of England, bound both to love and instruct her. These ought to be the ruling principles of all artists and poets. Flaxman and Blake thought it a still higher honour to be celebrated for their innocence and beauty of sentiment, than for a mere sensual representation of forms. Their internal e.thetic produced a similar external, not by any means inferior to the mere form-painter, and in this respect superior, that there was a Promethean fire which glowed in their productions, purifying the soul from the gross imperfections of the natural mind. . . .

This grand combination of art succeeded in every particular, painting being the flesh, poetry the bones, and music the nerves of Blake's work.

The figures surrounding and enclosing the poems, produce fresh delight. They are equally tinged by a poetical idea, and though sometimes it is difficult to understand his wandering flights, yet the extraordinary power developed in the handling of both arts astonish[es] as well as delight[s]. Here and there figures are introduced, which, like the spirits in Macbeth, pass quickly from the sight; yet they every one of them have been well digested in the brain of a genius; and we should endeavour rather to unlock the prison-door in which we are placed, and gain an insight into his powerful mind than rail and scoff at him as a dreamer and madman.

For instance, Albion, with which the world is very little acquainted, seems the embodying of Blake's ideas on the present state of England; he viewed it, not with the eyes of ordinary men, but contemplated it rather as a province of one grand man, in which diseases and crimes are continually engendered, and on this account he poured forth his poetical effusions somewhat in the style of Novalis, mourning over the crimes and errors of his dear country: and it is more extraordinary still that, like Novalis, he contemplated the natural world as the mere outbirth of the thought, and lived and existed in that world for which we are created. Horrid forms and visions pervade this Albion, for they were the only representatives, in his opinion, of the present state of mankind. No great genius wrote without having a plan, and so in this, a light is frequently thrown across the pictures, which partly discover the interior design of the Poet. We are perfectly aware of the present state of public opinion on this kind of men, but we know at the same time, that every genius has a certain end to perform, and always runs before his contemporaries, and for that reason is not generally understood.—This is our candid opinion with respect to Blake, but we hope that hereafter his merits will be more generally acknowledged.

We now proceed to the other poems.

A CRADLE SONG

Sweet dreams form a shade
O'er my lovely infant's head;
Sweet dreams of pleasant streams
By happy, silent, moony beams.

Sweet sleep, with softest down
Weave thy brows an infant crown;
Sweet sleep, angel mild,
Hover o'er my happy child.

Sweet smiles in the night
Hover over my delight,
Sweet smiles, mother's smiles,
All the livelong night beguiles.

Sweet moans, dovelike sighs,
Chase not slumber from thine eyes!
Sweet moans, sweeter smiles,
All the dovelike moans beguiles.

Sleep, sleep, happy child,
All creation slept and smil'd,
Sleep, sleep, happy sleep,
While o'er thee the mother weep.

Sweet babe, in thy face
Holy image I can trace;
Sweet babe, once like thee
Thy Maker lay and wept for me:

Wept for me, for thee, for all,
When he was an infant small;
Thou his image ever see,
Heav'nly face that smiles on thee:

Smiles on thee, on me, on all,
Who became an infant small,
Infant smiles are his own smiles,
Heav'n and earth to peace beguiles. . . .

['The Divine Image' and 'The Garden of Love']

This ['The Garden of Love'] is a curious and mystical poem, which
as yet can be but partially understood—but at the same time it is highly

poetical. Now approaching a new subject, the elegant dream of Thel, which seems born in the perfume of the lily, so charming, so fairy-like, are all its illustrations, there is only one work that we remember like it in elegance, the Sakontola, for it wears all the freshness of Indian simplicity and innocence.

THEL.

The title-page of this mazy dream contains a specimen of his utmost elegance in design:—two beautiful figures are chasing one another in gentle sport, and the Peri Thel is looking on the fairy land. A few specimens of this poem will suffice to show its merit.

A Speech address to Thel by a Cloud.

Virgin, know'st thou not our steeds drink of the golden springs
Where Lovah doth renew his horses? Look'st thou on my youth,
And fearest thou, because I vanish and am seen no more:
Nothing remains? O maid, I tell thee, when I pass away,
It is to tenfold life, to love, to peace, to raptures holy;
Unseen descending, weigh my light wings on balmy flowers,
And court the fair-eyed dew to take me to her shining tent:
The weeping virgin, trembling kneels before the risen sun,
Till we arise linked in a golden band and never part—
But walk united, bearing food to all our tender flowers.

Dost thou, O little cloud? I fear I am not like thee;
For I walk through the vales of Har, and smell the sweetest flowers,
But I feed not the little flowers; I hear the warbling birds,
But I feed not the warbling birds, they fly and seek their food:
But Thel delights in these no more, because I fade away,
And all shall say, without a use this shining woman lived,
Or did she only live to be at death the food of worms?

The cloud reclined upon its airy throne, and answered thus:
Then if thou art the food of worms, O virgin of the skies,
How great thy use, how great thy blessing; every thing that lives,
Lives not alone, nor for itself: Fear not, I will call
The weak worm from its lowly bed, and thou shalt hear its voice:
Come forth, worm of the silent valley, to thy pensive queen!
The helpless worm arose, and sat upon the lily's leaf,
And the bright cloud sailed on to find his partner in the vale.

This little work is the fanciful production of a rich imagination, drawing, colouring, poetry, have united to form a beautiful whole; all the figures teem with elegance, and convey sentiments which are noble, though veiled under a fairy tale. With this last extract we conclude for the present, earnestly recommending the works of our author to the attention of the English nation, whereby their taste may be improved in the fine arts, as well as gratification derived from the perusal of his poetry.*

Why cannot the ear be closed to its own destruction,
    Or the glittering eye to the poison of a smile?
Why are the eyelids stored with arrows ready drawn,
    When a thousand fighting men in ambush lie?
Or an eye of gifts and graces, showing fruits and coin'd gold,
    Why a tongue impressed with honey from every wind,
Why an ear, a whirlpool fierce to draw creations in,
    Why a nostril wide, inhaling terror, trembling, and affright?
Why a tender curb upon the youthful burning boy,
    Why a little curtain of flesh on the bed of our desire!

The virgin started from her seat, and with a shriek,
Fled back unhindered, till she came into the vale of Har.

* Blake and Coleridge, when in company, seemed like congenial beings of another sphere, breathing for a while on our earth; which may easily be perceived from the similarity of thought pervading their works. [Reviewer's note.]

41. Anon., 'The last of the supernaturalists'

1830

Fraser's Magazine, vol. II (March 1830), pp. 217–35.[1]

The anonymous essay in *Fraser's Magazine* entitled 'The last of the supernaturalists'[1] is strikingly rambling, derivative, and uninformed. Of its approximately 14,500 words, over 4,000 are irrelevant to Blake or to supernaturalism; some 6,500 words are repeated from Cunningham's biography; and statements like the one that Blake 'wanted in early life . . . a true friend' simply ignore the facts (such as his early and true friendships with Flaxman, Stothard, and Cumberland). Blake is simply the occasion here for some cheap iconoclastic criticism.

The world is, without contradiction, a fitting habitation for spirits of only a like order. This truth, which is obvious to many, was a secret to William Blake to the hour of his death: it was a true sibylline leaf to his uninitiated sense. Happy for him had it been otherwise!

The history of this much-canvassed individual is, indeed, a 'psychological' curiosity, according to the favourite term, in writing as well as speaking, of Samuel Taylor Coleridge. By all the world Blake was thought a madman: this is the fate of those who differ in thought, word, or action, from the every-day sillinesses of visible life. Thus we have heard it said that Jeremy Bentham was a madman . . . [as well as] Samuel Taylor Coleridge . . . Professor Wilson . . . De Quincey . . . Wordsworth . . . Byron . . . Thomas Campbell. . . . Let, then, the sentence which asserts that

'Great wits to madness are allied,'

be placed amongst the most drivelling pieces of nonsense that have been uttered by the charnel-fuming lips of the *persifleur* and scoffer. . . .

[1] On somewhat implausible evidence, the article has been attributed to Carlyle (J. A. S. Barrett, 'Carlyle on Blake and Vitalis', *TLS*, 26 April 1928, p. 313) and to John Abraham Heraud or William Maginn (T. M. H. Thrall, *Rebellious Fraser's* [1934], p. 268).

And now, having described the only species of madman whom we are pleased to recognise, that is, those of the inferior order of created beings, we come to the true subject of our paper—William Blake, the mystic, the spiritualist, the supernaturalist. Was he a madman? In our opinion he was not. Did he, then, purchase his exemption by participating in the fraternity of exalted talent? He had not part or parcel in that high order. What is, then, our meaning? may well be demanded by the wondering reader. Have a moment's patience, very courteous sir, and you shall hear.

Nature, in her bounty, had done her part generously and nobly by William Blake—Art had done nothing. (Understand us well, good reader; by ART we do not mean the *art* of copperplate engraving, or painting.) When that combination is perfect, you will have a perfect man ... [like] Göthe. Had the circumstances of life favoured the formation of nature in William Blake, he, too, would have been a perfect man, and, yielding in merit to few of his prophetic brethren, would have been honoured by them and by mankind as a truly inspired *Vates*. But, alas! the boy exceeded his condition of life: he anticipated the generation of his family. The part in him which Nature had bestowed she sedulously fostered and perfected, and his imagination grew to its fulness of strength, and was competent to attain the highest and loftiest landmarks which the most adventurous and daring of men had ever set for the attainment of their comprehension. But the part which art and parental anxiety had taken in his education was trifling in the extreme. Heaven poured on the tender plant its genial sunshine; but without sufficient moisture in the soil, the plant could not grow to maturity; and earth—its parent earth—refused it the waters of the smallest rill or gushing fountain. When Blake grew up, he felt a secret pain—a gnawing—a sense of weakness, though indescribable, in his body. His mind prompted him to action—his limbs collapsed with weakness at the moment of trial: he was like the chained Titan. . . .

Blake was, in secret longing, like the student Anselmus of Hoffman's tale: he felt that the earth, as it is at present peopled, was no fitting habitation for one of his order; here all was cold selfishness and empty folly. Had he known of the history of that student of Dresden, he too, with the fervour of the romance-writer, would have exclaimed:— 'Ah, happy Anselmus! who hast cast away the burden of weekday life. . . .'

William Blake was a man who stood alone in the world: men laughed at him, and scoffed him, as they would treat some paltry, petty, conjuror and sleight-of-hand trickster at a country fair. Yet the good man bore up with patience, and even apparent cheerfulness, against all the contumelies of the never-thinking world. Had men examined his case,—had they investigated the poor creature's heart—his principles of thought,—had they traced the stream of imagination through its green savannas, its tangled brakes, its overhanging precipices, and interminable forests, to its primal source, they would have found wherewithall to startle their weak, pre-conceived notions of geological aptitude,—a fountain of the sweetest and Blandusian waters issuing from a rock of salt more detestable to the taste than the ashy apples of the Asphaltic lake. The Psalmist has wisely and beautifully said, 'It is good for me to have been in trouble, that I might know THY precepts.' Adversity was the bitter, every-day food of the good old man; yet to him it was of the divinest support; for it enabled him to attain those things which are the most glorious of earthly possessions, undying hope, universal charity, inextinguishable love for God. Ministers of state, men in affluence, 'dominations, princedoms, powers,' pause ye in your career of earthly nothingness, and gaze and ponder over the dying scene, the last words, the expiring utterance of this glorious piece of mortality. Thus is it most simply described by his biographer [Cunningham, paragraphs 46–7]. . . .

But adversity has the same tendency as prosperity: it disturbs the serenity of the mind, and makes that which should be, as it were, a translucent lake, shewing the beautiful azure of the heavens, and every luxuriant bush and leaf that hangs enamoured over the banks, a spectacle of 'dismal and foaming brine!' Where, in this land, and among the great ones of her metropolitan Babel, shall we see a human being calm and undisturbed at the temptations of his prosperous circumstances, as was the poor, bed-ridden, starving, aged, yet happy, William Blake, in his sorry crib and his wretched lodgement? . . .

Let us now descend to the facts of Blake's life.

William Blake was the son of a hosier. What! do you start in wild amaze, my young limb of fashion and sentiment—my formless fly-blow of college education? Gape on, and stare with your ugly goggle eyes in open wonder. Ay, we repeat it, and repeat it with pride, William Blake was the son of a hosier—Robert Burns was an untutored clown—James Hogg was an uncouth shepherd boy—John Clare is a Northamptonshire peasant. . . .

The following extract from Allan Cunningham's biography will introduce the subject fully before the reader [paragraphs 2–8]. . . .

And this was the boy whom Fortune had bound down to daily toil for the supply of the daily necessaries of life. Alas! for her crocketty caprices and her wanton favours! While some longeared lordling is lolloping his asinine length upon the sofa, complaining of the difficulty he has in killing that worst of enemies, Time . . . the poor children of misery and misfortune, such as Heyne, Vitalis, Blake, lie in their ricketty garrets, have not wherewithall to warm their frosty blood into a wholesome circulation, save the agonising pangs of disappointment shooting with electric rapidity along their veins and sinews, and burning with the woful flame of consuming fire. And yet the crumbs which fell from the very servants' table of the above-named '*laudator temporis acti*' at hunts, *coulisse*-intrigues, and green-rooms, racing grounds and platter-and-dish dalliance, would have been ample for the food of those wretched and starving sons of genius, and sent them in gladness of heart, and with a fervent blessing on their lips, to pursue the stony path that leads to the temple of renown, where that soul only

> 'Shall enter, which hath earned
> The privilege by virtue!'

Vitalis, however, was a man of sterner, ruder materials, than our William Blake; the misery of life could not bend into submission his too stubborn heart, but its strings burst in twain even with the very effort of resistance. William Blake had a calmer, quieter, more gentle, tractable spirit, and he lived onward to a ripe old age, a happy, cheerful man, though one engaged in daily struggles with poverty. Both wanted in early life the one thing essential to every individual, of whatever nature or degree of intellect,—a kind, compassioning adviser;—a true friend;—one who would have chided gently and en-couraged much: who would have listened to the tale of sorrow: not checked by coldness or sarcasm the tear struggling for a passage through the lowered fringes of the strained, blood-shot eye: and with quiet movement and soothing speech taught the young gladiators with self, how to struggle with error: instructed these inexperienced mariners how to trim their vessels, avoiding all the shoals and quicksands of a siren-thronged world: how to repair into the tranquil haven, how to produce their freight, and deal in an advantageous traffic with the inhabitants on shore, thereby gaining uncountable riches! . . . The secrets of existence, however, are dark—dark and unfathomable; yet the lives of Vitalis and Blake proclaim this manifest moral: 'Youth, arise, and be a-doing in the path marked out for thy career of life by the omniscient and omnipotent Taskmaster in heaven!'

Enough of this: Allan Cunningham next comes to speak of Blake's marriage. The process of love-making and pairing was characteristic of the man [paragraphs 9–12, 14–28]. . . .

The singularity of the man attracted public attention; yet he never had a companion, save one person, well enough known for his eccentricity. This eccentricity, however, we have the very best reason in the world for knowing, was assumed for the purpose of getting a name, in which he has partially succeeded, and has thereby put certain golden guineas into his pockets by the exercise of his profession. But this individual had not that transcendental perception into the supernatural, which would have given him the privilege of claiming kin and brotherhood with Blake. One was the genuine, true, and all-convinced mystic; the other was like the superficial tyro, waiting by his master to hear his words of wisdom, to note down the words explanatory of the esoteric doctrines of what he, in his ignorance, thought to be mere craft. . . . This man, therefore, is a buffoon and knave, 'not by spherical predominance,' but by artifice, that he may put money in his purse, and get rich.

But it was otherwise with poor William Blake. That he was no knave, will appear from the following anecdote, which must bring us to a conclusion directly the contrary of what it appears likely to induce. In other men, this conduct manifested on Blake's part would have proved the existence of a mendacious spirit [Cunningham, paragraph 28]. . . .

Now, no man in his mortal senses would have asserted what Blake is described to have done, without a conviction that the assertion was founded on truth. But it was wholly false, and yet Blake kept on persisting in its correctness, though accumulated evidence from almost every quarter of the town could be, and was, immediately brought forward to prove its nothingness. If Blake had been really an impostor, he would have calculated the chances of detection. This he never seems to have done: by no process of prudent conduct would a man deliberately write himself down a liar, when exposure was easy and certain. What shall we say, then, in Blake's extenuation? Simply this, that by severe abstraction, Blake's brain became fevered: he mistook the dreams of fancy for reality. Poor, unfortunate, ill-fated son of genius!

Therein lies the whole mystery of the man's existence; and the mystery yields and is unravelled by the slightest investigation. Had

Blake been perfect in mind, as he was in body (which combination alone makes the first-rate character), it had been well for him: had he been an educated man, and a man of the world, it had been well for him: had he been the pupil or the friend of a strong-minded, well-educated man, and a man of the world, it had been well for him. But he was deficient in all these necessaries for the Voyage of life. The world's neglect, the want of a friend, turned him to abstract speculations. Had vigour of mind *then*, as it were by some sudden revelation, come upon him, the milk of human love around his heart would have been curdled from disgust to gall and bitterness; and the young artist would have become an inveterate, irrecoverable sceptic. But blindness of faith is the usual comforter of weak minds in affliction; the poor youth, rejected of men, turned his thoughts and devotion from worldly concerns to the worship of his Maker; and, well aware of the all-lovingness of God, and, in his frenzied adoration, forgetting the weakness of mortal flesh, he imagined that his bruised and broken soul had found refuge in the bosom of the One True and Universal Friend. This was his spirit, indeed, regenerated, and with mortal utterance it spoke of the immortal wonders of another and a better world. To such a pass did the world's neglect, and the victory of disappointment, bring this man, the whiteness of whose soul was as immaculate as new-fallen snow upon mountain-tops. Thus very excess of virtue became in him an evil; yet he proceeded in his fatal error:—for how were it otherwise? William Blake had, for the voyage of life, neither Compass nor Ballast: he had, for the trials of life, neither Friend nor Adviser! Nevertheless was the suffering transcendentalist happy, gay, and unsubdued, even to the last, by the cares of this world of grief. His mind was constantly active—not a brook or a stone—not a leaf, a flitting shadow, or a gleam of sunshine, but carried to his head a silent, and consolatory meaning. How well do Burton's lines apply to him!

> 'When to myself I act and smile,
> With pleasing thoughts the time beguile,
> By a brook-side, or wood so green,
> Unheard, unsought for, and unseen;
> A thousand pleasures do me bless,
> And crown my soul with happiness:
>   All my joys besides are folly,
>   None so sweet as melancholy.

★   ★   ★   ★   ★

'Methinks I hear, methinks I see,
Sweet music, wondrous melody;
Towns, palaces, and cities fine,
Here now, then there, the world is mine;
Rare beauties, gallant ladies shine,
Whate'er is lovely or divine:
    All other joys to this are folly,
    None so sweet as melancholy.'

Stronger beings than Blake have believed in the supernatural. Johnson's theory has been put into the mouth of the sage Imlac, and is sufficiently known. What man that exists but has in his mind a faint adumbration of supernatural agency? This is the constant accompaniment of conscience; and so long as that monitor shall be active in the breast of man, so long will the sense of supernatural agency remain with him. But though a sense of the supernatural accompanies conscience, springing from the perpetration of evil; yet is it also the associate of Love for the purposes of good, as was the case with William Blake. Thus was it with Max. in Schiller's *Wallenstein*. . . .

Blake, it appears, published a catalogue of his pictures, in which he set forth the principles of his art according to his conception. All this is well described by our friend Allan Cunningham [paragraphs 29–34]. . . .

The following extracts are descriptive of some paintings which we ourselves have seen. Let the reader give his earnest attention to it [paragraphs 36–9, 41]. . . .

Blake had now arrived at a good old age, and felt himself to be dying. Still he kept touching and retouching his favourite painting. At last, he 'threw it from him, exclaiming, "There! that will do! I cannot mend it." He saw his wife in tears—she felt this was to be the last of his works. . . .'

This woman, says the writer of this singular piece of biography, is still alive, 'to lament the loss of Blake—and *feel* it.' Ye self-styled saints on earth, and ye distributors of private charity, ye need not go far in search of a fitting object on whom to bestow the golden guineas in your purses. Behold her here.

For the facts relative to Blake contained in this our paper, we are indebted to Allan Cunningham's volumes, entitled 'The Lives of English Painters,' &c., and forming a portion of the *Family Library*, published by Don John Pomposo [i.e., Murray], of Albemarle-street.

Gentle reader, go and purchase these Lives; or, if you will, the whole collection, for they are well worth every farthing of the money which you will pay.

As for Blake—peace to his sacred ashes!—his soul is now far beyond the sound of the jeers and the mockery of his earthly detractors: and for those detractors, we will quote some words from a book of which perhaps they know little—it is worth their perusal: 'CAST OUT THE BEAM OUT OF THINE OWN EYE; AND THEN SHALT THOU SEE CLEARLY TO CAST OUT THE MOTE OUT OF THY BROTHER'S EYE.'

42. Frederick Tatham, 'Life of Blake'

?1832

Tatham's 'Life of Blake'[1] was composed about 1832, in part to advertise for sale *Jerusalem* (copy E), with which it is bound, and other unsold copies of Blake's works which Tatham acquired at Mrs Blake's death in October 1831. The punctuation, paragraphing and continuity are eccentric. Tatham knew Blake better than any of Blake's other biographers, and Blake's widow lived with him for a time, but his own vigorously naïve piety influenced his diction and distorted his thought. His admiration for Blake was clearly that of a disciple for his master, but his dispraise of *Poetical Sketches* and his enthusiasm for the *Songs* and *Jerusalem* may be determined in part by his commercial interest; he had copies of the latter for sale. The critical extracts which follow are incidental to what is essentially a biographical account.

Blake pursued his Task [in Westminster Abbey as an apprentice, 1772–9] & his absorption gathered to itself impressions that were never forgotten. His Imagination ever after wandered in a cloister, or clothing itself in the dark Stole of mural sanctity, it dwelt amidst the Druid terrors. His mind being simplified by Gothic Forms, & his

---

[1] The text, first printed in A. G. B. Russell's edition of Blake's *Letters* (1906), is given here as in the manuscript in the possession of Mr Paul Mellon.

Fancy imbued with the livid twilight of past days, it chose for its quaint Company, such sublime but antiquated associates as the Fearful Merlin, Arthur & the Knights of his Round Table, the just & wise Alfred, King John, and every other hero of English History & Romance. These Indigenous Abstractions for many of the following years occupied his hand, & ever after tinctured his thoughts & perceptions. The backgrounds of his pictures, nearly always exhibited Druidical Stones & other Symbols of English Antiquity. Albion was the Hero of his Pictures, Prints & Poems. He appeared to be the Human Abstract of his mystical thoughts. He recounted his deeds, he exhausted the Incidents of his History & when he had accomplished this 'he then imagined new.' He made him a spiritual Essence— representing the Country of Brittain under this one personification he has made him the Hero of nearly all his Works—[.] He has connected Albion with Jerusalem & Jerusalem with other mysterious Images of his own fancy, in such a manner, as will be difficult to unravel, but not entirely impossible, it is imagined, after reading the remainder of his writings, which will absorb time & pains[,] much indeed of both for his pen was quite as active in his indefatigable hand, as was his Graver or his Pencil; he used all with equal temerity & complete originality.

Between the age of 12 & 20 he wrote several poems afterwards published by the advice & with the assistance of Flaxman, Mrs Matthews & others of his friends—they are succinct[,] original, fanciful & fiery but as a general criticism, it may be said that they are more rude than refined, more clumsy than delicate. Two of them are equal to Ben Johnson [*sic.*]

Song. ['How sweet I roamed'] . . .

Song

'Love & Harmony combine,
　　And around our souls entwine,
　While thy branches mix with mine,
　　And our roots together join.

2

Joys upon our branches sit,
　　Chirping loud & singing sweet,
　Like gentle streams beneath our feet,
　　Innocence & virtue meet;

3
Thou the golden fruit dost bear,
    I am clad in flowers fair.
Thy sweet boughs perfume the Air,
    And the Turtle buildeth there.

4
Then she sits & feeds her young
    Sweet I hear her mournful Song,
And thy lovely leaves among,
    There is love I hear his tongue.

5
There his charming nest doth lay,
    There he sleeps the night away,
There he sports along the day,
    And doth among our branches play.'

The others although well for a lad are but moderate. His blank verse
is prose cut in slices, & his prose inelegant, but replete with Imagery.
The following [from 'Contemplation'] is a specimen[:]

'Who is this with unerring step doth tempt the Wilds; where only
natures foot hath trod. 'Tis Contemplation, daughter of Grey Morning.
Majestical she steppeth & with her pure quill on every flower writeth
Wisdoms name. Now lowly bending, whispers in mine Ear, O man
how great how little art thou. O man slave for each moment, Lord of
Eternity, Seest thou where mirth sits on the painted cheek; doth it not
seem ashamed & grow immoderate to brave it out. O what a humble
Garb true Joy puts on. Those who want happiness must stoop to find it,
it is a flower that grows in every Vale. Vain foolish man that roams on
lofty rocks! where because his garments are swollen with wind he
fancies he is grown into a Giant.' The Aphorism on happiness is worthy
of his after days,—he seems at this time to have sighed after something
invisible for he complains in these words[:] 'I am wrapped in Mortality,
my flesh is a prison & my bones the Bars of Death.'

About this time Blake took to painting, & his success in it being a
matter of opinion it will require some care to give a fair account. Oil
painting was recommended to him, as the only medium through which
breadth, force, & sufficient rapidity could be obtained; he made several
attempts, & found himself quite unequal to the management of it; his
great objections were, that the picture after it was painted, sunk so
much that it ceased to retain the brilliancy & luxury that he intended,

& also that no definite line, no positive end to the form could even with the greatest of his Ingenuity be obtained, all his lines dwindled & his clearness melted, from these circumstances it harassed him, he grew impatient & rebellious, & flung it aside tired with ill success & tormented with doubts. He then attacked it with all the Indignation he could collect, & finally relinquished it to men, if not of less minds of less ambition. He had Michael Angelo on his side without doubt & a great many of the old genuine painters. Desiring that his colours should be as pure & as permanent as precious stones, he could not with Oil obtain his End. . . . Blake seemed intended for the 15 Century, when real energy of mind gained the appropriate rapidity of hand, and when the Vehicle, if not such as he invented was in much better command for sublime compositions. . . . The Author has seen pictures of Blakes in the possession of Wm Butts Esqre Fitzroy Square, that have appeared exactly like the old cabinet pictures of the 14 & 15, Century where he has touched the lights with white compound of whiting & glue, of which material he laid the ground of his Panel. Two of these pictures are of the most sublime composition & artistlike workmanship: they are not drawings on Canvas as some of his others, but they are superlative specimens of genuine painter-like handling & force, & are little inferior in depth, tone & colour to any modern Oil picture in the Country. . . . Blake painted on Panel or canvass covered with 3 or 4 layers of whitening & carpenters Glue; as he said the nature of Gum was to crack, for as he used several layers of colour to produce his depths, the Coats necessarily in the deepest parts became so thick, that they were likely to peel off. Washing his Picture over with glue in the manner of a Varnish, he fixed the Colours, and at last varnished with a white hard varnish of his own making. It must however be confessed that his pictures mostly are not very deep, but they have an unrivalled tender brilliancy. He took infinite pains with them, coloured them very highly & certainly without prejudice, either for or against, has produced as fine works, as any ancient painter. He can be excelled by none where he is successful. Like his thoughts his paintings seem to be inspired by fairies & his colours look as if they were the bloom dropped from the brilliant Wings of the Spirits of the Prism. This may appear too much to be said of the mad Blake as he was called by those too grovelling & too ignorant to discern his merits. Mr Butts' collection is enough in all conscience to prove this & more & whoever does not perceive the beauties of this splendid collection ought indeed to find fault with modesty & censure with a blush.

... He always asserted that he had the power of bringing his imagination before his minds Eye, so completely organized, & so perfectly formed & Evident, that he persisted, that while he copied the vision (as he called it) upon his plate or canvas, he could not Err; & that error & defect could only arise from the departure or inaccurate delineation of this unsubstantial scene. He said that he was the companion of spirits, who taught, rebuked, argued, & advised, with all the familiarity of personal intercourse. What appears more odd still was the power he contended he had, of calling up any personage of past days, to delineate their forms & features, & to converse upon the topic most incidental to the days of their own existence: how far this is probable must be a question, left either to the credulity or the faith of each person: it is fair however to say that what Blake produced from these characters, in delineating them, was often so curiously original, & yet so finely expressed, that it was difficult if prejudices were cast away, to disbelieve totally this power. It is well known to all enquiring men that Blake was not the only individual who enjoyed this peculiar gift.

... These visions of Blake seem to have been more like peopled imaginations, & personified thoughts, they only horrified where they represented any scene in which horrors were depicted as a picture or a Poem. ...

Again in reference to the authenticity of Blakes Visions, let any one contemplate the designs in this Book [*Jerusalem*]; Are they not only new in their method & manner; but actually new in their class & origin. Do they look like the localities of common circumstances, or of lower Worlds? The combinations are chimerical, the forms unusual, the Inventions abstract, the poem not only abstruse but absolutely according to common rules of criticism as near ridiculous, as it is completely heterogeneous. With all that is incomprehensible in the poem, with all that might by some be termed ridiculous in the plan, the designs are possessed of some of the most sublime Ideas, some of the most lofty thoughts, some of the most noble conceptions possible to the mind of man. You may doubt however the means, & you may criticise the peculiarity of the notions, but you cannot but admire nay 'wonder at with great admiration' these Expressive, these sublime, these awful diagrams of an Etherial Phantasy. Michael Angelo, Julio Romano or any other great man never surpassed Plates 25, 35, 37, 46, 51, 76, 94, and many of the stupendous & awful scenes with which this laborious Work is so thickly ornamented.

'Visions of glory spare my aching sight
Ye unborn ages crowd not on my Soul.'

Even supposing the poetry to be the mere Vehicle or a mere alloy for
the sake of producing or combining these wonderful thoughts it should
at all events be looked upon with some respect. . . .

Fuseli was very intimate with Blake & Blake was more fond of
Fuseli, than any other man on Earth: Blake certainly loved him, & at
least Fuseli admired Blake & learned from him as he himself confessed,
a great deal. Fuseli & Flaxman both said, that Blake was the greatest
man in the Country & that there would come a time when his works
would be invaluable. Before Fuseli knew Blake he used to fill his
Pictures with all sorts of fashionable ornaments & tawdry Embellishments. Blake's simplicity imbued the minds of all who knew him.
His life was a pattern, & has been spoken of as such from the Pulpit.
His abstraction from the World, his powers of self denial, his detestation
of hypocrisy & gain, his hatred of Gold & the things that perish,
rendered him indeed well able to have exclaimed,

'In innocency I have washed my hands[.]'

His poetry (& he has written a great deal) was mostly unintelligible,
but not so much so as the Works written in the manner of this present
one. Generally speaking, he seems to have published those [which were]
most mysterious. That which could be discerned was filled [with]
Imagery & fine Epithet. What but admiration can be expressed of
such Poetry as this[:]

London
'I wander thro' each chartered Street,
'Near where the winding Thames does flow,
'And mark in every face I meet,
    'Marks of weakness, marks of woe.

2
'In every cry of every man,
    'In every infants cry of fear,
'In every voice of every ban,
    'The mind Forged Manacles I hear.

3
'How the chimney sweepers cry,
    'Every blackening church appals,

'And the hapless soldiers sigh
'Runs in blood down palace Walls;

4

But most through midnight streets I hear,
How the youthful Harlots curse,
Blasts the new born infants tear:
And blights with plagues the marriage hearse.

———

The Tiger. . . .

A beautiful Stanza selected from the following Work [*Jerusalem*, pl. 27]

— — — — —

The Rhine was red with human blood,
The Danube rolled in purple tide,
O'er the Euphrates Satan stood,
And over Asia stretched his pride

— — — — —

Another [*Jerusalem*, pl. 52]

— —

For a tear is an Intellectual thing
And a sigh is the sword of an Angel King
And the bitter groan of a martyrs woe
Is an Arrow from the Almighty's Bow[.]

It may well be said of such poetry as this[,] such thrilling lines as these that they are 'Thoughts that breathe & words that burn'[.] There is another very tender—

The Lamb [from *Innocence*]. . . .

There is another in which is beautifully related the tender & exquisite circumstance of a mother looking on her Sleeping Infant which he calls a cradle Song [from *Innocence*]. . . .

These quotations are from the Songs of Innocence & Experience Engraved on Type plates which work the Author of this is now in possession of by the kindness of Mrs Blake who bequeathed them to him as well as all of his Works that remained unsold at his [i.e., her] Death being writings, paintings, & a very great number of Copper Plates, of whom Impressions may be obtained.

Frederick Tatham

PART VI   FORGOTTEN YEARS
REFERENCES TO WILLIAM BLAKE
1831–62[1]

For a quarter of a century after Catherine Blake's death in October 1831, few except Blake's own friends showed much interest in him except for those titillating rumours of the mad painter's visions. Then in 1855 a young man named Alexander Gilchrist began working vigorously on a biography of Blake, writing letters to Blake's friends and verifying all the accounts of him he could discover. When Gilchrist died suddenly in 1861, his work was almost finished, and the last touches were added by his widow Anne and an informal syndicate of the Pre-Raphaelite Brotherhood.[2] When Gilchrist's biography was published, the public image of Blake abruptly changed from that of an obscure eccentric to that of a major literary and artistic figure with just enough eccentricity to lend mystery and enchantment.

The index that follows of references to Blake from 1831 to 1863 is intended merely as a guide to Blake's flickering reputation in the forgotten years until Gilchrist rescued it for all time.[3]

18–19 Oct. 1831   In his journal, John Linnell wrote:

Tuesday 18 [October 1831] . . . Mrs Blake died at 7 in the morning
Wed 19 to F. Tatham &c—see F. Tatham's letters[4]

probably to see whether any letters in Tatham's possession were conclusive as to the ownership of the property Catherine had left, particularly Blake's Dante designs.

---

[1] For other accounts of the forgotten years, see particularly (1) Louis W. Crompton, 'Blake's Nineteenth Century Critics', University of Chicago Ph.D. (1954); (2) Valerie W. Rance, 'The History of William Blake's Reputation from 1806 to 1863', Reading University M.A. (1965); (3) Deborah Dorfman, *Blake in the Nineteenth Century* (1969); (4) Suzanne R. Hoover, 'Fifty additions to Blake bibliography: further data for the study of his reputation in the nineteenth century', *Blake Newsletter*, vol. v (1971–2), pp. 167–72; and (5) S. R. Hoover, 'William Blake in the wilderness: a closer look at his reputation 1827–1863' in *William Blake: Essays in Honour of Sir Geoffrey Keynes*, ed. Paley and Phillips (1973), pp. 310–48. Mrs Hoover's *festschrift* essay is by a visible margin the most 'comprehensive' treatment of the subject up to 1973, but it seems to omit the (mostly minor) references to Blake

22 Nov. 1831 A copy of *Job* is inscribed:
This work, remarkable both for genius and extravagance, is the gift of
Amelia Opie to her Friend [the sculptor Pierre Jean] David, whose own
genius will make him prize the former, while his eminent taste makes
it impossible for him to imitate the latter—Paris, 14me No. 22me 1831[1]

[1] Quoted from a clipping from an unidentified catalogue in a scrapbook in the possession of Mr Paul Mellon; I have not traced the copy of *Job* itself. The work was also inscribed: 'j'ai acheté ce livre à la vente de feu David le Statuaire, H. D. T[riqueti] 1856'.

---

below dated 18, 19 October, 22, 30 November (G. Hamilton), December 1831; 1831
(Knowles); 7, 14 April, 15 May, 29 June, July, 20 August, 8 September, 12, 19 December
1832; 1832 (Linnell); 1 March, 1, 4, 16, 18, 26 July, 21 November, 27 November, 16 Dec-
ember 1833; 1833 (Tatham); 1833 (Thorpe); 1833 (*Gallery of Portraits*); March, July, 18, 23
July, 8 December 1834; 1834 (Lowndes); May, 6, 19 May, 8 August 1835; 1835 (Nagler);
27 April, 4, 21 August, 23 October 1836; 1836 (Southey); 1836 (Hacket); 21 July 1837; 1837
(Ebert); 1837 (Partington); February, 8 February, 9, 19 April, 8 August, August, 7, 26
September, 2 October, November 1838; 1 January, 6 February, 5 March, 8 April, 20, 21
August 1839; 1839 (Jackson and Chatto); 1839–40; March, July, 7 December 1840; 1840
(Douce); 1840 (Ruskin ALS); May 1841; 1841 (Bohn); 1841 (Hazlitt); September, 1
October, 13 December 1842; 6, 14 February, September, December 1843; 1843
(Raimbach); 1843 (Leslie); 1843 (Péricaud); 18 January, 27 September, 8 November 1844;
1844 (Scott); February, July–August, 14 September 1845; 15 June, September 1846; 1846
(Durfee); 1846 (Linnell); October 1847; 1847 (Bohn); 5 February, April, 16, 25, 27 April,
9, 17, 20, 24, 24, 26 May, 27 July, 10 August, 21 October, 12 November 1848; 1848
(Milnes); 15 February, 5 March 1849; 1849 (Chatto); 1849 (Hobbes); 27 May 1850; 1850
(Rose); 17, 18 January, August 1851; 1851 (Wilkinson); 1851 (Arvine); 1851 (Bray); 20
January, 14 July, 27 October 1852; 1852 (Romney); 1852 (Palgrave); January, February, 29
June, 28 November 1853; 1853 (Spooner, *Biographical Dictionary*); March, March, 8 March,
May, 7–30 June, December 1854; 1854 (Pearson); 1854 (Montgomery); 1854 (*Nouvelle
Biographie Universelle*); 17, 23, 25, 27 April, June, 16, 17, 20, 23, 28 June, 23 August 1855;
1855 (Sotheby); 1855 (Leslie); 8 January, 31 August, 15 October, 3 November, 30 Decem-
ber 1856; 25 August, 4, 11, 18 December 1858; 1 March, 15 May, 29 December 1859. . . .

[2] His widow followed the advice which D. G. Rossetti gave her in a letter of 1863: 'I
think the whole *Life* should go in your Husband's name simply' (*Letters of Dante Gabriel
Rossetti*, ed. O. Doughty and J. R. Wahl [1965], vol. II, p. 478). For other D. G. Rossetti
letters cited below, see vol. I, pp. 96–7, vol. II, pp. 229, 396, 409, 412, 418, 420, 424, 439–41,
445, 451–9, 461–2.

[3] I omit simple reprints of works like Mrs Hemans's poem on Blake (see February
1832) and sales of minor Blake works. Of the MSS. frequently cited here, Linnell's Journal
and 'Cash Books' are in the Ivimy MSS., and Crabb Robinson's Diary, Reminiscences and
Correspondence are in Dr Williams's Library, London; for more details, see *Blake Records*
(1969). The references to dates before 1831—e.g., 'see 30 May 1815'—allude to *Blake Records*
(1969), where all the contemporary references to Blake up to 1831 then known are collected, together with such posthumous references as seem to have unique authority or interest. These 'Forgotten Years' form, as it were, Part VII of *Blake Records*, for which it was
written in 1963.

[4] Quoted from the MSS. of Mrs Joan Linnell Ivimy Burton, whose friendship and
generosity continue to rejoice me. For an extended account of the quarrel between Linnell
and Tatham over Blake's surviving property, see *Blake Records* (1969), pp. 413–18: 'Post-
script: "God Protect Me from My Friends": 1831–3'.

30 Nov. 1831 H. C. Robinson wrote in his Diary for 30 November that Cunningham 'has softend down the more offensive parts in the biography' of Blake, Fuseli, and Barry; 'I have a strong impression in favor of *Blake* as a man but as a painter his works are to me un-attractive. . . .'

30 Nov. 1831 On 30 November appeared part 31 of G. Hamilton's *The English School*,[1] with an engraving (no. 181) by '*Normand fils*' after Blake's design of 'Death's Door. La Porte du Tombeau', accompanied by an explanation:

This composition is the work of an artist whose productions,[2] though often disfigured by conceit and extravagance, and sometimes un-intelligible, occasionally present much grace, beauty,[2] and originality. It is one of a series of 'inventions,' as Blake called them, illustrative of Robert Blair's poem, 'The Grave,' which were purchased of the artist by Cromek, whose admiration of their excellence induced him to place them in the hands of Louis Schiavonetti, by whom they were ably transferred to copper; and they were introduced to the world in a splendid edition of the poem accompanied by some observations on their design and execution from the pen of Fuseli, whose almost unqualified praise, stamped with the assent of the most distinguished professors and judges of Art, renders all farther commendation superfluous.

The subject is taken from the concluding lines of the poem: [six lines of which are quoted]. . . .

In the explanation, which the symbolic nature of these compositions rendered necessary, we find the following description of Death's Door. 'The Door opening that seems to make utter darkness visible; Age,

---

[1] G. Hamilton, *The English School: a Series of the Most Approved Productions in Painting and Sculpture; Executed by British Artists from the Days of Hogarth to the Present Time. Selected, Arranged, and Accompanied with Descriptive and Explanatory Notices in English and French* [including a French title page] *Engraved in Outline upon Steel*. 4 vols. London: Charles Tilt [or 'Bossange, Barthés and Lowell' in a variant title page], Paris: Chez Hamilton et Chez Audot [plus, in vol. III, La Librairie Etrangère], 1831-2. An advertisement in vol. I dated 10 March 1831 says that 'arrangements have been made' to issue 'future numbers every fortnight', and implies that the first number appeared in July 1830. *If*, as seems likely, this advertisement accompanied the last number (no. 12) of vol. I, and *if* the announced schedule was adhered to, the thirty-first number should have appeared on 30 November 1831 and the forty-sixth (also with a Blake plate) on 29 June 1832.

Hamilton's book was generously pointed out to me by Sir Geoffrey Keynes.

[2] In the accompanying French version of these comments, it is Blake's 'pensée' (rather than 'productions') which shows 'conceit and extravagance', and it is 'noble' rather than showing 'beauty'.

on crutches, hurried by a tempest into it. Above is the renovated man seated in light and glory.'

Dec. 1831 An anonymous review of Cunningham ('Memoir of Flaxman the Sculptor') in *New Jerusalem Magazine*, vol. v (Boston, December 1831), pp. 153–4, mentions 'the mad imaginations of Blake' and says of Flaxman, 'With Blake, in particular, he loved to dream and muse' (see *Blake Records* [1969], p. 480, n. 10).

1831 John Knowles, in *The Life and Writings of Henry Fuseli* (1831), summarizes the (abortive) plan for Blake to engrave Fuseli's Milton designs (see 1 September 1791, 29 May 1792) and an early prospectus for Blake's designs for Blair's *Grave* (only recently rediscovered—see *Modern Philology*, spring 1974).

Jan. 1832 In Anon., 'Memoirs of William Blake', *New Jerusalem Magazine*, vol. v (January 1832), pp. 192–9, paragraphs 8–10, 14–41, 47, most of the paragraphs of Cunningham are given 'for the sake of the contrast between him [Blake] and Flaxman', Flaxman being 'a model of order and rationality', that is, a receiver of Swedenborgian truth, while Blake was a man of 'unregulated enthusiasm' and 'wild phantasy' who could not understand 'these [Swedenborgian] truths'.

Feb. 1832 Mrs [Felicia Dorothea] Hemans's poem, 'The Painter's Last Work.—A Scene' in *Blackwood's Edinburgh Magazine*, vol. xxxi (February 1832), pp. 220–1, was 'Suggested by the closing scene in the life of the painter Blake; as beautifully related by Allan Cunningham'.[1] The poem is better than one might expect.

7 April 1832 According to his Journal, Linnell went on 'Sat 7 [April 1832]—to Mr Callcott/ to Mr Rogers left Blake's Drawings of Paradise Reg^d for him to look at'. Linnell had purchased the *Paradise Regained* series of drawings from Blake in the autumn of 1825 for £10 and had previously offered them to the sculptor Sir Francis Chantrey for £20 and to the painter Sir Thomas Lawrence for £50 in February 1827,[2] but they remained in Linnell's family until long after his death.

[1] The poem was reprinted in the *Philadelphia Album and Ladies Literary Port Folio*, vol. vi (31 March 1832), p. 97; *Godey's Lady's Book*, vol. v (July 1832), p. 32; *Scenes and Hymns of Life* (Edinburgh and London, 1834), pp. 157–64; *The Poetical Works of Mrs. Felicia Hemans* (Philadelphia, 1836), pp. 371–2; *Works of Mrs Hemans* [ed. Mrs Hughes] (Edinburgh and London, 1839), vol. vii, pp. 210–15; *The Poetical Works of Mrs. Felicia Hemans* (Philadelphia, 1842), pp. 371–2; *The Complete Works of Mrs. Hemans*, ed. [Mrs Hughes] (New York and Philadelphia, 1847), vol. ii, pp. 490–2; *The Poems of Felicia Hemans* (Edinburgh and London, 1849), pp. 595–6; and in 1865, 1866, 1872, 1912, 1914, 1920.

[2] *Blake Records* (1969), pp. 606, 338–9.

14 April 1832 On 'Sat 14 [April, Linnell went] to Mr Rogers bro<u>t</u> away Blake's Drawings of Paradise reg<u>d</u>'.

15 May [*?1832*] It was perhaps in 1832[1] that the poet Samuel Rogers wrote:

5 Hanover Terrace
Regent's Park
May 15th

My dear Miss [Caroline] Philips

I return the beautiful specimen of that most eccentric Artist, Blake, with many thanks for the pleasure it has afforded me: it recalled to my recollection that I had a copy of the same work in my library, but as there is some slight difference in the design as well as in the coloring, I send it thinking it may interest you to compare them:—Should you not have the opportunity of returning it before you quit London, be so obliging as to leave it in Hertford St. and my friends there will forward it to me: With repeated thanks for the trouble this kind loan has occasioned you—

Believe me
Yours very truly
S. Rogers[2]

29 June 1832 Part 46 (no. 271) of Hamilton's *The English School* (vol. IV) probably appeared on 29 June 1832 (see 30 November 1831), bearing an engraving of Blake's 'Death of the Strong Wicked Man Mort d'un Réprouvé' by Normand fils and an explanation:
[fourteen lines from Blair's *Grave*]
This composition, one of the series alluded to in the account of Death's Door in No. 31, is thus noticed by Cromek[:] 'Extent of limb . . . share his fate.'[3]

It has been objected to this design that it is fearful and extravagant: admitting the truth of the observation, it may be remarked, that the first qualification, being derived from the poem, belongs to the subject,

[1] The year assigned here (1832) is a pure guess; almost any other year before the writer's death in 1855 would do as well.

[2] Quoted from a transcript of the letter in the possession of Mr Paul Mellon. Rogers was sending his *Innocence* (C) to be compared with the curious MS. facsimile (copied from Hanrott's *Songs* [P]) with the bookplate of 'Caroline Philips' (now in the possession of Mr Mellon). His correspondent may have been the daughter of Thomas Phillips, and the sister of Henry Wyndham Phillips whose bookplate is in *Songs* (I).

[3] The description of the design quoted here from Blair's *Grave* (1808) is anonymous.

the extravagance is characteristic of Blake, and is found more or less in almost all his productions.

July 1832 Anon., 'British school of engraving.—no. II.', *Library of the Fine Arts*, vol. IV (July 1832), pp. 5, 13, contains incidental references to Blake as the 'dupe of visionary fancies' and as the occasion of some of Schiavonetti's best work.

20 Aug. 1832 According to his journal, on 'Monday 20 [August 1832, Linnell] . . . sent to Sussex Hotel for Mr Lizars . . . a Book of Job plain 2.2.0 . . .'[1]

8 Sept. 1832, 1833 Anon., '*Major's Cabinet Gallery of Pictures: with Historical and Critical Descriptions and Dissertations*, by Allan Cunningham. No. 1', *Athenaeum*, no. 254 (8 September 1832), p. 482, gives *in toto* the 'capital anecdote of Blake' from Cunningham's book which was published in parts and then collected in January 1833:

Blake, who always saw in fancy every form he drew, believed that angels descended to painters of old, and sat for their portraits. When he himself sat to Phillips [4 April 1807] for that fine portrait so beautifully engraved by Schiavonetti, the painter, in order to obtain the most unaffected attitude, and the most poetic expression, engaged his sitter in a conversation concerning the sublime in art. 'We hear much,' said Phillips, 'of the grandeur of Michael Angelo; from the engravings, I should say he has been over-rated; he could not paint an angel so well as Raphael.' 'He has not been over-rated, Sir,' said Blake, 'and he could paint an angel better than Raphael.' 'Well, but' said the other, 'you never saw any of the paintings of Michael Angelo; and perhaps speak from the opinions of others; your friends may have deceived you.' 'I never saw any of the paintings of Michael Angelo,' replied Blake, 'but I speak from the opinion of a friend who could not be mistaken.' 'A valuable friend truly,' said Phillips, 'and who may he be I pray?' 'The arch-angel Gabriel, Sir,' answered Blake. 'A good authority surely, but you know evil spirits love to assume the looks of good ones; and this may have been done to mislead you.' 'Well now, Sir,' said Blake, 'this is really singular; such were my own suspicions; but they were soon removed—I will tell you how. I was one day reading Young's Night Thoughts, and when I came to that passage

---

[1] This appears in Linnell's *Job* accounts under August 1832 as £2 10s. and £2 12s. 6d., specifying that it was obtained by 'H. W. Lizars Edinburgh for a friend' (*Blake Records* [1969], pp. 597, 600).

which asks "who can paint an angel," I closed the book and cried, "Aye! who can paint an angel?" A voice in the room answered, "Michael Angelo could." "And how do *you* know," I said, looking round me, but I saw nothing save a greater light than usual. "I *know*," said the voice, "for I sat to him; I am the arch-angel Gabriel." "Oho!" I answered, "you are, are you; I must have better assurance than that of a wandering voice; you may be an evil spirit—there are such in the land." "You shall have good assurance," said the voice, "can an evil spirit do this?" I looked whence the voice came, and was then aware of a shining shape, with bright wings, who diffused much light. As I looked, the shape dilated more and more: he waved his hands; the roof of my study opened; he ascended into heaven; he stood in the sun, and beckoning to me, moved the universe. An angel of evil could not have *done that*—It was the arch-angel Gabriel.' The painter marvelled much at this wild story; but he caught from Blake's looks, as he related it, that rapt poetic expression which has rendered his portrait one of the finest of the English school.

12 Dec. 1832 The Sotheby sale of the late William Ensom's effects on 12 December 1832 included Ensom's 'Portrait of W. Blake, R.A.' for which he had won the silver medal from the Society for the Encouragement of Arts, Manufactures, and Commerce on 30 May 1815.

19 Dec. 1832 The following letter to Linnell in the Ivimy MSS. was written on 19 December 1832:
If not inconvenient Mrs Törrens would be much obliged by your sending by the bearer the *'Book of Job'*, as you kindly promised to do, before we left town: You may depend that all care will be taken of it—

[*?1832*] The biography of 'William Blake' among the 'Memorials of Engravers that have exercised the art in Great Britain' (BM Add. MSS. 33, 397, ff. 140–2) by Thomas Dodd (1771–1850) is drawn chiefly from Cunningham except for some original information about Blake's engravings. It was probably written about 1832 to continue Dodd's *Connoisseur's Reportorium*, which left off in the middle of the letter B in 1831—see 'An unknown early biography of Blake', *The Times Literary Supplement*, 16 March 1962, p. 192.

[*?1832*] About 1832 John Linnell wrote in a notebook in the Ivimy MSS. labelled 'Engravings Subscribers Accounts' of an unidentified Subscriber: 'query did I send any Book of Job[?]'

Jan. 1833 For the collected edition of Cunningham's *Cabinet Gallery of Pictures*, published in January 1833, see September 1832 above.

March 1833 For the somewhat impressionistic account of Blake's visions in Anon., 'Bits of biography. No. I. Blake, the vision seer, and Martin, the York Minister incendiary', *Monthly Magazine*, vol. xv (March 1833), pp. 244–5, see December 1824, 27 January 1829.

1 March 1833 For Tatham's two letters about the disputed ownership of Blake's Dante drawings to Linnell of 1 March 1833 (Ivimy MSS.), and John Linnell Jr's comments on them, see *Blake Records* (1969), p. 414.

[?1833] For Tatham's undated letter offering Blake's works for sale to Sir John Soane of about 1833 (Sir John Soane Museum), see *Blake Records* (1969), p. 413.

July 1833 For an unacknowledged translation and corruption of the March 1833 *Monthly Magazine* account of Blake's visions in Anon., 'Hôpital des fous à Londres', *Revue Britannique*, 3rd S., vol. iv (July 1833), pp. 183–6, see *Blake Records* (1969), p. 299, n. 1.

1833 An account consisting almost entirely of quotations from Cunningham was published by Mrs D. L. Child as 'Mrs. Blake, Wife of William Blake', *Good Wives* (Boston, 1833), pp. 128–33; *Biographies of Good Wives* (New York and Boston, 1846), pp. 125–8; (1847); (London and Glasgow, 1849), pp. 123–8; (Boston and New York, 1850); (1855).

July 1833 Anon., 'Art. VI.—Works of Mrs. Child...', *North American Review*, vol. xxxvii (July 1833), pp. 138–64, quotes in passing Mrs Child's anecdotes in her *Good Wives* about the fairy's funeral and about Blake's deathbed.

1 July 1833, 4 July 1833 Linnell recorded in his journal that he went on 'Monday 1st [July 1833] to Mr Geo Stephen[,] Coleman[?] St. to meet Miss Blake @ Administering to her Brothers Effects with Mr S. & Miss B— to Proctors. &c'.[1] And three days later he went on 'Thursday 4 ... to Miss Blake, Painters [or ?Pimlico] &c'.

[1] The discovery of Linnell's journal itself reveals that the transcripts by A. H. Palmer quoted in *Blake Records* (1969) were inaccurate in minute particulars; in some cases (such as the entries for 1 and 4 July 1833—the latter given in *Blake Records* as 7 July) this warrants reprinting the journal entries in corrected form.

16, 18 July 1833 At Evans's sale of the collection of P. A. Hanrott on 16 and 18 July 1833, 'Blake's America [G], Europe [B], and Jerusalem [B], Prophecies, *coloured plates,* . . . 1793' were sold to French for £4; 'PICKED PROOFS' of *Job* went to Bohn for £3 3s.; *Songs* (P) *'with Singular Designs'* and *For Children: The Gates of Paradise* (A) went to Thorpe for £2 10s. and £1 16s.

26 July 1833 On 'Friday 26 [July 1833 Linnell went] to Lisson Grove to look at F. Tatham's effects on sale', presumably including his Blakes inherited from Catherine Blake.

25 Oct. 1833 For FitzGerald's letter of 25 October 1833 about the copy of Blake's *Songs of Innocence* which he had just bought, see No. 12g above.

21 Nov. 1833 On 'Thursday 21 [November 1833, Linnell] . . . sent in the Evening by Mr Ns[?] messenger . . . 1 Book of Job . . . to Colnaghi'.

Nov. 1833 [Amédée Pichot,] 'Artiste, poète et fou. (La vie de Blake)', *Revue de Paris,* vol. LVI (November 1833), pp. 164–82 (reprinted in Pichot's 'Le Visionnaire Blake', *Revue Britannique,* vol. V [1862], pp. 25–47) is a piece of casual journalism, based on a distant acquaintance with Cunningham, Young's *Night Thoughts,* and Blair's *Grave,* which both compares Blake to Wordsworth (pp. 170–1) and produces the following delightful bit of distorted dialogue: when Catherine says she pities Blake for having been jilted: 'Vous me plaignez? reprit Blake, oh! alors vous daignerez bien *poser* pour moi?—Volontiers.' (In Cunningham's account from which this is derived—*Blake Records* [1969], p. 481—was: '"Do you pity me?" said Blake, "then I love you for that." "And I love you" . . . .')

27 Nov. 1833 L[ucy] H[ooper] used the anecdote of the fairy funeral Blake saw (as reported by Cunningham) as the basis for 'The Fairy's Funeral', *Long Island Star,* 27 November 1833, p. 1 (reprinted in *The Poetical Remains of the Late Lucy Hooper,* ed. J. Keese [New York, Philadelphia, and Boston, 1842], pp. 174–6). The poem could be worse.

16 Dec. 1833 On 16 December 1833 Allan Cunningham told Thomas Keightley, author of *Faery Mythology*: 'You will find a fanciful account of a Faery funeral in my "Life of Blake" in the "Lives of the Painters."' (A. Cunningham, *The Lives of the Most Eminent British Painters,* ed. C. Heaton [London, 1879], vol. I, p. *xx.*)

1833   In his catalogue for 1833, Thomas Thorpe offered 'William Blake, Artist, Autograph Dedication of his Visions to the Queen, in Verse, 4*s*.'

1833   Anon., *The Gallery of Portraits: with Memoirs* (London, 1833), vol. I, p. 28, contains a reference to Flaxman's 'intimacy with Blake and Stothard'.

1833   In an account of Blake's visions [from Cunningham] in [Josiah Holbrook,] *A Familiar Treatise on the Fine Arts, Painting, Sculpture, and Music* (Boston, 1833), pp. 96–7, the poet is introduced to 'young readers' in three paragraphs as 'a man whose fancy over-mastered his reason'.

March 1834   Anon., 'Past and present', *New England Magazine*, vol. VI (March 1834), pp. 235–6, is about a travelling dreamer who was able 'to study the individual countenances of Romans, whom I called up at will, as Blake, the painter, was wont to do when he would draw them'.

April 1834   [T. H. Lister,] 'Art. III. *Lives of the most Eminent British Painters, Sculptors, and Architects. By Allan Cunningham. 6 vols. 12mo. London: 1830–1–2–3*', *Edinburgh Review*, vol. LIX (April 1834), pp. 53, 64, remarks on the partiality Cunningham showed by including 'the able, but, alas! insane' Blake, who 'could scarcely be considered a painter', in his lives of *Eminent British Painters*.

April 1834   Anon., 'Art. XI. *Illustrations of the Bible*. By John Martin . . .', *Westminster Review*, vol. XX (April 1834), p. 464, remarks in passing of Martin, 'His pictures are opium dreams, a phantasmagoria of landscape and architecture, as Fuseli's and Blake's designs were of human beings'.

July 1834   In July 1834, Mrs S[arah] Austin (1793–1867) wrote to Crabb Robinson:
Dear Sir
    Mr Linnell the friend of Blake & the present possessor of the copies of 'Job' wishes much to make this work known in Germany where he thinks it might find some sale.
    I send a copy w^h I would thank you to give Mrs Jameson[1] begging

---

[1] Mrs Anna Brownell Jameson (1794–1860) may be the 'German friend of Mrs Austin' who appears in Linnell's *Job* accounts for one copy plain (*Blake Records* [1969], p. 602). For her published praise of Blake, see 1848.

her to do what she can to forward Linnells views. I will write to her very shortly—Pray give my kindest regards to her.

I suppose you will find her at Vienna. . . .

P.S. I need not ask you to speak of Blake—knowing your sentiments about him—

18 July 1834 Perhaps it was in furtherance of this campaign that Robinson sent to Dr Julius, the translator of his essay on Blake (1811), a book marked

The mad genius of Blake:	Memoriæ Causa
The philanthropy of Bet-	scripsit
tina v. Arnim	18th July 1834
The passionless wisdom	H. C. Robinson
of Goethe	Plowden Buildings
To Dr Julius	Temple
	London[1]

23 July 1834 On 23 July Mrs Austin wrote again: 'Dear Sir, / It was to serve Linnell that I ventured to trouble you with the "Job". He wd be glad to make it known in Germany. Do as you think best with it. . . .'

8 Dec. 1834 Among the 54,534 lots sold by Evans from the Heber Collection in December 1834 was no. '99 Blake's (W.) Poetical Sketches [F], *red morocco*, 1783', which sold on the 8th for 2s. This was Nancy Flaxman's copy, which Heber had probably bought at the Reed sale—see 5 December 1807.

1834 In William Thomas Lowndes, *The Bibliographer's Manual of English Literature*, 4 vols (London, 1834), Blake is mentioned under Blair and Young; in the eleven-volume edition (ed. [H. G. Bohn], London, 1857–61), a separate Blake entry was added, a list (in 1857) of eleven titles, with sales records.

1834 John Gould's *Biographical Sketches of Eminent Artists comprising Painters, Sculptors, Engravers, and Architects, from the Earliest Ages to the Present Time; Interspersed with Original Anecdotes* (London, 1834), pp. 48–9, described Blake with facts derived from Watkins and Shoberl, *Biographical Dictionary of Living Authors of Great Britain and Ireland* (1816) and the *Gentleman's Magazine* obituary of Blake (October 1827).

[1] Quoted from H. G. Wright, 'Henry Crabb Robinson's "Essay on Blake"', *Modern Language Review*, vol. XXII (1927), p. 139n, citing only 'a book' in the State and University Library of Hamburg.

1834 In *The Philosophy of Sleep* (New York, 1834), pp. 227–8,[1] Robert Macnish quotes from Cunningham's accounts of Blake's visions to demonstrate that 'his wild imagination . . . totally over-mastered his judgment, and made him mistake the chimeras of an excited brain for realities'.

28 Feb. 1835 Anon., 'Enthusiasm of an artist', *Atkinson's Saturday Evening Post*, 28 February 1835, p. 2, is an account from Cunningham of Blake's colouring of his 'Ancient of Days' for Tatham on his deathbed.

May 1835 James Weal's note in the 'most elaborately finished copy of the Songs of Innocence & Songs of Experience [*X*] . . . executed by the highly gifted artist expressly for his friend, Mr Wainewright', dated May 1835, will be found under 8 August 1820.

On 6 May 1835, George Cumberland sold part of his library (doubtless in part because he was going blind) through Christie's, including *America* [F], *Visions* (A), *Europe* (D), *Song of Los* (D), and Blair's *Grave* for £3 18s. to Butts, and *Job* and *Thel* (A) for £3 13s. 6d. to Bohn.

19 May 1835 On Beckford's copy of *For Children: The Gates of Paradise* (C) is written: 'A present from H. G. Bohn 19 May 1835'.

24 July 1835 For Isaac D'Israeli's letter to T. F. Dibdin of 24 July 1835 (given in T. F. Dibdin, *Reminiscences of a Literary Life* [1836], pp. 784–9), see No. 16u above.

8 Aug. 1835 A letter from Eliza Aders to John Linnell postmarked 8 August 1835 (Ivimy MSS.) mentions that Linnell recently bought 'Blakes Songs of Innocence &c [copy AA from the Aderses] at 6G^s'.

1835 Dr G. K. Nagler's article on 'Blake, William' in *Neues allgemeines Kunstler-Lexicon* (Munich, 1835), vol. 1, pp. 519–22, is an ambitious account which is naturally derived chiefly from Cunningham.

Jan. 1836 For the Blake references in T. F. Dibdin's *Reminiscences of a Literary Life*, which was published in January 1836, see No. 16i above.

27 April 1836 The second edition of William Carey's *Critical Description and Analytical Review of Death upon the Pale Horse*, with its long

---

[1] The Blake account does not appear in the earlier edition (Glasgow, 1830), but it does appear in later ones: (1836); (Glasgow and London, 1838), pp. 258–60; (Glasgow, London, and Edinburgh, 1845), pp. 296–8; (Glasgow and London, 1859), pp. 152–3. Mrs Hoover (p. 320) refers to a corrected edition of Boston, 1835 which I have been unable to trace.

eulogy of Blake's *Grave* designs, was published 27 April 1836; see 31 December 1817.

4 Aug. 1836 For Crabb Robinson's conversation with Samuel Palmer about Blake's insanity reported in his diary on 4 August 1836, see 8 January 1828.

21 Aug. 1836 Crabb Robinson's letter to Thomas Robinson of 21 August 1836 (Dr Williams's Library) refers to his meeting with '*Palmer* an admirer of *Blake* . . .'.

23 Oct. 1836 In his letter to William Bodham Donne of 23 October 1836 (*A FitzGerald Friendship*, ed. C. B. Johnson and N. C. Hannay [London, 1932], p. 6), Edward FitzGerald wrote that he had 'also got Blake's book of Job for you to see: terrible, awful, and wonderful—'.

1836 For the abortive Blake collection which (according to J. Forster, *Walter Savage Landor* [1869], vol. II, pp. 322–3) Walter Savage Landor began in 1836, see 24 July 1811.[1]

1836 For Southey's quotation in *The Works of William Cowper, Esq.*, ed. R. Southey (1836), vol. III, p. 238, of a letter from Hayley citing Blake's report of the universal admiration for Flaxman's monument to Cowper, see January 1804.

1836 In a list of sixty-five 'Patrons and Admirers of the science and doctrine of Astrology' in J. T. Hacket, *The Student's Assistant in Astronomy and Astrology* (London, 1836), p. 119, only 'Mr. Blake, Nov. 28, 7h. 45' p.m. 1757' is identified with more than the year of his birth. The information probably derives from the article on Blake in *Urania*—see December 1825.

21 July 1837 In the Sotheby catalogue, 21 July 1837, of William Young Ottley appeared Blake's *Jerusalem* (?A), '*one hundred engravings from wood*', which was sold to Bohn for £3 18s.

1837 F. A. Ebert's *Allgemeines Bibliographisches Lexicon* (1821) with its references to Blake (largely borrowed from Crabb Robinson's 1811 essay) was translated by Arthur Brown as *A General Bibliographical Dictionary* in 1837—see 1821.

---

[1] Landor's MS. note, 'Blake, never did a braver or a better man carry the sword of justice', has been erroneously associated with the poet (e.g., by Keynes, *Bibliography of William Blake* [1921], p. 335, and Hoover [1973], p. 328), but, as R. H. Super wrote to me in 1967, the Landor note is appended to his Imaginary Conversation on the Cromwellian Admiral Robert Blake. The Blake in the note is therefore Robert, his bravery is nautical, and his sword is real.

1837   Charles F. Partington's conventional paragraph on Blake in *The British Cyclopaedia of Biography* (London, 1837), vol. I, p. 223 (part of his *British Cyclopaedia of Arts and Sciences*), merely says that his 'strange eccentricity' marred his talent.

1837   In *Lives of Eminent and Illustrious Englishmen, from Alfred the Great to the Latest Times*, ed. George Godfrey Cunningham (Glasgow, Edinburgh, and London, 1838), vol. VIII, p. 310, the account of Flaxman quotes one sentence from Cunningham's description (1830) of Flaxman with Blake.

Feb. 1838   In a little book listing subscribers to engravings (Ivimy MSS.), John Linnell noted that he had sold to James Bohn, King William Street, Strand, in February 1838, 'One Copy of Job India paper [which sells for £]5 [for the dealer's price of £]4—'; 'one D Dante by Blake 1.10—'; 'two Job India 8—'; and '(Dante?) 1 10'.

9 April 1838   Edward Evans told Linnell in a letter of 9 April 1838 (Ivimy MSS.) that they had sold all the copies of *Job* they had and needed two more copies.

19 April 1838   On 19 April 1838 Evans wrote again (Ivimy MSS.) to say that they needed a small paper copy of *Job* instead.

20 May 1838   For the literary gossip about Blake given in Crabb Robinson's diary account of his breakfast on 20 May 1838, particularly W. S. Landor maintaining 'Blake to be the greatest of poets', see No. 8d above.

22 May 1838   According to Crabb Robinson's account in his reminiscences of the conversation at his delightful literary breakfast on 22 May 1838, 'Talleyrands recent death and the poet Blake were the subjects. Tom Moore had never heard of Blake—at least not of his poems—[1] Even he acknowl^{d} their beauty.'

Aug., Nov. 1838   In 1838 Linnell recorded in his book of 'Engravings Subscribers Accounts' (Ivimy MSS.), f.18, that he had sent the dealer John Bohn 'one Copy of Job—india in Boards 5.5—one d^{o} of Dante 2.2.' and 'two India of Job unb^{d} 10 10', and in the same book (f.19) he recorded under Henry Bohn 'Aug^{t} [1838] to exchange also 3 Copies

---

[1] As late as 1874, Trelawny had never heard of Blake (*Some Reminiscences of* [i.e., by] *William Michael Rossetti* [London, 1906], vol. II, p. 378), but in 1881 he spoke with 'great admiration' of Blake and recited 'London' (S. Colvin, *Memories & Notes of Persons & Places 1852–1912* [1921], p. 250).

of Blake's Dante for Flaxmans outline of Eschylus, Homers Illiad & Oddysie'.[1] H. G. Bohn paid 17s. 6d. 'for the binding & deb[d] to Dante in separate prints unbound'. A separate Linnell account of '1838' with James Bohn (Ivimy MSS.) lists

one D° [copy] Blake's Job India			4—
One D°	D°	Dante	1.10
. . .			
Two Job India			8—
One Dante—			1.10

In Linnell's 'Cash Book' '1837 to 1848' (Ivimy MSS.) under 1 November 1838 he recorded his receipt from the dealer 'Evans for Dante—[£]1.1'.

8 Aug. 1838 For Bernard Barton's letter to Linnell about Blake of 8 August 1838 (given in A. T. Story, *The Life of John Linnell* [1892], 1, p. 179), see No. 33h above.

7 Sept. 1838 According to his journal, on 'Friday—7 [September 1838, Linnell] exchanged with Mr Hilly [?] Bookseller King S[t][?]—C[ovent] Gardens 6 plain Copies of Job for Encyclopedia Britan . . .'.

26 Sept., 2 Oct. 1838 Among Linnell's receipts (Ivimy MSS.) is one from Dixon & Ross for a bill of 26 September 1838 for printing '25 of each of 7 Plates Dante India 2.15.0', that is, Blake's Dante engravings. In the same collection is another Dixon & Ross receipted bill dated 2 October 1838 for printing '95 Imp[rs] of 7 Plts. Dante India 1[0].10 0'. The daybook of Dixon & Ross (now trading as Thomas Ross & Son), reported to me kindly by Mr Iain Bain, gives the same information.

6 Nov. 1838. On 6 November 1838 J. J. G. Wilkinson[2] wrote: A few days ago I was introduced by my friend Mr Elwell to a Mr. Tathans [i.e., Tatham], an artist, who possesses all the drawings left by Blake. . . . [see No. 16ff above.]

?1838 About 1838, R. M. Milnes wrote to Aubrey de Vere: 'Have you ever seen any of Blake's poetry? I think of publishing some selections from him which will astonish those who are astoundable by

[1] *Compositions from the Tragedies of Aeschylus Designed by Iohn Flaxman, Engraved by Thomas Piroli, and Frank Howard* (1831); *The Iliad* [and *Odyssey*] *of Homer Engraved from the Compositions of Iohn Flaxman Sculptor* (1805).
[2] C. J. Wilkinson, *James John Garth Wilkinson* (London, 1911), pp. 29–30.

anything of this kind.'[1] Milnes was perhaps disappointed by de Vere's reply, for he never published anything of Blake's, though he did collect his works.

1838 [Richard Henry Horne,][2] 'British artists and writers on art', *British and Foreign Review*, vol. VI (1838), pp. 610–57, remarks: 'William Blake's estimate of himself as a man of genius (visions inclusive) was a just one. If he saw no faults in his works, it has been a pleasant occupation for others to discover them for him' (p. 626).

1838 The sentence about Blake (1759–1827) in Samuel Maunder, *The Biographical Treasury, a Dictionary of Universal Biography, Intended as a Companion to 'The Treasury of Universal Knowledge'* (London, 1838), p. 96, said merely that he was 'a highly gifted but very eccentric artist and writer' who had published *America, Europe, Songs of Experience,* 'and an infinity of admirable engravings'.

1 Jan. 1839 According to its inscription, Blake's copy of Swedenborg's *Divine Love and Divine Wisdom* (now in the British Museum) was bought from Tatham on 1 January 1839; see 4 July 1833.

6 Feb. 1839 In his 'Cash Book' '1837 to 1848', Linnell recorded receipt 'of Bryant for 2 plain Copies Book of Job 2 10' on 6 February 1839.

8 Feb. [?1839] Among Linnell's receipts (Ivimy MSS.) is one from the Rev. C. Aitken dated 8 February (?1839) for, among other things, '15 Blakes dante Imp folio joints at 4.9 each 3 11 3'.

5 March 1839 In a letter of 5 March 1839 from Rome to his father-in-law John Linnell, Samuel Palmer wrote: 'I never till the other day knew the full stretch of Rafaelle's power—. . . The Shepherds coming to the manger is the loveliest composition I ever saw—a group in the wise mens' offering has all the fury of Blake. . . .'[3]

8 April 1839 Hannah Palmer wrote to Mr and Mrs John Linnell (her parents) from Rome on 8 April 1839 that her return home will be 'a

---

[1] T. W. Reid, *The Life, Letters, and Friendships of Richard Monckton Milnes, First Lord Houghton* (London, Paris, Melbourne, 1890), vol. I, pp. 220–1.

[2] The author (Richard Henry Horne) is identified by H. B. de Groot in 'R. H. Horne, Mary Howitt and a mid-Victorian version of "The Ecchoing Green"', *Blake Studies*, vol. IV (1971), p. 82n.

[3] This and the next letter, from the Ivimy MSS., were generously pointed out to me by Mr Raymond Lister.

foretaste of Heaven & I think to me it will be like Mr Blakes print of the meeting of a family there' [in his designs for Blair's *Grave*].

9 July 1839   Garth Wilkinson's little edition of the *Songs* (based on Tulk's copy [J]) was evidently published in London on 9 July 1839,[1] the date of the published preface. For the preface itself, see No. 12h above.

17 July 1839   On 17 July 1839, Garth Wilkinson wrote a letter about Blake given as No. 10 above.

20 Aug. 1839   Mary Ann Linnell wrote on 20 August 1839 to her daughter Hannah (Samuel Palmer's wife) in Italy, mentioning in passing 'Mr. Blake who used to say how much he preferred a cat to a dog as a companion because she was so much more quiet in her expression of attachment'.[2]

21 Aug. 1839   In the book with the names of subscribers to his engravings (Ivimy MSS.), Linnell made a note that on 21 August 1839 he had sent to Evans '1 proof of plate of Blake Dante in Exchange to M.A.C. [?Michael Angelo copperplate] of Pisa'.

1839   Most of Cunningham ¶ 17 is quoted in John Jackson [and William A. Chatto], *A Treatise on Wood Engraving, Historical and Practical* (London, 1839), pp. 715–17, to demonstrate that Blake's technique in his Illuminated Books was very like wood-engraving, and that, because of this, the process of 'printing [his works] was necessarily slow'. A second edition of the book was printed in 1861.

1839   Lady Charlotte Bury's account of her dinner with Blake on 20 January (?1818) and of 'the perfect simplicity of his mind and his total ignorance of all worldly matters' was published in her *Diary Illustrative of the Times of George the Fourth*, ed. J. Galt (1839), vol. III, pp. 345–8; in her *Court of England under George IV* (1896), vol. II, pp. 190–1; and in her *Diary of a Lady-in-Waiting*, ed. A. F. Steuart (1908), vol. II, pp. 213–15.

---

[1] C. J. Wilkinson, *James John Garth Wilkinson* (London, 1911), p. 26. The draft preface, bound with the first state of the edition (BM) was dated 8 June 1839. Tulk had lent Wilkinson his Copy of the *Songs* (J) in 1838 (*Wilkinson*, p. 25). Garth's brother William provided the funds and found the subscribers for the edition.

[2] Quoted from the MS. (which I have not seen) in the possession of Mrs Joan Linnell Ivimy Burton by R. Lister, 'References to Blake in Samuel Palmer's Letters', in *William Blake: Essays in Honour of Sir Geoffrey Keynes*, ed. M. D. Paley and M. Phillips (1973), pp. 308–9.

1839–40   Under P. and C. Colnaghi in his subscription book (Ivimy MSS.), Linnell wrote in the autumn of 1839 '1 Blake's Dante'; and under the same account he wrote in 1840: 'Remaining in Colnaghi's hands on sale or return' '1 Blake's Dante—28—1.10.6 1 Book of Job—1.2.6'. A letter from Colnaghi to Linnell (Ivimy MSS.) of 12 November(?) 1840 indicates indebtedness for the 'Book of Job—1.2.6' sent in 1838 and 'Blake Dante—1–10.6' sent in 1839, both of which were still in Colnaghi's hands at the time of the letter.

March 1840   In an anonymous article headed 'Reminiscences of Charles L—' in a series called 'Sketches of Life and Manners, from the Autobiography of an English Opium-Eater' in *Tait's Edinburgh Magazine*, vol. VII (March 1840), p. 166, Thomas De Quincey wrote that 'Death was indeed to him [Charles Lloyd], in the words of that fine mystic, Blake the artist, "a golden gate"—the gate of liberation from the captivity of half a life', quoting from Blake's dedication for Blair's *Grave* (1808).

July 1840   A copy of Wilkinson's edition of the *Songs* (1839), inscribed 'J. Ogle, from the Editor, J. J. G. Wilkinson, July, 1840', is in the collection of Sir Geoffrey Keynes, according to his *Bibliotheca Bibliographici* (1964). My own copy is inscribed:

R T Kinnaird the gift of E Barrett Esq.

On admirable Blake.

Blest man, blest, gifted, happy man!
'With master hand, and poets fire,'
Who didst adorn the gloomy 'Grave',
And rais'd our human fame the higher,
'Sleep on, and take your rest,'
After your well-spent life.

R T K.

7 Dec. 1840   In his 'Cash Book' '1837 to 1848', Linnell noted his receipt on '7 [December 1840] of Mr Richmond for a plain set of Blake's Job—[£]2 2'.

1840   Allan Cunningham included in his revised version of Matthew Pilkington's *General Dictionary of Painters* (London, 1840), pp. *xcii–xciii*, 52–3, brief, admiring accounts of Blake summarized responsibly from his own biography. The Blake sections were not significantly altered in the new editions of 1852 and 1857.

1840 The *General Catalogue of the Printed Books and Manuscripts bequeathed by Francis Douce, Esq. to the Bodleian Library* (Oxford, 1840), p. 32, records Douce's gifts of *Thel* (I), *Designs to a Series of Ballads* (1802), and the *Descriptive Catalogue* (H).

1840 Benson J. Lossing included a brief discussion of Blake's engraving technique in his *Outline History of the Fine Arts* (New York, 1840), pp. 301–3; (New York, 1843), pp. 301–3.

?1840 John Ruskin wrote 'about 1840'[1] to George Richmond to ask about returning the portfolio of Blake drawings which he had bought for £100 from the dealer Joseph Hogarth; the works included 'The Horse' (for Hayley's *Ballads* [1805]—see 25 November 1855), 'The Owls' ('Hecate', colourprint), 'Newton' (colourprint), 'Nebuchadnezzar' (colourprint), 'Satan and Eve' (for *Paradise Lost*), 'The Goblin Huntsman' (for Young's *Night Thoughts* [1797], p. 70), and 'The Search for the Body of Harold' (*The Letters of John Ruskin* [vol. xxxvi of *The Works of John Ruskin*, ed. E. T. Cook and A. Wedderburn] [London and New York, 1909], vol. i, pp. 32–3).

?1840 A second letter from Ruskin to Richmond of the same period suggests that Hogarth will 'arrange it to my satisfaction' (*ibid.*).

?1840 Ruskin's letter of about 1840 to Flaxman's sister-in-law, Maria Denman, about her copy of Blake's *Songs* is given under No. 12j above.

May 1841 Jane Porter's account of Blake's visionary heads of William Wallace and Edward I in her *Scottish Chiefs* (May 1841) will be found under October 1819.

1841 The reference to Blake's visions in W. C. Dendy's *Philosophy of Mystery* (1841) will be found in No. 5a above.

1841 Henry G. Bohn's *Catalogue of Books* (London, 1841) offered two copies of *Job* at £1 10s. and £3 3s., *Thel* (?A) at £1 5s., *Jerusalem* (?A) at £5 5s., *Songs* (?V), with no price given, and *Milton* (D) and *Thel* (O) bound together, with no price given.

1841 Hazlitt's *Lectures on the English Poets* with its apparent echo of a passage in Blake's *Descriptive Catalogue* (see spring 1818) and his *Plain Speaker* with its passing statement that Blake was 'a profound mystic' (see 12 May 1826) were reprinted in 1841.

---

[1] Quoted from a reproduction of the MS. in Houghton Library, Harvard.

Sept. 1842 'The Lamb' from *Innocence* was quoted in the *New Jerusalem Magazine*, vol. XVI (September 1842), p. 40.

1 October 1842 In his Reminiscences of 1 October 1842, Crabb Robinson said he went to thank Miss Denman for her presents of 'Blake's Catalogue & Poems'.

13 Dec. 1842 Linnell obtained *Songs* (X) from Mr White on 13 December 1842, according to his note in it. In his 'Cash Book' '1837 to 1848' Linnell recorded this as December '13 to Mr White for a Copy of Blakes Songs Cold 10 — —'.

[?1842] Emily Dickinson's teacher, Thomas Wentworth Higginson, wrote in his copy of the *Songs* (1839): 'I read these about 1842' (E. J. Rose, 'The 1839-Wilkinson edition of Blake's Songs in transcendental America', *Blake Newsletter*, vol. IV [1971], p. 80).

21 Jan. 1843 Henry Cole's account of the 'derision' Blake's Virgil woodcuts roused among professional wood-engravers, which he gave in his review of Mulready's illustrations to *The Vicar of Wakefield* in the *Athenaeum*, 21 January 1843, p. 165, may be found at No. 31a above.

6, 14 Feb. 1843 Linnell recorded in his 'Cash Book' '1837 to 1848' that he received on 6 February 1843 'of Mr Dilke for a Copy of Dantè 1.12 & Job 1.10 [£]3 2', and on the 14th 'of Mr Dilke by Mr Cole for a Copy of Job—[£]1 10' (see also 8 November 1844).

Sept. 1843 Mrs Elizabeth J. Eames's inferior poem 'Love's Last Work', in the *Southern Literary Messenger*, vol. IX (September 1843), pp. 559–60, is probably patterned after Mrs Hemans's very similar poem (see February 1832); it does not mention Blake, but it is clearly related to Cunningham's account of his death.

18 Nov. 1843 For George Darley's obituary of William Seguier in the *Athenaeum*, 18 November 1843, with its reference to his having been '"taught" by the celebrated William Blake', see 1809–10.

Dec. 1843 In his book of subscribers to engravings (Ivimy MSS.), Linnell listed 'Book of Job India proof 5.5.0' under 'Books in Exchange' with Longman & Co. in December 1843.

1843 In a note on James Parker in his *Memoirs and Recollections of the Late Abraham Raimbach, Esq. Engraver*, ed. M. T. S. Raimbach (1843), Raimbach referred to 'the insane genius Blake'.

1843 The *Songs* were printed about 1843 (the date of the watermark in the paper), and in one copy, now in the British Museum, is the following note:

This copy of Blake's *Songs of Innocence and Experience* was printed by M! Charles Augustus Tulk, a Friend of Blake's, and a dear friend of my Wifes and mine;—and spaced as in the Original, in order that any who chose, might copy in the paintings with which the original is adorned. Twelve copies only were printed.

J. J. Garth Wilkinson April 9, 1886

1843 For the anecdote of Blake and Constable in C. R. Leslie's *Life of John Constable* (1843, 1845), see 12 September 1818.

?1843 Blake's 'Cradle Song' from *Innocence* was printed in *The Little Keepsake for 1844*, [ed. Mrs S. (Pamela Chandler) Colman] (Boston [?1843]), p. 94.

1843 Val. P[éricaud]'s article on 'Blake (Guillaume)' in [J.F.] Michaud's *Biographie Universelle* (Paris, 1843), vol. IV, was apparently taken from the *Gentleman's Magazine* obituary of 1 November 1827.

1843 'On Another's Sorrow', 'Night', and 'The Little Black Boy' from *Innocence* were printed in *Poetry for Home and School* [ed. Mrs Anna Cabot Lowell] (Boston, 1843), pp. 68–9, 74–5, 85–6; the book was republished as *Gleanings from the Poets, for Home and School* (Boston, 1855), pp. 49, 52, 61; (Boston, 1862), pp. 49–50, 52–3, 61–2.

18 Jan. 1844 According to his book of subscribers to engravings (Ivimy MSS.), Linnell took a book 'in exchange for a french paper Copy of Job' on 18 January 1844.

27 Sept. 1844 On 27 September 1844 Linnell wrote to C. W. Dilke: 'I have sent you a couple of proofs [of the *Job* engravings] before the Borders as a curiosity, because the borders were an afterthought, and designed as well as engraved upon the copper without a previous drawing.'[1] And Sir Charles Dilke replied in an undated letter:

Dear Sir   I return the Duplicates with thanks & return £3 2 for the copies retained.[2]

---

[1] See *Illustrations of the Book of Job*, ed. P. Hofer (1937), p. 8. Sir Geoffrey Keynes, who owns the letter itself, supplies the date.

[2] 'Mr. Dilke was a great admirer of the work of Fuseli, Haydon's friend, and of Blake, who was also the friend of both. He formed one of the best collections of Blake's drawings, and was one of the earliest admirers of his poems' (*The Papers of a Critic Selected from the Writings of the Late Charles Wentworth Dilke*, with a Biographical Sketch by his Grandson

I shall be most happy to have another morning with Blake. Mr Cole writes to me that he has named next Tuesday morning & to breakfast with you. . . .[1]

In his 'Cash Book' '1837 to 1848' Linnell entered his receipt on 8 November 1844 'of C. W Dilke for two copies of Job—3 3' (see also 6, 14 February 1843).

1844 David Scott's manuscript note of 1844 written in his copy of Blair's *Grave* in high admiration of its designs was printed in A. Gilchrist, *Life of William Blake*, '*Pictor Ignotus*' (London and Cambridge, 1863), vol. 1, p. 377—see No. 129l above. It was sent by W. B. Scott to W. M. Rossetti, who sent it to D. G. Rossetti, who wrote on 19 December 1862 that he had inserted it in Gilchrist's book.

Feb. 1845 In February 1845, F. T. Palgrave wrote to his mother from Balliol College, Oxford, where he was an undergraduate a letter which is given under No. 33i above.[2]

July, Aug. 1845 In his ledger for 1819–54 (Ivimy MSS.), f. 95^v, Linnell recorded payment from Messrs Payne & Foss, Booksellers of Pall Mall,[3] for

| July [1845] one Blakes Job | 5 5 |
| one Dante | 2 2 |

and in his 'Cash Book' '1837 to 1848' he noted that he had received on 7 August 1845 'of Mr Richmond for book of Job—4.4.'

14 Sept. 1845 In the autumn of the same year, on 14 September, Samuel Palmer wrote to his three-and-a-half-year-old son Thomas More Palmer encouraging him with his reading: 'If I had not taught you your letters every day—you could not now have read a chapter in the Bible nor the Pilgrim's Progress nor Sandford and Merton nor the

---

[1] Quoted from a transcript in an exercise book in the Ivimy MSS. headed 'J Linnell Correspondence General', p. 1.

[2] G. F. Palgrave, *Francis Turner Palgrave* (1899), p. 27.

[3] Under January 1846 (f. 96^r) for the same firm Linnell wrote 'one Job one Dante on Sale' without giving the price and '1848 P. & F returned M[ichael] A[ngelo] prints by Linnell] Job & Dante'.

Sir Charles Wentworth Dilke [1875], vol 1, p. 51). Dilke also owned at least (1) *Innocence* (K), (2) *Urizen* (E), (3) 'Illustration to the 85th Psalm', (4) 'The Crucifixion', (5) 'Queen Katherine's Dream', (6) 'The Stoning of Achan', and (7) 'Satan Tormenting Job', nos 3–4 bought at the Butts sale at Sotheby's of 26–7 March 1852, lots 150–1, 166 (nos 4–7 were sold at Christie's on 11 April 1911, lots 125–8).

Songs of Innocence nor any of your pretty story books.'[1] Since Palmer is not known to have owned an illuminated copy of *Songs of Innocence* or *Songs of Innocence and of Experience*, the copy from which his son was learning to read was presumably either the conventionally printed edition of 1839 or a manuscript transcript.

?1845 A passing reference to 'un fou appelé Blake, surnommé *le Voyant*' in Bedlam, taken from the *Revue Britannique* of July 1833, was printed in A. Brierre de Boismont, *Des Hallucinations* (Paris, ?1845, 1852), pp. 94–6; *Hallucinations* (Philadelphia, 1853), pp. 85–7; *A History of Dreams* (1855), pp. 85–7; *On Hallucinations* (London, 1859), pp. 83–5; *Des Hallucinations* (Paris, London, New York, and Madrid, 1862), pp. 89–91.

1845 'The Little Boy Lost' and 'The Little Boy Found' from *Innocence* were printed in *Child's Gem*, ed. Mrs S. Colman (Boston, 1845), p. 69.

1845 For the account of Blake and the A. S. Mathew salon in J. T. Smith's *Book for a Rainy Day* (1845, 1845, 1861), see 1784.

15 June 1846 At the Evans sale of the property of William Upcott on 15 June 1846, Evans bought *Experience* (?H) for £1 14*s*. and *America* (H) and *Europe* (D) with 'some original drawings' (the Large [A] and Small [A] Books of Designs) for £7 2*s*. 6*d*., all of which went to the British Museum Print Room.

9 July 1846 Robert Browning wrote to Elizabeth Barrett Barrett on 9 July 1846 about the painter B. R. Haydon, who had committed suicide on 22 June:

There is the serene spot attained, the solid siren's isle amid the sea; and while *there*, he was safe and well . . . but he would put out to sea again, after a breathing time I suppose: though even a smaller strip of land was enough to maintain Blake, for one instance, in power and glory thro' the poor, fleeting 'sixty years'— . . .[2]

Sept. 1846 William H. C. Hosmer's dull first-person poem called

[1] Quoted, from a transcript belonging to Mr A. H. Palmer II, by R. Lister, 'References to Blake in Samuel Palmer's Letters' in *William Blake: Essays in Honour of Sir Geoffrey Keynes*, ed. M. D. Paley and M. Phillips (1973).

[2] *The Letters of Robert Browning and Elizabeth Barrett Barrett 1845–1846*, ed. E. Kintner (1969), vol. II, p. 861. The influence of Blake on Browning has been seen in his 'Karshish' and 'Transcendentalism' by R. D. Havens, 'Blake and Browning', *Modern Language Notes*, vol. XLI (1926), pp. 464–6, T. L. Hood, 'An Allusion to Blake', *Nation*, vol. XCIII (1911), p. 240, and T. L. Hood, 'Browning and Blake', *Trinity Review*, n.s., vol. II (1948), pp. 42–50.

'Blake's Visitants' in *Graham's Magazine*, vol. XXIX (September 1846), p. 151, was based on Cunningham.

31 Oct. 1846 'On Another's Sorrow' from *Innocence* was printed in the *Harbinger*, vol. III (31 October 1846), p. 333.

1846 In *The Panidea* (Boston, 1846), p. 63,[1] 'Theoptes' (i.e. Job Durfee) says that Cunningham's biography indicates Blake was 'an extraordinary instance' of the power of the mind to see retinal images.

1846 Copy O of *Descriptive Catalogue* is inscribed 'John Linnell / 38 Porchester Terrace / Bayswater /—/ 1846', presumably indicating when he acquired it.

30 April 1847 Dante Gabriel Rossetti, who as a very young man was 'already a hearty admirer of William Blake's *Songs of Innocence and Experience*',[2] wrote in Blake's manuscript *Notebook* (now in the British Museum):

I purchased this original M.S. of [Samuel Palmer's brother William] Palmer, an attendant in the Antique Gallery at the British Museum,[3] on the 30ᵗʰ April, 1847. Palmer knew Blake personally, and it was from the artist's wife that he had the present M.S. which he sold me for 10ˢ [and for which Dante's brother William supplied the cash.] Among the sketches, there are one or two profiles of Blake himself . . . [2 1/2 lines erased and illegible.]

Dante's brother explained that 'His ownership of this truly precious volume . . . conduced to the Praeraphaelite movement . . . [and its contents] were balsam to Rosetti's soul, and grist to his mill. The volume was moreover the origin of all his after-concern in Blake literature. . . .'

---

[1] Reprinted in *The Complete Works of the Hon. Job Durfee, LL.D.*, ed. [Thomas Durfee] (Providence and Boston, 1849), p. 391.

[2] *Dante Gabriel Rossetti: His Family-Letters*, ed. W. M. Rossetti (London, 1895), vol. I, p. 109, which also provides some of the interpolated information below. W. M. Rossetti gives essentially the same account in *Anne Gilchrist: her Life and Writings*, ed. H. H. Gilchrist (London, 1887), p. viii (except that here the price for the *Notebook* is 10s. 6d.) and in *Some Reminiscences of* [i.e. by] *William Michael Rossetti* (London, 1906), vol. I, pp. 302–3.

[3] B. P. C. Bridgewater, Secretary of the British Museum, informed me that William Palmer of 69, Harrison Street, Gray's Inn Road, London, WC, was employed as an attendant in the Department of Antiquities in the British Museum from 3 July 1837 to 13 January 1862. In a letter dated only Monday, Mary Ann Linnell wrote to her husband: 'Mʳ William Palmer has got a situation at the British Museum which is for life. He will receive 22ˢ/- per week at first and in time may be advanced which I think is very well as he will scarcely have anything to do but lounge about in the Sculpture room and read the newspapers &c' (Ivimy MSS.).

Oct. 1847   The 'Introduction' to *Innocence* was quoted from Cunningham in an anonymous review of 'Works of Hans Christian Andersen', *Blackwood's Edinburgh Magazine*, vol. LXII (October 1847), p. 389, to demonstrate that Blake and Andersen were 'of somewhat kindred nature'.

15 Nov. 1847   According to his Reminiscences, Crabb Robinson called on the Longs on 15 November 1847 and read to them some of Blake's *Songs of Innocence*. 'Long could not I expect enjoy them[.] He is altogether without imagination . . . .'

20 Nov. 1847   Anon., 'Death's Door. By William Blake', *Howitt's Journal*, vol. II (20 November 1847), pp. 321-2, reproduces Blake's *Grave* design engraved by H. Harrison, and uses Cunningham's anecdotes (without acknowledgment) to demonstrate that Blake was 'one of the most spiritual-minded and original men that ever lived'.

1847, 1858   Blair's *The Grave, a Poem With Illustrations, from Designs by William Blake* (New York: A. L. Dick, 1847; reissued by Sanford & Delisser in New York, 1858) included twelve reduced-size engravings by A. L. Dick, omitting 'The Meeting of a Family in Heaven' (perhaps because of the enthusiasm of the embraces depicted) and decorously draping the genitals of the previously naked gentlemen on pls. 1 and 8. Both editions include a new biography of 'William Blake' (pp. v–vi) compiled chiefly from Cunningham.

1847   In Henry G. Bohn's *Catalogue of Books* (London, 1847), vol. I, p. 259, were offered Blake's *Job* at £2 12s. 6d., Dante at £1 16s., *America* (?C) at £3 3s., and *Milton* (D) and *Thel* (O) bound together (£10 10s.) and 'finished in colours, in the style of Drawings, expressly for his principal patron, Mr. [James] Vine of the Isle of Wight'. Vine was obviously not Blake's principal patron.

1847   Southey's references to Blake in *The Doctor* (1847) will be found under No. 14c above.

1847   [John Greenleaf Whittier,] *The Supernaturalism of New England* (London, 1847), pp. 25-6, obviously derived his reference to 'the mad painter, Blake, [who] saw the funeral of the last of the little people' directly or indirectly from Cunningham, though no source known to me says the funeral Blake saw was for 'the last' of the fairies.

1847   'The Tiger' from *Experience* and 'The Little Black Boy' from *Innocence* were printed in *The Estray* [ed. Henry Wadsworth Longfellow] (Boston, 1847), pp. 36-7, 103-4.

5 Feb. 1848   Crabb Robinson took the Lambs to Blake's exhibition on 11 June 1810 and bought four copies of the *Descriptive Catalogue*, one of which he gave to Lamb, who was delighted with it, especially its criticism of Chaucer. Lamb had his copy bound with 'Lord Rochester's Poems, Lady Winchelsea's poems, C. Lamb's Confessions of a Drunkard, with Corrections, &c., Southey's Wat Tyler, &c. 12 Tracts, with MS. List of Contents'. After Lamb's death in 1834, his books were kept by his sister; on her death in 1847, they went, by Lamb's directions, to his friend Edward Moxon, who destroyed all of them but about sixty, which he sold to an American dealer.[1] The tracts including the *Descriptive Catalogue* were listed in an anonymous article (by Evert A. Duyckinck, the editor of the journal?) in 'Charles Lamb's library in New York', *Literary World*, vol. III ([New York] 5 February 1848), pp. 10–11, and an offprint served as the *Catalogue of Charles Lamb's Library*, for sale by Bartlett & Welford, Booksellers and Importers, 7 Astor House, New York, on 5 February 1848, lot 54, priced at $4.50.

April 1848   According to George W. Curtis, 'Jenny Lind', *Union Magazine*, vol. II (April 1848), pp. 155–9, Jenny Lind and Correggio 'recalled in their best meaning' Blake's 'Introduction' to *Innocence*, which he quotes.

12 April 1848   Crabb Robinson reported in his Reminiscences that at a party at the Fields' on 16 April 1848, Emerson, Wilkinson, Chapman, Field, and Robinson 'talked only abo^t Blake'.[2]
According to Wilkinson's account of the dinner, Robinson

knew Blake well. After tea, he singled me out by miracle, and entertained me beyond measure about the great artist. It was he who gave Blake 25 guineas for the 'Songs of Innocence.' He warmly invited me to call upon him, when he will show me several of Blake's originals, both poems and pictures.[3]

[1] *A Descriptive Catalogue of the Library of Charles Lamb* (New York: The Dibdin Club, 1897), p. 1, a reprint of the February 1848 catalogue, which is also reprinted in Anon., 'Books of Charles Lamb's library in America', *Historical Magazine and Notes and Queries*, vol. IX ([New York,] 1865), pp. 45–9; in [W. C. Hazlitt,] 'Charles Lamb's library in New York', *Publisher's Weekly*, vol. LI (15 May 1897), pp. 817–20, and in *Mary and Charles Lamb*, ed. W. C. Hazlitt (London, 1874), pp. 297–307.

[2] Some of these Blake references in Crabb Robinson's 1848 diary are alluded to in Mark L. Reed, 'Blake, Wordsworth, Lamb, etc.: further information from Crabb Robinson', and in M. Phillips, 'Blake's corrections in *Poetical Sketches*', *Blake Newsletter*, vol. III (1970), p. 81, vol. IV (1970), p. 47.

[3] C. J. Wilkinson, *James John Garth Wilkinson* (1911), p. 52. The date of the dinner is given as April *17th*. According to Robinson's Diary of 18 February 1826, he paid £5 5s. (not £26 5s.) for *Songs of Innocence and of Experience* (Z) (not *Songs of Innocence* only).

?April 1848 In his 'Journal Gulistan [?April] 1848', Ralph Waldo Emerson wrote: 'I cannot remember J.[ones] Very without being reminded of Wordsworth's remark on William Blake, 'There is something in the madness of this man that interests me more than the sanity of Lord Byron and Walter Scott'.[1]

25 April 1848 Robinson mentioned in his Reminiscences for 25 April 1848 that Wilkinson 'is a great lover & admirer of Blake'.

27 April 1848 According to his Reminiscences for 27 April 1848, Crabb Robinson gave the gift copy of Wilkinson's edition of the *Songs* to Hare and ordered other copies for himself at Moxon's.

9 May 1848 In his Reminiscences, Robinson said that on 9 May 1848 he read in bed Wilkinson's 'very curious' preface to Blake's poems.

13 May 1848 On 13 May 1848 Robinson reported in his Reminiscences that he found Wilkinson's 'love of Blake . . . delightful'.

17 May 1848 According to his Diary for 17 May 1848, Crabb Robinson 'left at Fields a copy of Blake's poems', presumably the 1839 *Songs*.

20 May 1848 On 20 May 1848 Crabb Robinson wrote to his brother Thomas that 'W[ilkinson] & I are both great lovers of *Blakes* poems which he has also republished—'.[2]

24 May 1848 In his Diary for 24 May 1848 Robinson recorded that he 'wrote . . . To Wilkinson desiring[?] him to keep Blakes Poet[1] Sketches [?*A*], as I find I have a second copy [?*O*] bound in a Vol. of tracts'.

To this J. J. G. Wilkinson replied on the same day:
I cannot tell you how much I am obliged by your kind gift of Blake's Poetical Sketches, of which I shall thankfully constitute myself a Trustee until Such time as the public is of age to enter upon them. Yesterday I was with a publisher who, I think, will in all probability bring out an Edition of Blake's Poems.

---

[1] Quoted from p. 136 of the MS. (no. 108) in Houghton Library, Harvard, by S. R. Hoover, 'Fifty additions to Blake bibliography', *Blake Newsletter*, vol. v (1972), p. 168. The information probably came from Crabb Robinson, for Wordsworth had said something similar to Robinson on 24 May 1812, and Emerson had been seeing Robinson in April 1848.

[2] This and other Robinson correspondence quoted here are in Dr William's Library, London.

26 May 1848 In his letter of 26 May 1848 to his brother Thomas, Robinson mentioned that Wilkinson is 'editor of Blake'.

24 June 1848 'To Spring', 'To Summer', 'To Autumn', and 'To Winter' from Blake's *Poetical Sketches* were published in the *Harbinger*, vol. VII (24 June 1848), p. 57.

8 July 1848 'To the Evening Star', 'To Morning', 'How Sweet I Roam'd', 'My Silks and Fine Array', and 'Love and Harmony Combine' from *Poetical Sketches* were printed as 'Selections from Blake's poems' in the *Harbinger*, vol. VII (8 July 1848), p. 73.

27 July 1848 On 27 July 1848 Quillinan wrote to Crabb Robinson that Moxon had just sent Wordsworth a new edition of Blake's poems, and that he, Quillinan, found some 'sound very like nonsense-verses', though 'others have a real charm in their wildness & oddness'.[1] His information about Blake derived chiefly from Cunningham.

10 August 1848 To this Robinson replied on 10 August 1848:
You speak more slightingly than I should [have] expected of *Blake*.[2] Recollect they are not to be considered as works of art, but as fragments of a shattered intellect. Lamb used to call him a 'mad Wordsworth'[.][3] Enquire of Mrs. W: whether she has not a copy of his *Catalogue*.[4] If she has not, enquire of me hereafter. Many years ago Mr. W: read some poems which I had copied and made a remark on them which I would not repeat to every one. 'There is no doubt that this man is mad, but there is something in this madness which I enjoy more than the Sense of W[alter]: Sc[ott]: or Lord B[yron]:—[']⁵ I had lent him when he died the 8vo Edit in 2 Vols: of W.W's poems. They were sent me by his widow with the pencil marginalia which I inked over. He admired W: W: 'tho an atheist' And when I protested against this sentence it was thus supported. 'Who ever worships nature denies God, for nature is the Devils work.'⁶ I succumbed, for he always

---

[1] *The Correspondence of Henry Crabb Robinson with the Wordsworth Circle*, ed. E. J. Morley (Oxford, 1927), vol. II, pp. 675–6.

[2] Quillinan underlined 'Slightingly' and wrote in the margin: 'as usual a mistake of friend Crabbe's'.

[3] This does not appear in Robinson's Diary or Reminiscences.

[4] The Wordsworth's are not known to have had a copy of Blake's *Descriptive Catalogue* (1809).

[5] Robinson reports this idea in different words in his Diary for 24 May 1812 and gives virtually these words in his Reminiscences (*Blake Records* [1969], p. 536).

[6] Blake's comments on Wordsworth's poems (1815) are given in similar terms in Robinson's Reminiscences (*Blake Records* [1969], p. 545).

beat me in argument. He almost went into a fit of rapture at the platonic ode.[1]

21 Oct. 1848 Charles Lamb's copy of Blake's *Descriptive Catalogue*, offered for sale in February 1848, was sold on 21 October 1848 from the *Catalogue of a Private Library* (James T. Annan's) auctioned by Cooley, Keese & Hill, 191 Broadway, New York, lot 376, for $4.25 to Campbell.[2]

12 Nov. 1848 An untitled poem by Christina Rossetti, beginning 'Sleep, sleep, happy one' and dated 12 November 1848, has an epigraph

> Sleep, sleep, happy child;
> All creation slept and smiled.
> Blake ['A Cradle Song', *Innocence*, ll. 17–18][3]

1848 In his *Life, Letters, and Literary Remains of John Keats* (London, 1848; New York, 1848), p. 190, Richard Monckton Milnes said that the omitted stanzas of Keats's 'Melancholy', with its 'bark of dead men's bones', was 'as grim a picture as Blake or Fuseli could have dreamed or painted'.

1848 Mrs [Anna Brownell] Jameson, *Sacred and Legendary Art* (London, 1848), vol. I, pp. 50–1, found that Blake, who was 'somewhat mad', had yet provided 'The most original, and, in truth, the only new and original version of the Scripture idea of angels' in his *Job* designs. (For her introduction to *Job*, see July 1834.)

15 Feb. 1849 Edward Evans wrote to Linnell on 15 February 1849 (Ivimy MSS.) to say that 'We have a good supply of Blake's works at present'.

5 March 1849 On 5 March 1849 William Bell Scott wrote his name and the date on the title page of the copy of Blair's *Grave* (1808) which had been his father's; perhaps at the same time he wrote a sonnet on a flyleaf entitled 'On seeing again after many years William Blake's

[1] Robinson records this rapture in his Journal for 24 December 1825 and a letter of 19 February 1826.

The letter to Quillinan above is quoted from the MS. in Dove Cottage by Mark L. Reed, 'Blake, Wordsworth, Lamb, etc.: further information from Henry Crabb Robinson', *Blake Newsletter*, vol. III (1970), p. 78.

[2] The auction catalogue was also printed in *A Descriptive Catalogue of the Library of Charles Lamb* (1897), pp. 15–16. Lamb's copy of Blake's *Descriptive Catalogue* has not been traced since.

[3] Bodleian Library (Don. e. 1/5), kindly pointed out to me by my colleague Professor Hans de Groot.

Designs for "The Grave"', and perhaps David Scott's MS. note on the designs, written on the verso of the dedication leaf and dated 1849, was written at the same time.[1]

16-18 Aug. 1849 On 16 August 1849 William Allingham talked with Patmore at the British Museum about Blake; on the 17th he talked with Slater, the publisher, 'about a new edition of Blake's poems: civil, and seems inclined to publish'; and on the 18th he and Patmore tried 'to look up Blake [at the British Museum], but without success; they seem to have nothing of his'.[2] Consequently the publishing project came to nothing.

25 Aug. 1849 [Henr]Y [Jame]S reprinted and discussed 'The Little Vagabond' from *Experience* in 'William Blake's Poems', *Spirit of the Age*, vol. I (25 August 1849), pp. 113–14.

1849 William Allingham, 'Some chat about William Blake', *Hogg's Weekly Instructor*, n.s., vol. II (1849), pp. 17–20, surveys Blake's life and work sympathetically, finds the *Poetical Sketches* 'very, very extra-ordinary', and quotes 'To the Muses' and the Prologue to Edward III from *Poetical Sketches* and the 'Introduction' to *Innocence*, all from Cunningham and all without acknowledgment.

1849 The account of Blake in Michael Bryan's *Biographical Dictionary of Painters and Engravers*, rev. George Stanley (London, 1849), is largely derived from Cunningham.

1849 William A. Chatto, *Gems of Wood Engraving* (London, 1849), p. 28, included a paragraph about Blake's etching technique silently taken from Cunningham.

1849 Ruskin wrote a paragraph comparing the 'two magnificent and mighty' geniuses of the nineteenth century, Turner and Blake, but omitted it from the printed version of his *Seven Lamps of Architecture* (1849).[3] See No. 16gg above.

1849 James R. Hobbes, *The Picture Collector's Manual* (London, 1849), vol. I, p. 41, remarked on Blake's 'singular taste and flight of imagina-tion, . . . [which] produced some strange and wonderful pictures'.

---

[1] Sotheby's sale catalogue of 3 December 1962, lot 90; I have been unable to trace the book itself. Perhaps David Scott's note is that printed in W. B. Scott's *Memoir* (1850) of him. See also 1844, 1850.

[2] *William Allingham: A Diary*, ed. H. Allingham and D. Radford (London, 1907), p. 53.

[3] *The Seven Lamps of Architecture* (London and New York, 1903), p. 256 (vol. VIII of *The Works of John Ruskin*, ed. E. T. Cook and A. Wedderburn).

27 May [1850]   On 27 May [1850], John Ruskin wrote to Mrs Hugh Blackburn about the German love of horror and surprise: 'We have had one grand man of the same school—William Blake—whose "Book of Job" fail not to possess yourself of—if it comes in your way; but there is a deep morality in his horror—as in Dante's . . . .'[1]

6 Oct. 1850   On 6 October 1850, Crabb Robinson went, as he recorded in his Reminiscences, to Wilkinson's house to see 'three [drawings *del*] works by Blake which he offers me for £5 but I cannot bring myself to give so large a Sum'.[2]

1850   In his *Memoirs of David Scott, R.S.A.* (Edinburgh, 1850), p. 238, William B. Scott printed a random note of his brother's which read: 'Blake touched the infinite in expression or signification . . . but [was] very defective in execution.' (Perhaps this is the note in Blair's *Grave* [1808]; see 5 March 1849.) He also quoted Blake's dedication 'To the Queen' for his *Grave* designs.

1850   Hugh James Rose, *A New General Biographical Dictionary* (London, 1850), vol. IV, p. 284, summarized the *Annual Biography* obituary of Blake (see 11 March 1828) by saying that because he was 'eccentric . . . he lived and died in deep poverty'.

1850   The brief anonymous account of Blake 'The Visionary Painter', *The Brilliant, 1851*, ed. T. S. Arthur (New York, 1850), pp. 120–6, is taken almost entirely from Cunningham.

17 Jan. 1851   On 17 January 1851 D. G. Rossetti wrote to William Allingham:
I was looking the other day over my Blake MS., and it struck me more forcibly than ever as affording good materials for an article, which I resolved I would do as soon as leisure permitted. May I therefore beg that, should you in fact fulfil your intention [of writing a paper on Blake], you will not make use of any of those extracts which you took from my book at the time I lent it to you?[3]

[1] Ellen C. Clayton, *English Female Artists* (London, 1876), vol. II, p. 406 and *The Letters of John Ruskin* (vol. XXXVI of *The Works of John Ruskin*, ed. E. T. Cook and A. Wedderburn) (London and New York, 1909), vol. I, p. 110; the latter supplies the conjectural year.

[2] Keynes, echoed by Hoover (1973), p. 335, supposes that the 'three works' were *Thel*, *Songs*, and *America*, but the deleted 'drawings' and the price indicate that they were much less extensive works.

[3] Rossetti did not write the article.

Allingham's transcript is presumably the one now in the Alexander
Turnbull Library (Wellington, New Zealand) headed:
Extracts from a Manuscript Book of William Blake's. (Purchased by
Mr D. G. Rossetti from Palmer an attendant in the British Museum,
who knew Blake personally, & was given the M.S. by Mrs Blake. It is
a rough note-book, containing drafts of many of his published poems
and numerous sketches with pen & pencil, along with a crowd of
strange jottings & memoranda.
  Blake seems to have possessed almost all the high qualities of the
human mind—unstrung, as it were.)

W.A.[1]

18 Jan. 1851   Crabb Robinson met Ruskin at 'a very genteel dinner'
on 18 January 1851, according to his *Reminiscences*, and 'interested
him abo[t] Blake'.

Aug. 1851   A copy of Blake's *Songs* (1839) is inscribed by Ellen (Epps)
in 1845 to her brother William Bell Scott, and with it is a section
entitled:
Sketches traced by W.B.S. from a MS. notebook by Blake in the
possession of D. G. R[ossetti]. August 1851 [and] Poems, Epigrams, etc.
by William Blake, from a MS. book in his own writing in the possession of D. G. Rossetti. Copied out by W. M. Rossetti, Newcastle
August 1851[2]
with notes indicating he thought the poems 'fine but odd', or,
occasionally, 'decidedly to be given', apparently another step towards
an article on Blake.

1851   'The Human Form' (i.e. 'The Divine Image') was given in
chapter v on 'The Human Form' in J. J. G. Wilkinson's *The Human
Body and its Connection with Man* (London, 1851), pp. 319–20.

1851   Kazlitt Arvine, *Cyclopaedia of Anecdotes of Literature and the Fine
Arts* (Boston, 1851), pp. 240, 487, gives two brief accounts of Blake
based on Cunningham.

1851   The account of the boating expedition, in which Blake, Stothard,

---

[1] The Turnbull also has Allingham's transcripts of (1) the *Songs* (1839), including the
dedication to Blair's *Grave*; (2) 'Extracts ["Edward III"] from Volume [*Poetical Sketches*]
(published about [1783])'; (3) *Poetical Sketches* transcribed May 1854 (q.v.), and (4) 'Spring',
'Laughing Song', and 'The Lamb' 'From Blake's "Songs of Innocence" ', in a different
hand.
[2] Sotheby's sale catalogue of 3 December 1962, lot 91; I have been unable to trace the
book.

and Ogleby were arrested as French spies, from Mrs A. E. Bray's biography (1851) of her father-in-law, Thomas Stothard, will be found under September 1780.

20 Jan. 1852   At a miscellaneous book sale at Sotheby's on 20 January 1852, lot 45, *Songs* (?T), was bought for £4 14s. by Evans, and lot 186, *Urizen* (G), for £8 15s. by Milnes.

Feb. 1852   An anonymous review of Mrs Bray's 'The Life and Works of Thomas Stothard, R.A.', *Gentleman's Magazine*, n.s., vol. XXXVII (February 1852), pp. 149–50, quotes Cromek's letter to Blake of May 1807, and remarks on the omission from Mrs Bray's biography of any reference to Blake's picture of 'The Canterbury Pilgrims', which, however, is called 'a sorry performance'.

26 March 1852   At the Sotheby sale of 'an Amateur' (Thomas Butts) on 26 March 1852, ten of Blake's works in Illuminated Printing fetched an average of £5 6s. 8d. apiece, while twenty-five of his watercolour drawings brought £1 18s. 3d. each. In the copy of *Songs* (E) sold then was a manuscript poem 'written [according to the catalogue] in a playful style . . . in the autograph of the artist'. The poem itself, called 'A Song of Innonsense' and *not* in Blake's hand, is a mere *jeu d'esprit;* see 'A piper passes: the earliest parody of Blake's "Songs of Innocence"', *Notes & Queries*, vol. CCIX (1964), pp. 418–19.

12 June 1852   An inaccurate, conventional account of Blake from Cunningham in Anon., 'Death and immortality', *Illustrated Magazine of Art*, vol. I (12 June 1852), pp. 369–71, including W. J. Linton's woodcut of Blake's 'Death's Door' plate and 'To the Queen', was reprinted in *The Ladies' Drawing Book* (New York, 1852), pp. 15–16.

14 July 1852   On 14 July [1852], R. M. Milnes wrote to Crabb Robinson to say he had been
lately finding[?] many[?] works of that great genius whom you introduced to me—Blake.—Would you lend me your copy of his 'catalogue'[?]—& you would add to the favour if you would call on me any morning & see which I have got[.]—

19 July 1852   According to his Reminiscences, Robinson replied to Milnes on 19 July 1852 urging him to prepare 'an edition of Blakes Poems' and mentioning that he (HCR) had brought together his recollections of Blake's conversations.

27 Oct. 1852 In an exercise book in the Ivimy MSS. headed 'Job Revise I', A. H. Palmer transcribed Linnell's letter to Edward Evans of 27 October 1852 in which he said: 'There has not been any more printed of the book of Job since the first when the plates were just finished by Mr Blake'.

1852 Ch[arles] Romney's account of 'Blake (William)' in *Dictionnaire de la Conversation et de la Lecture* (Paris, 1852), vol. III, pp. 265–6, is long but conventionally inaccurate.

[?1852] Blake's design of 'The Body of Christ Borne to the Tomb' is inscribed '*W. Blake.* Bought of Mr. Butts of Fitzroy Square—about 1852. F. T. Palgrave.'[1]

Jan. 1853 Blake's engravings for Young's *Night Thoughts* were admired in passing in Anon., 'Poetry and painters', *Illustrated Magazine of Art*, vol. I (January 1853), p. 48.

Feb. 1853 A casual reference to the charity children, in 'St. Paul's Cathedral, London', *Illustrated Magazine of Art*, vol. I (February 1853), pp. 109–11, is the occasion for quoting 'Holy Thursday' from *Innocence*.

29 June 1853 The Foster & Son catalogue of works from the collection of Thomas Butts, sold 29 June 1853, quite rightly called the 110 drawings and paintings and the two books offered for sale a 'perhaps, matchless Assemblage of the Works of this highly gifted Artist'.

28 Nov. 1853 On 28 November 1853, Mrs L. M[?] Maculloch wrote to Crabb Robinson saying she was anxious to return 'that precious book of Blake's to its fortunate possessor'.

1853 The brief and inaccurate references to Blake given by Shearjashub Spooner in his *Biographical Dictionary of Engravers, Sculptors and Architects* (New York, 1853), p. 106, and in his *Anecdotes of Painters, Engravers, Sculptors and Architects, and Curiosities of Art* (New York, 1853), vol. I, pp. 3–4, vol. II, p. 79, are taken from Cunningham. (The *Anecdotes* was reprinted in 1854.)

March 1854 In his diary for March 1854, G. P. Boyce said William Allingham showed him the *Job* 'plates of the "Sublime Madman",

---

1 M. Butlin, *William Blake: A Complete Catalogue of the Works in the Tate Gallery* (1971), p. 44.

Blake' (R. Davies, 'William Blake', *The Old Water-Colour Society's Club Twenty-Second Annual Volume* [1944], p. 11).

March 1854 An anonymous account of the 'Death of Blake, the Painter', [T.S.] *Arthur's Home Magazine*, vol. III (March 1854), p. 220, is silently adapted from Cunningham as 'one of the most touching scenes in the history of art'.

8 March 1854 The nineteen Blake drawings offered by Foster & Son [from the Butts collection] on 8 March 1854 brought an average of 4s. 4d. apiece.

May 1854 Much of *Poetical Sketche* was 'Copied May' 54 / W[illiam] A[llingham]' in a manuscript now in the Turnbull Library.

7-30 June 1854 Among the 7,761 lots offered in the Southgate & Barret catalogue, 7-30 June 1854, of the stock of Joseph Hogarth were seventy-eight drawings by Blake.

Dec. 1854 In December 1854, Sotheby's sold *Jerusalem* (D), *Thel* (D), and *The Marriage* (I), according to Lowndes, *Bibliographer's Manual* (see 1834); I have not been able to trace this sale.

1854 According to the remarkably inaccurate anonymous account of 'Blake, William' in *The Encyclopaedia Britannica* (Edinburgh, 1854), vol. IV, p. 153, Blake

was born in Ireland . . . [but because of] his [early] natural bias . . . [for] the fine arts . . . [he was] sent to London, where he . . . received instructions in drawing from Flaxman and Fuseli; and . . . compose[d] many odes, sonnets, and ballads, which gained him a temporary reputation in the world of letters.

The passage quoted here (about half the article on Blake) is almost entirely fictional.

1854 *Urizen* (C) was offered for sale in 1854 in the catalogue of John Pearson for £55.

1854 All but the first stanza of 'The Ecchoing Green' was reprinted under the title 'A Summer-Evening on a Village Green' in *Pictorial Calendar of the Seasons Exhibiting the Pleasures, Pursuits, and Characteristics of Country Life for Every Month in the Year*, ed. Mary Howitt (London, 1854), pp. 274-5.

1854 Montgomery's impressions of Blake's *Grave* designs, published by Holland & Everett in their *Memoirs of the Life and Writings of James Montgomery* (1854) will be found under No. 29m above.

1854   The anonymous account of 'Blake, Guillaume' in the *Nouvelle Biographie Universelle*, ed. [Ferdinand] Hoefer (Paris, 1854), vol. VI, pp. 178–9, is remarkable only for its insistence that Blake died in 1828.

17 April 1855   On 17 April 1855, Alexander Gilchrist wrote to John Linnell thanking him for his letter and asking permission to call on the 20th.[1] Probably in preparation for this call, Linnell drew up the memorandum about Blake which will be found under 24 December 1825.

23 April 1855   On 23 April Gilchrist wrote again, asking Linnell to look through J. T. Smith's account of Blake ' & to mark in the margin anything which strikes him as inaccurate[.][2] "The first virtue of Biography is entire veracity[.]"'

25 April 1855   On 25 April Gilchrist wrote again (Ivimy MSS.) to say that he had only begun to collect material about Blake and would probably not begin writing for several months. He had so far been in touch only with Linnell, Palmer, and Richmond. 'With M.[r] Tatham I fear I shall have some difficulty. He has not yet replied to a note' sent two weeks before. Gilchrist said he especially needed information about Blake's early years, and was anxious to hear again Linnell's reminiscences of 'so remarkable & lovable a man: a man who attracts the more of my sympathy, the better I understand him. It is fullness of *detail* which to Biography imparts life & reality.'

27 April 1855   On 27 April Gilchrist wrote yet again, thanking Linnell for the parcel of Blake materials ' & especially for the *notes*, made by J.L., giving "modifications of statements already current" concerning Blake'.

June 1855   James Ward's letter of June 1855 to his son George Raphael Ward about Blake's sanity, his genius, and his 'being possessed . . . of spirits' (published in Gilchrist's *Life of William Blake*, 'Pictor Ignotus' [1863], vol. I, pp. 323, 325–6) will be found under 9 October 1820.

---

1 Unless otherwise noted, the following references to the relations between Gilchrist and Linnell, like this one, are taken from John Linnell Jr's 'List of John Linnell Senior's Letters and Papers' (Ivimy MSS.).

2 For Linnell's annotations to J. T. Smith's account of Blake, see *Blake Records* (1969), pp. 459, nn 1–2, 460, nn 1, 4, 461, n. 1, 463, n. 1, 464, n. 1, 466, n. 1; for Linnell's notes of 'April 1855' about Blake's early life, see p. 318, n. 2.

16 June 1855 On 16 June 1855 Gilchrist wrote to Crabb Robinson and asked permission to call on him to ask for information about Blake.

17 June 1855 On 17 June 1855 Samuel Palmer wrote to Robinson on Gilchrist's behalf, asking for assistance with the Blake biography, because his own 'gleanings in the field of memory have been scanty'.

20 June 1855 Robinson reported in his Reminiscences for 20 June 1855 that, before this 'formal introduction of Gilchrist', he 'took no notice of ... [Gilchrist's letter], but now I wrote in a friendly tone to him And asked him to breakf⸬ with me—And to Palmer more at length'.

23 June 1855 Three days later, on the 23rd, Robinson noted in his Reminiscences that he talked with Monckton Milnes about Gilchrist: 'M:M: has shewn him all his engravings & drawings by Blake'.

28 June 1855 On 28 June, Gilchrist and Robinson talked for four hours about Blake, according to Robinson's Reminiscences.
I read him my notes of a conversation with Bl. but I wo⁴ not trust him with the MS. . . . He was I dare say gratified by my attention to him— He is desirous to consider Bl: as an enthusiast not as an insane man—but such a question whe⁷ he were or not insane is a mere question of words—

23 Aug. 1855 Samuel Palmer's long letter to Gilchrist of 23 August 1855, printed in Gilchrist's *'Pictor Ignotus'* (1863), vol. 1, pp. 301–4, will be found under No. 1c above.

1855 In '1855', Sotheby's sold *Ahania* (Bb), *America* (B), *Songs* (P), and eight designs for *Comus*, according to Lowndes, *Bibliographer's Manual* (see 1834); I have not traced these sales.

1855 In his *Hand-Book for Young Painters* (London, 1855), p. 58, C. R. Leslie refers in passing to Blake's 'very singular mind', which permitted him to draw visionary portraits.

8 Jan. 1856 Rossetti commented irreverently on Blake's plates in Hayley's *Ballads* (1805), which Allingham had just sent him, in a letter of 8 January 1856—'The *Lion* seems singing a comic song with a pen behind his ear'.

31 Aug. 1856 *The Marriage of Heaven and Hell* (I) is signed by the Rev. 'Richard Edward Kerrick, August 31ˢᵗ 1856.'

15 Oct. 1856 Beaconsfield wrote a note in his copy of *Visions of the Daughters of Albion* (F) on 15 October 1856, remarking that the frontispiece was then missing.

3 Nov. 1856 J. H. Anderdon wrote a brief biography of Blake on 3 November 1856 ('11/3 56'), now with his papers in the British Museum Print Room, which seems to be derived exclusively from Watt's *Bibliotheca Britannica* (1819), with an addition 'In 1863' from the biography by Alexander Gilchrist, with whom 'I had some correspondence in regard to an autograph letter of much importance addressed by Blake to his great friend Ozias Humphrey' (of 1808), and he kept some 'proof sheets [of Gilchrist's chapter XXIV on "The Designs to Blair"] received from the publisher'.

30 Dec. 1856 On 30 December 1856, J. H. Chance wrote to his uncle John Linnell (Ivimy MSS.):
the Dante & Blake I have entirely on my own speculation being partial to them and if I can do any thing with them I shall be happy to enter into some agreements for 25 Copies by [i.e., ?but] when I have done the framing (you are kind enough to order of me) I may be better able to tell[.]
Evidently this indicates that Chance was publishing Blake's Dante engravings himself.

1856 In his *Modern Painters* (London, 1856), vol. III, pp. 103, 259, Ruskin said that 'Blake was sincere, but full of wild creeds, and somewhat diseased in brain' and that he 'fails always more or less as soon as he adds colour [partly] . . . because his subjects seem, in a sort, insusceptible of completion'.

1856 The respectful, anonymous account of 'Blake, William' in *The English Cyclopaedia*, ed. Charles Knight (London, 1856), vol. I, columns 716–17, remarked that some qualities of his poetry 'cannot easily be surpassed', although his visions suggest that he suffered from 'a species of chronic insanity'. The facts seem to come entirely from Cunningham.

1856 For the purchase of *Job* by H. de Triqueti in 1856, see 22 November 1831.

22 June, 5 Oct. 1857 Ruskin recommended that students should study Blake's *Job* in his *Elements of Drawing* (first edition 22 June, second edition 5 October 1857),[1] 342, and asserted that 'In expressing conditions of glaring and flickering light, Blake is greater than Rembrandt'.

1857 'The Tiger' (*Experience*), 'The Little Black Boy' (*Innocence*),

---

[1] T. J. Wise and J. P. Smart, *A Complete Bibliography of the Writings in Prose and Verse of John Ruskin, Ll.D.* (London, 1893), vol. I, pp. 76–81.

'My Silks' (*Poetical Sketches*), 'The Garden of Love' (*Experience*), and 'On Another's Sorrow' (*Innocence*) were printed in *The Household Book of Poetry*, ed. Charles A. Dana (New York, 1857).

1857 In the exhibition of British Art Treasures at Manchester in 1857 were two watercolours by Blake, no. 130, 'Oberon and Titania on a Lily' (i.e., the design analogous to *Song of Los*, pl. 5, called 'King and Queen of the Fairies', now in an anonymous collection) lent by William Russell Esq., and no. 130a, 'Vision of Queen Catherine' lent by C. W. Dilke, Esq.[1]

1857 A review of the exhibition in the *Manchester Guardian* paired Blake with R. Dadd 'as examples of painters in whom a disordered brain rather aided than impeded the workings of . . . fancy'.[2]

1 Aug. 1858 F. W. Fairholt, 'Tombs of English artists. No. 7.— William Blake', *Art Journal*, [vol. IV] (1 August 1858), p. 236, is a pedestrian article, with plates of Blake's house in Fountain Court (Strand), the 'Ghost of a Flea', and one of the Dante drawings.

25 Aug. 1858 Adam White of the British Museum wrote to Linnell on 25 August 1858 saying: 'I am collecting now, as opportunity occurs, everything about William Blake as man and artist'.[3]

4, 11, 18 Dec. 1858 In the late autumn of 1858, the editor of *Littell's Living Age*, on going through the books being prepared for the Christmas trade, came across the 1858 reissue of the 1847 Blair's *Grave* and was much struck by the plates after Blake's designs (vol. LIX, p. 784),

---

[1] *Catalogue of the Art Treasures of the United Kingdom* collected at Manchester in 1857 (London, 1857), cited by S. R. Hoover, 'Fifty additions to Blake bibliography', *Blake Newsletter*, vol. V (1972), pp. 168–9. She does not mention whether Blake appears in J. B. Waring, ed., *Art Treasures of the United Kingdom: from the Art Treasures Exhibition, Manchester* (London, 1858), which I have not seen. There is no Blake in *Photographs of the 'Gems of the Art Treasures Exhibition,' Manchester, 1857*, of Signori Caldesi and Mantecchi, [vol. I] Ancient Series [and vol. II: Modern Series] (London and Manchester, 1858).

[2] *A Handbook to the Water Colours, Drawings, and Engravings in the Art Treasures Exhibition* (London, 1857), pp. 12–13, 'a reprint of critical notices originally published in "The Manchester Guardian"' quoted by Mrs Hoover (previous footnote). (This sounds much like *A Handbook to the Gallery of British Paintings in the Art Treasures Exhibition Being a Reprint of Critical Notices Originally Published in 'The Manchester Guardian'* [London, 1857] which is listed in the BM catalogue but which I have not seen.) Mrs Hoover does not say which issue of the *Manchester Guardian* the Blake review is extracted from, nor whether Blake appears in *The Treasures Examined: Pictorial, Critical, and Historical Record of the Art Treasures Exhibition at Manchester Illustrated by Upwards of 150 Engravings on Wood by W. J. Linton, H. Linton, F. J. Smythe &c* (Manchester [1857]).

[3] Transcribed by A. H. Palmer in an exercise book in the Ivimy MSS. headed 'Blake Accounts', '27', 'Job'.

though 'we have never seen others' of Blake's designs (p. 912). He consequently reproduced plates of 'Death's Door', 'William Blake', and the 'Soul Exploring', with descriptive comment quoted from the 1858 *Grave*, on 4, 11, and 18 December 1858 (vol. LIX, pp. 721, 784, 785, 848, 849, 912).

1 March 1859   In his 'CASH' book for 1849–64, Linnell wrote that he had received 'March 1 [1859] of J H Chance for a copy of Blake's Job 2.2'.

15 May 1859, 24 Feb. 1860   In the Quaritch catalogues called *The Museum*, no. 147 (15 May 1859) and no. 156 (24 February 1860) were offered *Songs* (?G) bound with *The World Turned Upside Down* and other works for £10 10s. (1859) and £8 10s. (1860).

16 Dec. 1859   In a letter to W. B. Scott of 16 December 1859, Swinburne mentioned that he owned Blake's Dante and *Job* (*The Swinburne Letters*, ed. C. Y. Lang [New Haven, 1959], vol. I, pp. 27–8).

29 Dec. 1859   On 29 December 1859 Carlyle inquired of his neighbour Alexander Gilchrist about his success in discovering a publisher for his biography of Blake (*Anne Gilchrist: Her Life and Writings*, ed. H. H. Gilchrist [London, 1887], p. 74).

1859   S. Austin Allibone listed many of Blake's works and gave critical comments on Blake from Lamb (see Cunningham, 1830), Pilkington (1840), and Mrs Jameson (1848) in his *Critical Dictionary of English Literature, and British and American Authors* (Philadelphia and London, 1859), vol. I, p. 203 (reprinted 1877, 1891).

1859   Seventeen works by Blake are listed in Jean Georges Théodore Graesse, *Trésor de livres rares et précieux* (Dresden, Geneva, London, Paris, 1859), vol. I, p. 436.

5 Feb. 1860   W. M. Rossetti wrote to Anne Gilchrist about the Blake biography on 5 February 1860 (*Letters of William Michael Rossetti*, ed. C. Gohdes and P. F. Baum [Durham, 1934], pp. 14–15).

3 May 1860   For Samuel Palmer's letter to Gilchrist of 3 May 1860 about the orderliness and delightfulness of Blake's house, which Gilchrist printed in his *Life of William Blake*, *'Pictor Ignotus'* (1863), vol. I, p. 306, see *Blake Records* (1969), p. 565, n. 4.

1 Nov. 1860   On 1 November 1860 D. G. Rossetti wrote to Allingham saying that Gilchrist had asked to see Rossetti's Blake notebook, but that he, Rossetti, was putting him off for the moment, because both Allingham and D. G. Rossetti's brother William had spoken of editing it.

3 Nov. 1860 According to his Reminiscences, Crabb Robinson talked to Gilchrist for an hour on 3 November 1860 and 'promised to lend him some papers'.

24 Nov. 1860 On 24 November 1860 Gilchrist wrote to Linnell (Ivimy MSS.) saying that, though he understood that Linnell did not normally lend his books, he would particularly like to see *The French Revolution*.

28 Nov. 1860 Linnell replied on the 28th (Ivimy MSS.) that in this case he would oblige, though 'I have been terrified at lending anything of Blakes through having lost one[?] of his letters which I lent to Allan Cunningham'.

6 Dec. 1860 For Thomas Woolner's letter of 6 December 1860 to Rossetti about Blake and the pampered little girl (Library of Congress), see No. 6c above.

31 Dec. 1860 In a letter to George Richmond of 31 December 1860, Samuel Palmer recalled that Blake had once 'made a remark which is more decorously preserved in memory than committed to writing'.[1] Palmer was always conventionally cautious about indecorum. He told Anne Gilchrist: 'I should let no passage appear [in the biography] in which the word Bible, or those of the persons of the blessed Trinity, or the Messiah were irreverently connected . . .' (letter of 24 December 1862—see 24 December 1825), and he advised her to exclude from the transcripts of the *Marriage* 'an indecent word in the text—or at least a coarse one' (letter of 27 June 1862 in Yale).

1860 The 'Introduction' to *Innocence*, 'The Tiger' (*Experience*), 'The Blossom' (*Innocence*), 'The Angel' (*Experience*), and a 'Note' about Blake are printed in *Nightingale Valley* [ed. William Allingham] (London, 1860), pp. 54–5, 95–6, 116–17, 235, partly from the *Notebook*.

13 Jan., 2, 19, 22 Feb. 1861 On 13 January, 2, 19, 22 February 1861, Gilchrist wrote to Linnell and to John Linnell Jr about minor Blake matters (Ivimy MSS.).

---

[1] See R. Lister, *op. cit.*, p. 305, who thinks this 'an obvious reference to the poem, "Then old Nobodaddy aloft"' ('Let the Brothels of Paris be opened', *Notebook*, pp. 99–8), but Palmer's context seems to require a spoken rather than a written remark.

14 March, 28 July, 22 Aug. 17, 20 Sept. 1861 On 14 March, 28 July, 22 August, 17 and 20 September 1861 Linton wrote to Linnell about engraving some of Blake's works for Gilchrist (Ivimy MSS.).

31 March 1861 Gilchrist wrote to John Linnell Jr on 31 March about engraving some of Blake's 'Visionary Heads' (Ivimy MSS.).

April 1861 In April Samuel Palmer wrote to Gilchrist saying, among other things: 'You really overrate my contributions to the Blake Revival' (Yale MS.). He also
mention[ed] that in the late Sir R. Peel's copy of the Europe and America there is a pencil drawing by Mr Richmond—done soon after Blake's decease while the memory was fresh, & assisted by the cast [by Deville] of which I spoke, most probably this is the closest likeness existing.
Sir Robert Peel (1788–1850), prime minister, is not known to have owned any of Blake's writings. The reference to a 'copy of the Europe and America' suggests that the two works were bound together, as were *America* (B, G, N, P, Q) and *Europe* (C, B, I, M, L). Perhaps Sir Robert had one of these, or an untraced set. The Richmond portraits of Blake known to me are in the Fitzwilliam Museum (reproduced in *William Blake: Catalogue of the Collection in the Fitzwilliam Museum, Cambridge*, ed. D. Bindman [1970], pls 71–2, which stayed in the Richmond family) and the collection of Sir Geoffrey Keynes, inscribed 'William Blake from recollection after his death 1827'; the last seems to correspond with Palmer's description.

20 April 1861 Rossetti suggested to Gilchrist on 20 April 1861 that Mrs Edward [Burne-] Jones could copy Blake's drawings (Library of Congress MS.).

4 May 1861 In his diary for 4 May 1861, G. P. Boyce recorded that, with Rossetti, Swinburne, and Madox Brown at Gilchrist's, he 'Spent a most interesting evening looking over some books of Blake's showing marked originality and marvellous invention' (G. F. Boyce, 'Extracts from Boyce's Diaries: 1851–1875', *The Old Water-Colour Society's Club Nineteenth Annual Volume* [1941], pp. 9–71).

18 June, 11 July, 23 Aug. 1861, 15, 31 Jan., 2 March, 13, 22, 25 Sept., Oct., 4, 12, 13, 19 Dec. 1862 On 18 June, 11 July, 23 August 1861, 15, 31 January, 2 March, 13, 22, 25 September, 'Friday', mid-October, 4, 12, 13, 19 December 1862, D. G. Rossetti wrote letters to the Gilchrists with minor references to Blake.

28 July, 22 Aug., 17, 20 Sept. 1861 On 28 July, 22 August, 17, 20 September 1861, W. Linton wrote to John Linnell Jr about engraving Blake's works (Ivimy MSS.).

27 Aug. 1861 On 27 August 1861 D. G. Rossetti wrote to Gilchrist: 'I have been reading the Blake MS [*The Pickering or Ballads MS.*], and have made the enclosed copies of *Auguries of Innocence*, omitting parts and transposing others so as (to my thinking) the better to make its merits tell', and will return the MS. on the 28th.[1]

24 Oct. 1861 Gilchrist wrote to William Howitt on 24 October 1861 for information on Blake matters, asking in particular if Howitt's daughter had manuscript poems of Blake.[2]

19 Nov. 1861 On 19 November 1861, D. G. Rossetti wrote to Gilchrist that he had been reading 'the two first sheets of *Blake*'.

1861 The 'Introduction' to *Innocence* was printed as 'The Piper' in *Folk Songs*, ed. John Williamson Piper (New York, 1861).

1861 For the account of Blake's 'Demon Flea' and his 'sight of the devil in his coal-cellar' in Walter Thornbury's *British Artists from Hogarth to Turner* (1861), see October 1819 and winter 1826.

1861 The anonymous account of 'Blake, William' in *Chambers Encyclopaedia* (London and Edinburgh, 1861), vol. II, p. 142 (reprinted in 1874) is brief and uninteresting.

18 Jan. 1862 For Bulwer Lytton's 'Strange Story' with its conversation about Blake's 'astonishing and curious' *Night Thoughts* engravings, first published in *All the Year Round*, vol. VI (18 January 1862), p. 386, see No. 22f.

20 March, 28 April, 22 May, Aug., Sept., 22 Nov., 13 Dec. 1862 For the correspondence of Anne Gilchrist with the Rossettis on minor Blake matters on 20 March, April, 28 April, 22 May, August, Septem-

---

[1] In an undated letter of 1861 he wrote to Gilchrist: 'I am glad you approve of my rather unceremonious shaking up of Blake's rhymes' (vol. II, p. 420). On a Sunday in 1863, Rossetti wrote that he wanted to insert a sentence to the effect that 'In printing the hither-to unpublished poems, the manuscripts of which are seldom in what appears to be a final state, some licence has occasionally been taken as to omission or transposition of parts when such treatment seemed to assist clearness or avoid redundance' (vol. II, p. 469), but no such note was printed.

[2] Library of Congress MS. William Howitt (1792–1879) had well-known daughters named Margaret and Anna Mary (d. 1884), the second of whom married Alaric Watts, but none of the Howitts or Wattses is known to have owned Blake materials.

ber, 22 November, and 13 December 1862, see *Anne Gilchrist: Her Life and Writings*, ed. H. H. Gilchrist (1887), pp. 112–13, 122, 123, 123–4, 124–5, 126–7, 132–3, *Letters of William Michael Rossetti*, ed. C. Gohdes and P. F. Baum (1934), pp. 3–4, 10–12, and W. M. Rossetti, *Rossetti Papers* (London, 1903), pp. 6, 15.

11 April 1862   A portrait of Blake appeared in Christie's sale of Flaxman's drawings on 11 April 1862, lot 450.

27 April 1862   Samuel Palmer referred to Blake in his letter to Anne Gilchrist of 27 April 1862 (Yale).

29 April 1862   At an anonymous sale (probably of Frederick Tatham) on 29 April 1862, Sotheby's sold over two hundred minor Blake works, mostly sketches.

1862   Five designs by Blake were included in the International Exhibition of 1862 and were listed in *International Exhibition 1862: Official Catalogue of the Fine Art Department* (London, 1862), nos 221, 965–8—Blake and Stothard are compared on p. 46; in *Illuminated Guide to the International Exhibition* (London [1862]), nos 965–8; in Francis Turner Palgrave,[1] *Handbook to the Fine Art Collection in the International Exhibition of 1862* (London and Cambridge, 1862; second edition, revised, 1862), pp. 65–6, in the last of which Blake's 'penetrative imagination' is compared with Stothard's, though 'it is hardly as art that his strange creations appeal to us'; and in Tom Taylor, *Handbook of the Pictures in the International Exhibition of 1862* (London, 1862), pp. 73–6, in which we find that Blake 'was a poet of rare originality and sweetness', though his pictorial 'work is rather tame and lumpish', 'much beyond the pale of good art'.

17 May 1862   An anonymous review in the *Athenaeum*[2] remarked in passing that 'Blake's transcendantal fancies are freely [*sic*] seen'.

1 July 1862   An anonymous review of the 'International Exhibition, 1862: Pictures of the British School', *Art-Journal*, XXIV (1 July 1862), pp. 149–52, compared Stothard with 'the more shadowy and visionary'

[1] Mrs Hoover (p. 341n) cites Palgrave's *Official Catalogue of the Fine Art Department, International Exhibition* (London, 1862), p. 46, which I have not traced; her quotations indicate that it is similar in substance to his *Handbook* above.

[2] Anon., 'International Exhibition. The English water-colour pictures', *Athenaeum*, no. 1803 (17 May 1862), p. 663, reprinted in *What Do You Think of the Exhibition? A Collection of the Best Descriptions from the Leading Journals Concerning the International Exhibition*, ed. Robert Kempton (London, 1862), pp. 179–81.

Blake, 'who maintained spiritual converse with the Virgin Mary, [and] was scarcely likely to do justice to the "Wife of Bath"' (p. 152).

24 July 1862 On 24 July 1862 Samuel Palmer wrote to Mrs Gilchrist about Blake's *Marriage*:

I think the whole page at the top of which I have made a cross in red chalk would at once exclude the work from every drawing-room table in England. Blake has said the same kind of thing to me; in fact almost everything contained in the book; and *I* can understand it in relation to my memory of the whole man, in a way quite different to that roaring lion the 'press,' or that led lion the British Public.

Blake wrote often in anger and rhetorically; just as we might speak if some *pretender* to Christianity whom we knew to be hypocritical, were *canting* to us in a pharisaical way. We might say, 'If this is your Heaven, give me Hell.' We might say this in temper, but without in the least meaning that that was our deliberate preference.

This is the clue to much of Blake's paradox, and often it carries its own explanation with it. Where it does not, without presumptuously recommending you what to do, I will just say what course *I* should think best. I should let no passage appear in which the word Bible, or those of the persons of the blessed Trinity, or the Messiah were irreverently connected. . . . I should simply put *******, and in case of omitting a page or chapter, simply say 'The —th Chapter is omitted.' This sometimes gives zest—a twinge of pleasant curiosity to the reader, the more attentive through not having the whole. I should state where complete copies could be consulted, I suppose the British Museum. Thus I should be guilty of no injustice to Blake, nor would I ever omit without asterisks; for it is not just to any author, living or dead, to join clauses when *he* has words intervening.

Now I have nearly done, but this one thing more occurs to me, that I think it would explain matters somewhat if the public knew that Blake sometimes wrote under irritation. Nothing would explain some things in the MS.[1] Being irritated by the exclusively scientific talk at a friend's house, which talk had turned on the vastness of space, he cried out, 'It is false. I walked the other evening to the end of the earth, and touched the sky with my finger.'

In his quiet moments, he made the devil on the heath say what he

---

[1] Palmer wrote to the Rev. J. P. Wright in February 1869: 'Blake was I think misled by erroneous spirits' (quoted from the MS. in the possession of J. E. A. Samuels by R. Lister, 'References to Blake in Samuel Palmer's Letters', in *William Blake: Essays in Honour of Sir Geoffrey Keynes*, ed. M. D. Paley and M. Phillips [1973], p. 306).

(Blake) hated, and the angel among the haycocks, what he (Blake) loved.

His real views would now be considered extravagant on the opposite side to that apparently taken in the *Marriage*, for he quite held forth one day to me, on the Roman Catholic Church being the only one which taught the forgiveness of sins; and he repeatedly expressed his belief that there was more *civil* liberty under the Papal government, than any other sovereignty; nor did I ever hear him express any admiration for the American republic.

Everything connected with Gothic art and churches, and their builders, was a *PASSION* with him. St. Teresa was his delight.

If madness and absurdity be synonyms, which they are not, then Blake would be as 'mad as a March hare,' for his love for art was so great that he would see nothing *but art* in anything he loved; and so, as he loved the Apostles and their divine Head (for so I believe he did), he must needs say that they were all artists. We see a touch of this absurdity in his *Marriage*, where he makes the blessed Comforter the spirit of poetic invention. . . . *Talent* thinks, Genius *sees*; and what organ so accurate as sight. Blake held this strongly. His word was 'precision.'[1]

18 Aug., 13 Nov. 1862   Swinburne referred to Blake in his letters to R. M. Milnes of 18 August and 13 November 1862 (*The Swinburne Letters* (1959), vol. I, pp. 59, 62).

25 Aug. 1862   In a letter to her sister-in-law, Mrs Burnie, of 25 August 1862, Anne Gilchrist remarked that her husband had left the section on the Prophecies 'an absolute blank that *must* be filled in' (*Anne Gilchrist: Her Life and Writings* [1887], pp. 125–6).

25 Aug. 1862   In his letter to Anne Gilchrist of 25 August 1862, D. G. Rossetti said that 'Mr. Swinburne . . . has made, next to your husband, the most diligent research of any one into the most recondite side of Blake'.

Sept. 1862   Samuel Palmer told Anne Gilchrist that 'Blake *was* mad about languages' when he wrote to her in September 1862 (Yale; see A. H. Palmer, *The Life and Letters of Samuel Palmer* [London, 1892], vol. I, p. 248).

[1] A. H. Palmer, *The Life and Letters of Samuel Palmer, Painter & Etcher* (London, 1892), pp. 244–6; the original letter in Yale is dated 27 June 1862.

3 Oct. 1862 Anne Gilchrist told Rossetti on 3 October 1862 that 'It was no use to put in [the *Visions of the Daughters of Albion*] what I was perfectly certain Macmillan (who reads all the proofs) would take out again. He is far more inexorable against any shade of heterodoxy in morals than in religion.'[1]

6 Oct. 1862 In his letter to W. M. Rossetti of 6 October 1862 (*The Swinburne Letters* [1959], pp. 59–60), Swinburne said he had been solicited to discuss the Prophecies in Gilchrist's book, but Macmillan would not have the Prophecies printed, so Swinburne was writing his own book instead.

17 Oct. 1862 On 17 October 1862 R. Arnold wrote to Linnell about *Job* (Ivimy MSS.).

20 Oct. 1862 J. A. Froude, the editor of *Fraser's*, wrote on 20 October 1862 accepting a rather indiscreet offer (later withdrawn) of W. M. Rossetti to review Gilchrist's biography of Blake, and he went on: 'Blake . . . has always seemed to me to be an instance of the prodigal carelessness of Nature, which gives a man so often half the qualities which make up genius, and, by leaving out the others, makes them almost useless.' (W. M. Rossetti, *Rossetti Papers* [London, 1903], p. 15.)

1 Nov. 1862 On 1 November 1862, Anne Gilchrist wrote to Linnell on minor Blake matters (Ivimy MSS.).

2–3 Nov. 1862 On 2 November 1862 W. M. Rossetti wrote to Swinburne about getting at the Milnes collection of Blake's works, and on the next day Swinburne replied (*The Swinburne Letters* [1959], vol. I, pp. 61–2).

6 Nov. 1862 Tatham told W. M. Rossetti on 6 November 1862: 'I have sold Mr Blake's works for thirty years. . . . Mr Evans bought nearly all I had latterly' (W. M. Rossetti, *Rossetti Papers* [1903], p. 16; see also 1787).

9 Nov. 1862 For Anne Gilchrist's letter to W. M. Rossetti of 9 Novem-

[1] *Letters of Dante Gabriel Rossetti to William Allingham, 1854–1870* (1897), p. 259. On 7 November 1866 Swinburne told M. D. Conway that some of Blake's Prophecies were not yet 'published because of the abject and faithless and blasphemous timidity of our wretched English literary society; a drunken clerical club dominated by the spurious spawn of the press' (*The Swinburne Letters* [1959], vol. I, pp. 208–9). Between April and 24 October 1862 D. G. Rossetti wrote to W. Ireland, saying that he and his brother 'shall both be very glad to see her [Mrs Gilchrist, at Ireland's house] again & go over Blake business by word of mouth' (Thomas L. Minnick, 'A new Rossetti letter' *Blake Newsletter*, vol. V [1972], p. 181).

ber 1862 about Tatham's relationship with Blake, see *Blake Records* (1969), pp. 416–18.

30 Nov., 2 Dec. 1862 W. M. Rossetti wrote to John Linnell Jr about the Dante drawings on 30 November 1862 (Ivimy MSS.), and the reply was written on 2 December (W. M. Rossetti, *Rossetti Papers* [1903], p. 18).

8 Dec. 1862 For W. M. Rossetti's letter to Anne Gilchrist of 8 December 1862 (*Letters of William Michael Rossetti*, ed. C. Gohdes and P. F. Baum [1934], p. 5) about D'Israeli's Blakes, see *Blake Records* (1969), p. 234, n. 2.

10 Dec. 1862 John Linnell wrote to Anne Gilchrist on 10 December 1862 saying that Blake 'certainly never did paint a Fresco according to the exact meaning of the term'. He used watercolour on a plaster ground, 'literally glue & whiting'. He went on to ask who had written the account of Blake printing from millboards (it was Tatham) and of his heraldry (Mr Riviere), which was 'all new to me'.

I am anxious to know what is said about Mrs Blake & Her doings after Blake's Death, lest I sh^d feel called upon to publicly contradict some statements, a thing I sh^d be extremely sorry to be compelled to do ....

P.S. I believe that the first copy of Cennino [Cennini, *Trattato della Pittura* (Rome, 1821)] seen in England was the copy I obtained from Italy & gave to Blake who soon made it out & was gratified to find that he had been using the same materials & methods in painting as Cennini describes—particularly the Carpenters glue[.][1]

11 Dec. 1862 Mrs Gilchrist replied on the 11th (Ivimy MSS.) that she didn't want to identify the men who supplied the stories about the millboard process and the heraldry. She said that she didn't think Linnell would object to anything about Catherine in her husband's book, but that she would send him proofs anyway. She also mentioned that after Butts's death his Blake collection had simply been stored in the cellar.

11 Dec. 1862 On the same day she wrote to W. M. Rossetti about Blake's process of colourprinting (W. M. Rossetti, *Rossetti Papers* [1903], p. 19).

[1] Ivimy MSS; see also A. T. Story, *The Life of John Linnell* (London, 1892), vol. II, p. 126. The issues are displayed in Gilchrist, *Life of William Blake* (1863), vol. I, p. 376 (*Blake Records* [1969], pp. 33–4).

16 Dec. 1862 On 16 December 1862 W. M. Rossetti wrote to J. Linnell Jr about Blake matters (Ivimy MSS.) and on the same day John Linnell wrote to Anne Gilchrist protesting about the heraldry story[1] and saying that it would take too long to correct her account of printing from millboard (Ivimy MSS.). Also on the same day Frederick Tatham gave W. M. Rossetti the same account of Blake's last hours as he had to J. T. Smith (W. M. Rossetti, *Rossetti Papers* [1903], pp. 19–20 —see *Blake Records* [1969], p. 475). Also on the same day Samuel Palmer told Linnell that he too had never heard the heraldry or millboard stories before (Ivimy MSS.).

17 Dec. 1862 Fortified with this authority, Linnell wrote to Anne Gilchrist on 17 December 1862 to contradict confidently the stories about the millboard and the heraldry. They cannot be true because he never heard them, and Blake 'told me freely all about his early life his being apprenticed to Basire the antiquarian Engraver & his drawing Gothic monuments'. He clearly suspected that Tatham was the author of the stories, for he said: 'I have more to say on this subject than I choose to write' (Ivimy MSS.).

21 Dec. 1862 For Anne Gilchrist's letter of 21 December 1862 to W. M. Rossetti concerning the millboard process (W. M. Rossetti, *Rossetti Papers* [1903], p. 21), see 1787.

21 Dec. 1862 On the same day John Linnell Jr told W. M. Rossetti that they had Blake's twenty drawings for Virgil, and that 'three of them [were] cut by another' engraver (W. M. Rossetti, *Rossetti Papers* [1903], p. 20).

23 Dec. 1862 On 23 December 1862 W. M. Rossetti wrote to Linnell (Ivimy MSS.) '*in perfect confidence* that the authority for the statement of Blake's herald-painting is Mr [William] Riviere [1806–76] of Oxford, who I believe is (or considers himself to be) an artist . . . I don't at all know *how* Mr Rivière professes to have learned that incident about Blake.'

24 Dec. 1862 On the 24th Linnell replied to Rossetti, saying, 'I never heard of Mr Riviére before or any one of that name who knew Blake. . . . I can find no one who believes it' (Ivimy MSS.).

1862 The 'Introduction' to *Innocence* and 'The Tyger' from *Experience*

---

[1] Linnell wrote a verse note to Palmer asking what he knew of the heraldry story (A. T. Story, *The Life of John Linnell* [London, 1892], vol. II, p. 127).

were printed in *The Children's Garland*, ed. Coventry Patmore (London and Cambridge, 1862), pp. 1–2, 158–9.

1862   In his 'Journal WAR 1862',[1] R. W. Emerson transcribed some Remarks on Blake, apparently from Crabb Robinson.

At the end of 1862, D. G. Rossetti wrote to William Allingham asking for the loan of 'that *Bogie* poem book of Wilkinson's' (*Improvisations from the Spirit* [1857], with spirit-written poems), which he wanted 'to mention in a passage on Blake's poetry which I am writing for the *Life*'.

In 1863, two thousand copies of Gilchrist's biography of Blake were published with great éclat, and from that time on Blake has been part of the educated Englishman's literary heritage. After 1863, almost all references to the poet are traceable, directly or indirectly, to Gilchrist's biography, and possession of information about him is no longer an indication of arcane—and therefore publishable—knowledge. On 23 August 1878 Linnell told Dixon that 'the life [by Gilchrist] contains all that can be said about Blake or me' (Ivimy MSS.), and though this was not strictly true, as thousands of essays and books have tried (usually vainly) to show, yet it was true enough to satisfy those who had known Blake himself.

ADDENDA

21 June 1834   On 21 June 1834, the account in Macnish of 'The Fairy's Funeral' was reprinted and also transformed by 'A.' into sentimental 'poetic dress' in the *New-York Mirror*, p. 406.

24 April 1838   At the posthumous sale of James Vine's Pictures, Modern Drawings, and Books of Prints at Christie's, 24 April 1838, appeared Blake's *Job*, *Milton* (D) and *Thel* (O) together, *Jerusalem* (J) and *Songs* (V) as lots 296–9; all apparently went to Bohn—see his 1840 catalogue.

1847   In *Œuvres de Flaxman*, Recueil de ses Compositions Gravées par Reveil, avec analyse de la Divine Comédie du Dante et Notice sur Flaxman (Paris: Audot, 1847), p. 3, the anonymous editor says of Flaxman:

Ses amis principaux furent Blacke et Stothard. Dans les compositions sauvages du premier il vit plu d'élévation poétique.

----

[1] Houghton Library (Harvard) MS. no. 77, pp. 244–6, cited by S. Hoover, 'Fifty additions to Blake bibliography', *Blake Newsletter*, vol. v (1972), p. 169.

Bibliography

This short, select bibliography is of works listing, describing, or reprinting nineteenth-century criticism of William Blake.

BENTLEY, G. E., JR, and NURMI, M. K., *A Blake Bibliography* (Minneapolis, University of Minnesota Press, 1964) (an edition revised by G. E. Bentley, Jr, as *Blake Books* is in the press) lists almost all published comments on Blake; an essay on 'Blake's reputation and interpreters' is on pp. 3–30.

BENTLEY, G. E., JR, *Blake Records* (Oxford, Clarendon Press, 1969) reprints all the then-known comments on Blake, printed or in MS., up to 1831.

CROMPTON, LOUIS L., 'Blake's Nineteenth Century Critics', Ph.D. Thesis, University of Chicago (1954) (unpublished), surveys the field and reprints a number of early comments.

DORFMAN, DEBORAH, *Blake in the Nineteenth Century: his Reputation as a Poet from Gilchrist to Yeats* (New Haven, Yale University Press, 1969) discusses Blake's late-Victorian critics, particularly the books of Gilchrist (1863) and of Ellis and Yeats (1893).

HOOVER, SUZANNE R., 'William Blake in the Wilderness: a Closer Look at his Reputation 1827–1863', in *William Blake: Essays in Honour of Sir Geoffrey Keynes*, ed. M. D. Paley and M. Phillips (Oxford University Press, 1973), pp. 310–48.

KEYNES, GEOFFREY L., *A Bibliography of William Blake* (Grolier Club of New York, 1921) lists many and quotes some early printed reviews and comments.

Annotated index of names

For assistance with this annotated index of names, I am grateful to G. E. Bentley, Virginia Prewitt, and Jane Welch.

Works by Blake (both visual and verbal) are listed under their titles; works by other authors are listed under their author's names.

Singer, June K., *The Unholy Bible* (1970), 21

Slater, publisher, 249

Sloss, D. J., and Wallis, J. P. R., ed., *Prophetic Writings* (1926), 17

'Small Book of Designs' (1795), 63, 242

Smith, John Thomas (1766–1833), Keeper of Prints & Drawings in the British Museum, Blake's second biographer (1828), xvii, 3, 9, 11, 16, 25, 48, 52, 61, 70, 72, 74, 81, 147, 170, 195, 199, 255, 268, pl. 11; *Book for a Rainy Day* (1845, 1845, 1861), 72, 242, 268, pl. 11; *Nollekens and his Times* (1828), 39, 48–9, 51–2, 54, 63, 70, 72, 75, 82, 88, 141

Soane, Sir John (1753–1837), architect, 165, 227; Soane Museum, 227

Society for the Encouragement of Arts, Manufacturers, and Commerce, 226

Socrates (*c.* 470–399 BC), 31

Soho Square, 34

'Song: How Sweet I Roamed', *Poetical Sketches* (1783), 214

'Song: I love the jocund dance', *Poetical Sketches* (1783), 154

'Song: Love & Harmony combine', *Poetical Sketches* (1783), 214–15

'A Song of Innonsense', 252

Song of Los (1795), 46, 231, 258

Songs of Experience (1794), 44, 147, 156, 164, 199–200, 235, 242, 244, 249, 257–8, 260, 268

Songs of Innocence (1789), 8, 33, 44, 50, 78, 147, 156, 176–9, 192–3, 198–9, 219, 224, 228, 241–5, 248, 251–3, 257–8, pl. 1

Songs of Innocence & of Experience (1795), 6–8, 16–17, 23, 26, 30, 46, 51–61, 163, 175, 194, 199, 213, 219, 228, 231, 236–40, 243, 245–6, 250, 252, 256, 259, 269; *see also* individual titles; (1839), 16, 57–60, 239, 246, 251

Songs of Innocence and Experience [sic], ed. M. Bottrall (1970), 24

Sotheby's sale (1832), 226; (1837), 232; (1852), 25, 241, 252; (1854), 254; (1855), 256; (1862), 263; (1903), 25; (1932), 25; (1962), 249, 251

sources, Blake's, 21

Southern Literary Messenger (1843), 239

Southey, Robert (1774–1843), poet laureate and man of letters, friend of Coleridge and Wordsworth, one of the chief Romantic poets, 9–10, 40, 64, 69, 108, 232, 244; *The Doctor*, 65, 244; *Wat Tyler*, 245

Southgate & Barret catalogue (1854), 254

Spain, 136

Spilsbury, Mr, 97

Spinoza, Baruch (1632–77), philosopher, 30

'The Spiritual Form of Nelson guiding Leviathan', design, 184

'The Spiritual Form of Pitt guiding Behemoth', design, 184

Spooner, Shearjashub, *Anecdotes of Painters* (1853–1854), 253; *Biographical Dictionary of Engravers, Sculptors and Architects* (1853), 253

Staël, Anne Louise Germaine Necker, Baronne de Staël-Holstein (1766–1817), author, 200

Stanley, J. T., translator of Burger's *Leonora*, 86

Stephen, Sir George (fl. 1833), author, 227

stereotype, 52

Stevens, Richard John Samuel (1757–1837), composer, 149

Stevenson, W. H., ed., *Poems* (1971), 17

Volumes published and forthcoming